EDITIONS SR

Volume 15

Love and the Soul
Psychological Interpretations of the Eros and Psyche Myth

James Gollnick

Published for the Canadian Corporation for Studies in
Religion/Corporation Canadienne des Sciences Religieuses
by Wilfrid Laurier University Press

1992

Canadian Cataloguing in Publication Data

Gollnick, James Timothy
    Love and the soul

(Editions SR ; 15)
Includes bibliographical references and index.
ISBN 0-88920-212-5

1. Love. 2. Soul. 3. Eros (Greek deity).
4. Psyche (Goddess). 5. Apuleius. Metamorphoses.
I. Canadian Corporation for Studies in Religion.
II. Title. III Series.

BF575.L8G6 1992   152.4'1   C92-093173-1

1992 Canadian Corporation for Studies in Religion/
Corporation Canadienne des Sciences Religieuses

Cover design by Connolly Design Inc.

Printed in Canada

Love and the Soul: Psychological Interpretations of the Eros and Psyche Myth has been produced from a manuscript supplied in electronic form by the author.

Order from:
WILFRID LAURIER UNIVERSITY PRESS
Waterloo, Ontario, Canada N2L 3C5

Eros and Psyche embracing

—Photograph used by kind permission of l'Archivio Fotografico dei Musei Capitolini

To my wife,
Debbie

who teaches me much about love and the soul

Contents

Acknowledgements

I am grateful to David Seljak, Debbie Thurling-Gollnick and Helke Ferrie for their editorial assistance in preparing this manuscript.

I would also like to thank Professors William C. James and David Jobling of the Canadian Society for the Study of Religion and Sandra Woolfrey of Wilfrid Laurier University Press for their roles in bringing this work to publication.

This book has been published with the help of a grant from the Social Science Federation of Canada, using funds provided by the Social Sciences and Humanities Research Council of Canada. Additional support was also provided by a University of Waterloo/Social Sciences and Humanities Research Council General Research Grant.

Abbreviations

AA	Aspects of Apuleius' Golden Ass
AC	L'Antiquité Classique
AJP	American Journal of Philology
AP	Amor und Psyche
BAGB	Bulletin de l'Association G. Budé
CW	Collected Works of C. G. Jung
G+R	Greece and Rome
HSCP	Harvard Studies in Classical Philology
IL	L'Information Littéraire
JHS	Journal of Hellenic Studies
JTS	Journal of Theological Studies
LCM	Liverpool Classical Monthly
MPL	Museum Philologum Londiniense
OLZ	Orientalistische Literaturzeitung
PCPS	Proceedings of the Cambridge Philological Society
PLL	Papers on Language and Literature
REA	Revue des études anciennes
REL	Revue des études latines
RPh	Revue de Philologie
SE	Standard Edition of the Complete Psychological Works of Sigmund Freud
TAPA	Transactions and Proceedings of the American Philological Association
WJA	Wuerzburger Jahrbuecher fuer die Altertumswissenschaft
ZAS	Zeitschrift fuer Aegyptische Sprache und Altertumskunde
ZDMG	Zeitschrift der Deutschen Morgenlaendischen Gesellschaft
ZPE	Zeitschrift fuer Papyrologie und Epigraphik

Introduction

In the twentieth century there have been numerous psychological interpretations of the Eros and Psyche myth. Next to the Oedipus story there is hardly another which has received more attention from depth psychologists. These interpretations have generally followed either Freudian or Jungian theories about the nature of the psyche and its development in their attempts to understand this popular story. While these interpretations have shed considerable light on the psychological ramifications of this myth, on the whole they have tended to expound and emphasize Freudian and Jungian theory at the expense of the myth's own integrity and literary context.

This work is intended to provide serious students of psychology, religion and mythology with a detailed account and analysis of what has already been accomplished in the psychological interpretation of the Eros and Psyche myth. Most psychological interpreters of this myth seem to be unaware of the larger picture of interpretation which emerges from comparing their studies with what others have done. Both Freudians and Jungians have not related their understanding of this myth to what the other school has contributed. This book aims to correct this neglect.

In this study I shall examine the strengths and weaknesses of these psychological interpretations in order to lay the groundwork for an interpretation which 1) avoids the rigidity of both Freudian and Jungian dogma, and 2) restores the myth to its rightful literary and religious context, something which has been ignored by most of the psychological interpreters. I also wish to call attention to the tendency of psychological reduction which is evident in many of these interpretations. Although Freudian sexual theory and Jungian archetypal theory illuminate certain aspects of the Eros and Psyche myth, they often cloud the potential religious meaning of the story which is presented in Apuleius' *Metamorphoses*, the larger context within which this myth lies.

The first chapter of this work will examine the origins and nature of the Eros and Psyche story in order to gain some perspective on the setting in which it arose and the literary forms which have been attributed to it. Here we shall take note of folklorists who observe that hundreds of oral versions of the tale were spread throughout Europe and beyond and consider the possible connections between these stories and the one we have received from Apuleius. We shall study the arguments for treating the story as a legend, fairy tale, allegory, myth or some combination of these literary forms. Then we shall consider two of the oldest allegorical interpretations of this story to understand the interpretive background against which modern depth psychologists approach "Eros and Psyche." The final section of this chapter examines how recent scholarship has focussed on the literary context of the Eros and Psyche story in Apuleius' *Metamorphoses* in order to counteract the tendency to emphasize only its universal aspects at the cost of overlooking its particularity.

The second chapter investigates the general method of interpreting myths psychologically by showing how closely myth interpretation follows dream analysis in both Freudian and Jungian schools. Because psychoanalysis from its origins has tended to understand myths in a similar fashion to dreams, it has recognized that myths also reflect, by analogy or symbol, important aspects of human existence. Not only is the same basic method employed in analyzing myths and dreams, but some of the same pitfalls are also evident. The rest of this chapter presents five Freudian interpretations of the Eros and Psyche myth—those of Franz Riklin (1908), J. Schroeder (1917), Jacques Barchilon (1959), Bruno Bettelheim (1975) and Fritz Hoevels (1979). It is evident that the Freudians, with one exception (Riklin), understand the story as the fantasy or dream of a girl or young woman and that Freud's psychological theory and his understanding of the term Eros as the "love instinct" have greatly influenced how all the Freudians interpret Eros in a sexual way.

The third chapter considers six Jungian interpretations of the Eros and Psyche myth—those of Erich Neumann (1956), Marie Louise von Franz (1970), Ann Ulanov (1971), James Hillman (1972), Robert Johnson (1976) and Jean Houston (1987). This chapter illustrates how the Jungians generally interpret the story as a symbolic portrait of feminine development, whether that be considered in relation to women or to feminine aspects of men. One notices that half of these Jungian interpretations are open to the religious implications of the myth, but they do not relate this spiritual meaning to the context of the story in the *Metamorphoses*. Only von Franz thoroughly treats this myth in the context of Apuleius' novel, but she does not see how it might reflect Lucius' religious experience at the end of the *Metamorphoses*.

Throughout this work we shall observe in both the Freudian and Jungian interpretations how psychological theory determines the direction of interpretation much more than does the literary context of the myth. Not only does psychological theory determine how the overall story and the major characters of the myth are interpreted, but in some cases whether certain elements of the myth are considered at all. What depth psychologists judge to be the key symbols of the myth are frequently those which best express the dynamics of their own psychological theory. In all of these interpretations we shall observe how theory guides, and to a great extent, determines the reading of the text. The striking variety of interpretations demonstrates the tendency of depth psychologists to project their own theories and preoccupations onto myths as much as it illustrates the many levels at which symbols may simultaneously operate. In a book soon to follow, I wish to build on the analytical groundwork provided here in order to develop a psychological interpretation which takes into account the numerous insights of these past studies and at the same time is faithful to the literary and religious context of this myth as it appears in Apuleius' *Metamorphoses*.

1 Origins and Nature of the Eros and Psyche Story

Origins of the Story

The best-known story from Apuleius' famous second-century book, the *Metamorphoses*, is the tale of "Eros and Psyche" which has had a great influence on literature and art in the centuries following Apuleius' life.[1] Before discussing the origins of this tale, I shall present a brief summary of the story for those who may not be familiar with its main points.

Summary of Eros and Psyche Story

A king and queen have three daughters, the youngest of whom is called Psyche. She is so extraordinarily beautiful that many people believe she is the reincarnation of Aphrodite (Venus) and some, preferring to gaze at Psyche's mortal beauty, stop visiting Aphrodite's shrine and neglect her festivals. People even address Psyche with the sacred titles that belong only to Aphrodite herself. Because of Psyche's remarkable beauty no man dares to approach her. Psyche stays at home feeling miserable and she begins to hate the beauty for which she is renowned.

The king is upset that Psyche's less beautiful sisters have no trouble finding kings to marry, while his fairest daughter has found no one at all. Imagining that the anger of the gods is somehow involved in this strange situation, the king consults the ancient oracle of Apollo, who commands that Psyche be dressed for a funeral and placed on a mountain top as a bride for a terrifying serpent.

Psyche accepts her fate with grim resignation when she realizes that Aphrodite is behind the gruesome plan. She even tries to comfort her broken-hearted parents as the bridal procession moves slowly up to the mountain top. After all have departed Psyche is finally left alone, crying and fearful. Suddenly a friendly wind arises and carries her to a lovely valley at the foot of the mountain. When she wakes Psyche walks to a nearby woods, where she discovers a magnificent royal palace. Psyche is

5

entranced by this amazing place where she finds everything she could wish for. A disembodied voice tells her that all the treasures there are for her and that after she rests she should dress in her bridal costume in preparation for the wedding banquet. During the feast food and wine appear magically and she hears a choir and celestial music though she sees no one. After this ghostly banquet Psyche goes to bed and around midnight her unknown bridegroom climbs into bed beside her. She only knows him by touch and voice since there is no light in the room and he departs before sunrise.

Psyche makes herself at home in the palace and her husband continues to visit her in the dark of night without revealing his identity. One night he warns Psyche that her sisters, alarmed at a report of her death, will approach her but she should not respond. Alone in her palace-prison every day Psyche longs for human contact and finally she forces her husband to allow her to speak with her sisters. His only condition is that she must not reveal anything about him. Psyche entertains the sisters splendidly and gives them jewels to take home but she manages to keep the secret of her husband's identity even though she tells them that he is a handsome young man. On their return home the sisters grow more and more envious as they discuss Psyche's good fortune, in contrast to their own unhappy lives, and they resolve to ruin it.

Psyche's unseen husband warns her of the sisters' treachery. He tells Psyche that they will urge her to look at his face, though if she does so, she will lose him. He also informs Psyche that she is pregnant and if she keeps the secret of his identity, their child will be a god, otherwise it will be mortal. But Psyche begs to see her sisters again and this time, in answer to their questions about her husband, she invents a different story—that he is a middle-aged merchant. With these two conflicting descriptions of the mysterious husband, the sisters begin to think that Psyche has never seen him, in which case he must be a god. They grow even more jealous, imagining that Psyche's child might also be a god.

The third time the sisters visit Psyche they tell her that her mysterious husband is really the savage wild beast spoken of in Apollo's oracle and that he will devour her when she is far into pregnancy. Horrified by their story, Psyche forgets her husband's warning and listens to their advice. They tell her to hide a carving knife and lighted lamp so that when he is sleeping she can cut off his head. Even though Psyche wavers and has doubts about this plan, she resolves to carry it through.

That night, after making love, when her husband has fallen asleep, she uncovers the lamp and lights the bed. Psyche, overcome by the sight of Eros' beauty and what she has done, tries unsuccessfully to stab herself. Spellbound, she stares at Eros and while examining one of the arrows in his quiver at the foot of the bed, she pierces her thumb and draws a few drops of blood. When she passionately embraces him, the lamp she is still holding drops oil on the god's right shoulder. Eros leaps from the bed and tries to fly away but Psyche clings to his right leg and soars with him until her strength finally fails and she tumbles back to earth. Eros lights on a cypress tree and tells Psyche how he disobeyed Aphrodite's command by taking her for his own lover instead of making her fall in love with a worthless man. He reproaches her for ignoring his warnings and listening to her sisters' lies. Psyche's penalty is that Eros leaves her. Eros also vows that the sisters will pay for what they have done.

In despair Psyche throws herself in a river to end her sorrow but a gentle wave washes her ashore. The god Pan, meeting her there, tells her to make no further attempt at suicide but rather to try to win Eros back. Psyche wanders about until she comes to the city where her eldest sister is queen. She explains what has happened and adds that Eros wishes now to marry her, the eldest sister. The sister rushes off to meet Eros, but as she leaps into the air to catch the wind that should take her to Eros' palace, she falls onto the rocks below and is cut to pieces. Psyche finds her way to the other sister and tells her the same story, whereupon this sister also tries to reach Eros' palace and is killed in the same way.

When Aphrodite learns what has happened between Eros and Psyche she is furious, vows revenge, and sends Hermes (Mercury) to make a proclamation for Psyche's capture. Psyche continues to wander in search of Eros and when she is finally brought before Aphrodite, the goddess denounces her and imposes upon her four seemingly impossible tasks. First, Psyche must sort out a heap of mixed grains before nightfall. Psyche despairs, but ants pity her and come to her rescue by sorting all the grain for her. Angry at this, Aphrodite orders a second difficult task: Psyche is to bring back wool from dangerous rams. This time a kindly reed rescues Psyche by advising her to gather wisps of wool sticking to the briars where the sheep graze. When the sheep fall asleep in the afternoon, Psyche picks their wool from the briars and returns to Aphrodite with a whole lapful of the delicate wool. Again Aphrodite suspects someone of helping Psyche so she gives her an even more severe test. Psyche must climb to the top of a high mountain and fetch a jarful of dark-coloured water from the underworld stream that bursts out of the rock of the mountain top. She is almost killed by the dreadful waters of the Styx and the deadly dragons guarding the sacred water. Suddenly the eagle of Zeus (Jupiter), who owes Eros a favor, swoops down and fills Psyche's jar for her, thus accomplishing the third task.

Now angrier than ever, Aphrodite demands the ultimate task: Psyche must descend into the realm of Hades to get some of Persephone's (Proserpina's) beauty ointment. This is tantamount to a death sentence, so Psyche mounts a high tower to commit suicide by throwing herself off. But the tower speaks to her and gives detailed directions on how to enter the underworld and avoid the terrible obstacles there. Above all, the tower warns Psyche not to look into the box containing Persephone's ointment. With great care Psyche manages to do everything perfectly but in the end, she cannot resist looking into the box. She finds that the box contains no beauty at all but only a deadly sleep. She falls to the ground and remains there until Eros flies to her and removes the lethal sleep from her body. Thus Psyche is able to complete her fourth and final task.

Eros pleads successfully with Zeus to approve his marriage to Psyche, and Aphrodite finally agrees to the match. So Hermes escorts Psyche to heaven, where Zeus hands her the cup of nectar which makes her divine. Then, with all of the gods and goddesses present, Eros and Psyche are married and enjoy a great wedding feast. In time Psyche and Eros have a daughter, whose name is Voluptas.

There has been considerable debate over the meaning of this tale and its function within the overall context of the *Metamorphoses*. Even its genre is the subject of much scholarly debate, since some see it as a folk-tale and trace its origins to the folklore of surrounding lands and peoples, while others view it as a universal myth and subject it to the allegorical and psychological interpretations of myth. While this study seeks to concentrate primarily on the psychological interpretations of the Eros and Psyche tale, it begins with a historical perspective that describes what classicists and folklorists have told us about the origins and nature of this story.

First, folklorists have discovered that there are several hundred oral variants of this tale told throughout Europe, and some examples have been found in the Near East, India, North America and the Caribbean.[2] Many scholars believe that the widespread existence of this tale indicates that Apuleius derived his account from a common story which already existed in oral or written form. Louis Purser holds that "Eros and Psyche" is an ancient tale which Apuleius heard or read and elaborated in his own peculiar style.[3] Michael Grant speculates that while there is no trace of "Eros and Psyche" in

Greek or Latin literature before Apuleius, he may have used a now-lost Greek version of the tale, or he may have introduced the names of Eros and Psyche into a current folk-tale.[4] According to Jan Swahn, the trend of scholarly opinion clearly indicates that Apuleius related a current folk-tale which had been furnished with mythological additions.[5] Swahn strongly rejects the view that a myth of Eros and Psyche existing long before Apuleius' tale can be proved to have any motifs in common with Apuleius' version. Stith Thompson explains that no one knows where and when the first "Eros and Psyche" tale was told[6] so that scholars will continue to speculate about the relationship between Apuleius' version and its many variants.

Alex Scobie concludes from his folkloric study that Apuleius' version of "Eros and Psyche" derives from a folk-tale known to him through an oral source, or even possibly a written source.[7] Scobie believes that the structure of the tale, as well as the large number of folk-tale motifs contained in it, point to the likelihood of an oral source. He suggests that Apuleius may have adapted the previously known version of the tale to produce or emphasize thematic links between Lucius' adventures in the *Metamorphoses* and the Psyche tale.

One of the most intriguing studies of the origins of this tale was done in the early part of the twentieth century by Ernst Tegethoff.[8] Tegethoff prefers the view that the Psyche tale was, in its most elementary form, the result of a dream experience. Although the story is never actually found in this particular form, he believes that the core story was a woman's dream in which she is married to a superhuman lover until her happiness is interrupted by her breaking a taboo. While many appreciate Tegethoff's contribution to the study of folk-tales dealing with the "search for the lost husband" motif, his speculation on the dream origin of this tale has not found a receptive audience.[9]

Richard Reitzenstein tried to show from Hellenic and early Christian literature, as well as from Hellenic and Egyptian *Kleinkunst*, that Psyche was originally an Oriental-Hellenic goddess.[10] He argues that Apuleius adapted an ancient myth which had been depicted by various artists. Swahn, however, rejects Reizenstein's argument on the grounds that while *some* Psyche myth may be illustrated on Egyptian ointment-pot lids and perfume jars, there is no evidence that these figures relate to the Eros-Psyche tale of Apuleius' novel. Carl Schlam agrees with Swahn that Reitzenstein's reconstructions of Eastern myths move far beyond the Eros and Psyche tale of Apuleius' novel, but acknowledges that Reitzenstein established the importance of mythic and ritual elements in connection with the Eros and Psyche figures.

Karl Kerenyi examines the Eros and Psyche tale from a history-of-religions perspective. He carefully considers Reitzenstein's proposal that the origin of the story is to be found in Iranian myth and that Psyche may originally have been a goddess. Kerenyi states that the most important phases of Psyche's tasks are in fact not in the Iranian religious texts—in particular, Psyche's journey to the underworld in search of the water of life.[11] Though Kerenyi does not deny the possibility that the Eros and Psyche tale may ultimately have an Iranian source, he places more importance on the Egyptian elements of the story. He finds the Isis myth an important key to understanding both the *Metamorphoses* as a whole and the Eros and Psyche tale.

Reinhold Merkelbach follows Kerenyi's attempt to discover the religious roots of the Eros and Psyche tale. For Merkelbach, the *Metamorphoses*, like most Greek romances, grew out of the mystery cults. In fact, he interprets the *Metamorphoses* as a mystery text in transposed form: it presents a process of initiation which re-enacts the cult myth of Isis.[12] The initiate in the Isis mysteries symbolically imitates Isis' suffering. Merkelbach attempts to show that the Psyche myth is itself a version of the Isis myth.[13] Through a complicated reasoning process Merkelbach tries to demonstrate that the Psyche story actually portrays different aspects of the goddess Isis. In this interpretation Psyche herself represents the suffering Isis who wanders through the world seeking her lost love, Osiris, while Aphrodite (the Roman's Venus) represents Isis-Tyche or Fortuna whose difficult tests are meant to lead to salvation.[14] Merkelbach recognizes Isis as the great goddess who appears in many forms, just as she appeared to Lucius in Book 11.[15] In a sense, she is the *alpha* and *omega* of the world, as well as of the Eros and Psyche story. So, for Merkelbach, the ultimate origin of the Psyche myth is another myth, the Isis myth, which was re-enacted in Apuleius' own mystery religion. Apuleius saw how the Psyche myth was symbolized in his own experience of Isis, and he drew it into the *Metamorphoses* because it reflects the Isis myth and Lucius' own identification with this myth in his initiation in Book 11. Merkelbach's attempt has left many scholars less than convinced by his reasoning.[16]

Carl Schlam points out that while there is no literary evidence of the Eros and Psyche tale prior to Apuleius' novel, there are many artistic representations of these figures that can be traced back to at least the fourth century BCE. He tried to determine from a careful study of the ancient representations of Eros and Psyche whether they illustrate the story Apuleius tells and whether they illuminate the interpretation of the tale. Schlam finds that the monuments do not illustrate any narrative and, in particular, they do not provide evidence of a Greek narrative of "Eros and Psyche" from which

Apuleius may have drawn.[17] He concludes that the representations of Eros and Psyche are essentially independent of Apuleius' version of the tale: "Apuleius transformed a folk-tale into the literary center-piece of his novel, and built into it elements of philosophic and religious allegory. He was able to do this by using a pair of figures whose symbolic significance was established by a long tradition of artistic representations."[18] With such diverse opinions about the origins of the Eros and Psyche tale it is difficult to feel certain that any one of them provides the complete answer. There are clearly elements of fairy tale, myth and ritual involved in the story and the collective contribution of the authors just cited means there may be more than a single origin of the story.

Literary Genre

Not only is there disagreement about the origin of the Eros and Psyche tale, there is considerable debate over its literary genre. Scholars debate whether it is a fairy tale, a myth, a legend, an allegory or some combination of these forms. H. Rose considers "Eros and Psyche" a fairy tale:

> Apuleius appears to have started this story with the notion of making it an allegory; the names of the principal characters suggest the human Soul (Psyche) and the divine Love which is so prominent in Platonic philosophy. But it would appear that he soon forgot his didactic purpose, and went on to tell this loveliest of fairy-tales for its own sake.[19]

He distinguishes the fairy tale from both myth and saga in saying that while these latter forms intend to find or record a truth, the fairy tale aims only at amusement, accounting for the cause of nothing and recording no historical or semi-historical event.[20] Although Rose recognizes that any given story could contain elements of all three—myth, saga and fairy tale—he finds no evidence of myth or saga in the Eros and Psyche tale.

W. Halliday agrees completely with Rose on his characterization of Apuleius' Eros and Psyche story: "though it has been dressed up by the author ["Eros and Psyche"] is genuinely a folk-tale, not a mere allegory, there can be no doubt whatever."[21] Similarly, Alex Scobie argues that "Eros and Psyche" is a fairy tale on the grounds that it is non-historical, displays no geographical exactitude and employs only the third-person form of narration instead of the first-person form used in legends. Scobie contrasts the fairy-tale form of the Eros and Psyche tale with the characteristics of legend found in the framing narrative of Lucius' adventures.

For Louis Purser, the fairy-tale character is evident from the stereotyped form at the very beginning of the tale which he translates in the traditional way: "Once upon a time there were a king and queen. . . ."[22] For this same reason Michael Grant classifies Eros and Psyche as a fairy story:

> The very first words of Cupid and Psyche let us know by their familiarity, that the sort of folk-tale with which we are concerned is the fairy-story. Fairy-stories are easier to recognize than to define. . . . Or rather, this is not a single fairy-story, but a huge conglomeration of fairy-stories and other folk-tales, many of them paralleled all over the world. Apuleius' capacity for story-telling has made him one of the most remarkable of all literary intermediaries with the anthropologist's world that lies only just below the surface of his narrative.[23]

Jungian analyst Marie Louise von Franz also considers "Eros and Psyche" to be a fairy tale. She sees fairy tales as the purest and simplest expression of the collective unconscious compared with the more elaborate forms of myth and legend which have acquired an overlay of cultural material.[24] Recognizing that certain characteristics of both myth and fairy tale apply, Karl Kerenyi finds the question of determining the exact genre of the Eros and Psyche tale so clouded that he prefers simply to call it a story (*Erzaehlung*).[25] Also seeing this ambiguity, Bruno Bettelheim classifies the Eros and Psyche tale as a myth which contains some fairy-tale-like features.[26] He argues that Psyche's becoming immortal is a critical sign that this is a myth, as such things do not happen in fairy tales. According to Bettelheim, the presence and intervention of the gods also indicate that this a myth.[27] Similarly, Carl Schlam characterizes Apuleius' version of "Eros and Psyche" as a combination of myth and folk-tale.[28]

Approaching this question from a slightly different angle, Ward Hooker classifies the Eros and Psyche story as an "allegorical myth."[29] He sees it as a neo-Platonic myth based on Socratic doctrine and disagrees with Elizabeth Haight, who holds that the Eros and Psyche story owes little to Plato. According to Hooker, Plato's definition of love in *Symposium* and the myth of the soul's progress in *Phaedrus* are the sources of Apuleius' allegory.[30] Gisbert Kranz also classifies the Eros and Psyche story as a myth.[31] While not denying the allegorical elements in "Eros and Psyche," Kranz believes that the story is essentially a myth since it goes beyond all attempts to discover allegorical meanings. For him, myth has many meanings and is higher than allegory.

While it seems that most scholars agree "Eros and Psyche" is essentially a fairy tale and not a legend, it is more difficult to distinguish it as fairy tale from myth and allegory. Even by von Franz' definitions of myth and fairy tale, there is really no evidence to show that "Eros and Psyche" exists in the "purest and simplest" state which she reserves for fairy tales as opposed to culturally overlaid myths. As for the allegorical elements of the Eros and Psyche tale, they are difficult to overlook. Even Rose and Halliday, who treat the story as a fairy tale and not as mere allegory, do not deny the allegorical dimensions of the story. It seems that Schlam's view of "Eros and Psyche" as a mixture of folk-tale and myth and Hooker's term "allegorical myth" do the most justice to the complex form of this story.

Allegorical Interpretations

The interpretation of this story until modern times has been primarily allegorical. This is probably due in part to the appearance of the Eros and Psyche myth in written form in the midst of a story about the transformation of a man into an ass. It seems that the author literally invites the reader to see much of the *Metamorphoses* as an allegorical tale. Even in the previous discussion of the genre of this story we have seen how literary scholars have highlighted the obvious allegorical features of the tale. Another reason for the primacy of allegorical interpretation of the Eros and Psyche tale is that this seemed to the ancients the best way to understand a story of such universal significance, whether it was thought of as a myth or a folk-tale.

Plutarch, who lived a generation earlier than Apuleius and made a considerable impression on him, advised precisely this kind of allegorical interpretation of myth: "We must not treat the myths as wholly factual accounts, but take what is fitting in each episode according to the principle of likeness (to truth)."[32] Plutarch interpreted myths' analogies as resemblances to important life experiences.[33] Like dreams, metaphors and analogies, allegories operate on the principle of resemblances.[34]

Before dealing with two of the most famous allegorical interpretations of the Eros and Psyche myth, let us pause briefly to consider the various functions of myth in order to see why interpreters have been drawn to this myth as a magnificent expression of life's meaning. As stories about the gods, myths often help to explain social and religious customs or some phenomenon of nature. Joseph Campbell organizes the diverse functions of myth in the following way: 1) the *mystical*, which opens the world to the dimension of mystery by showing that people address the transcendent through conditions of their everyday world; 2) the *cosmological*, which shows the shape of the universe in such a way that the mystery comes through; 3) the *sociological,* which supports and validates a certain social order, and 4) the *pedagogical,* which shows how to live a fully human life under any circumstances.[35]

This last function, which might also be called the moral or *psychological* function, refers to the way myths put the mind in accord with nature, the body, and particular stages of human development.[36] In this regard myths allow people to get in touch with their own deepest selves which, ironically, may run contrary to social or ethical norms or even to the ideological role of myth which validates a particular aspect of society. Such conflicts between a person's deepest self and social demands are often the source of severe psychological problems but Campbell believes that it is possible to find a mythological counterpart to serve as a guide through these and other problems of human development.[37] This psychological dimension of myth operates in much the same way that dreams are said to lead a person through stages of difficulty. Campbell recognizes that dreams increasingly serve this function in a society which no longer has efficacious myths of passage and transformation: "In the absence of an effective general mythology, each of us has his private, unrecognized, rudimentary, yet secretly potent pantheon of dreams."[38] Therefore, when the myths of life and transition no longer guide human beings, dreams largely assume this crucial function. Dreams can take over this guiding role of myths because, Campbell argues, they originate from the same unconscious region or symbolic universe.

> Dream is the personalized myth, myth the depersonalized dream; both myth and dream are symbolic in the same general way of the dynamics of the psyche. But in the dream the forms are quirked by the peculiar troubles of the dreamer, whereas in myth the problems and solutions shown are directly valid for all mankind [sic].[39]

In these observations Campbell builds on the great contributions of various psychoanalytic schools. Later, when examining the psychological interpretations of myth, we shall see how the psychoanalytic tradition has viewed myth as a valuable source of knowing the collective human psyche in the same way that dreams are used to understand the individual mind. Here we have briefly considered the functions of myth in order to see why philosophically minded people have read the Eros and Psyche myth as a powerful symbolic statement of Christian and Platonic philosophy. They have used this myth to emphasize the mystical dimensions of human life and, in particular, to show the way to realize the most important values in life. This use of the Eros and Psyche story represents what Campbell has called the mystical and pedagogical functions of myth.

Now we shall consider briefly two of the best known of the allegorical interpretations of the Eros and Psyche myth: those of Fulgentius and Hildebrand.[40] In the fifth century CE, Fulgentius presented the first recorded allegorical interpretation of the Eros and Psyche tale, which was considered the standard for centuries.[41] For Fulgentius, Psyche's father and mother, the king and queen, represent God and matter; Psyche and her adventures symbolize the soul, while the other two sisters stand for the flesh and free will. That Psyche is the most beautiful of the daughters means that the soul is superior to the flesh and free will. He interprets Aphrodite as lust, which envies the soul and sends desire (Eros or the Roman Cupid) to ruin her. Eros himself is both good and evil desire and in this case falls in love with the soul rather than trying to seduce it.

When Eros tells Psyche not to look at him, Fulgentius understands this to mean that Psyche should not yield to the attractions of desire by giving in to the advice of her sisters, that is, to the flesh and the will in order to gratify her curiosity. According to Fulgentius, the light shed on Eros discloses the desire in the soul and the lamp oil that injures Eros indicates how desires burn in the soul and leave behind a stain of sin. In Fulgentius' obviously Christian interpretation, Psyche's sorrowful search for Eros and her perilous tasks all follow from the soul's giving in to desire, as this is the way of disaster. Fulgentius does not finish the details of the Eros and Psyche tale after he sets up the main allegorical elements. He leaves this task to the reader.[42]

A striking feature of Fulgentius' classical allegorical interpretation is how little material it needs from the Eros and Psyche story to propel itself. There is scant attention to the details of the original story, and to a large extent, a moral story is merely substituted for the dramatic action of the original tale.[43] Aside from the names, Eros (Cupid) and Psyche, there are very few clues from the story as to where Fulgentius found the hooks on which to hang his moral retelling of the tale. One wonders what qualities of the king and queen make them resemble God and matter, or the sisters resemble flesh and free will. Though such an understanding of the symbols in the Eros and Psyche story may have seemed evident to Fulgentius, Hildebrand, whose interpretation has been called a Platonic allegory, comes up with a very different interpretation.[44]

For Hildebrand, Psyche is the pure soul as it came down from heaven, Eros represents heavenly love, and Aphrodite is fate who sends base desires and envy in the form of Psyche's sisters to remove Psyche from her initially high place.[45] Influenced by these base impulses Psyche injures love, which leaves her. In all of her trials, the soul is upheld by her longing for reunion with love, which she finally enjoys again in heaven. The union of heavenly love with the soul is the fundamental point of Hildebrand's Platonic reading. Hildebrand also sees a connection between the Eros and Psyche tale and the mysteries of Isis,[46] a theme which Merkelbach develops in great detail.

Both Hildebrand and Fulgentius see Aphrodite as a negative force on the soul, though they portray this differently. To Fulgentius Aphrodite is simply lust, while to Hildebrand she is fate and as fate she is responsible for negative impulses which infect the soul. The key difference between these two allegorical interpretations is that, for Hildebrand, Eros represents heavenly love rather than both heavenly and earthly love in Fulgentius. Here Hildebrand's Platonic vision seems to be more optimistic about the soul's original state and its relation to divinity than Fulgentius' Christian version of the tale.

These two allegorical interpretations are related to later psychological interpretations in that they use a well-developed theoretical framework to interpret the main symbolic actors and events of the story. The difference lies chiefly in the nature of the theoretical frameworks employed. The Christian and Platonic theories do not describe the structure and dynamics of the psyche in terms of specific clinical observation but rather from general observations about the meaning of human existence. The psychological interpretations generally concern themselves more with the details of the Eros and Psyche story in order to show how the dynamics of certain aspects of human development are symbolized in that tale. For example, we shall see that Fritz Hoevels shows in great detail how the story illustrates the feminine Oedipus complex, sibling rivalry and the mechanism of projection, and how Erich Neumann highlights the development of female psychology in Psyche's experiences. Generally speaking, the psychological studies are also more explicit about their methodology in dealing with the story according to a particular theory of the mind.

One of the main criticisms of allegorical attempts to understand this tale is that each interpreter explains it differently.[47] If this criticism applies to allegorical interpretations, we shall see that it applies equally to the psychological interpretations, since both the Freudian and Jungian interpretations also show a great variety of opinion on the symbolic meaning of the figures and actions in the Eros and Psyche story. There is a debate as to whether this diversity of interpretation means that all of the interpretations will necessarily be arbitrary or whether it is simply the character of myths' symbolic expression which lends itself to being understood in many ways. The latter view seems to offer a more promising direction for trying to make sense of the extraordinary variety of interpretations of the Eros and Psyche myth.[48]

When interpreters of the Eros and Psyche myth have sought a universal meaning for the story (whether that be Christian, Platonic or other), they have tended to remove the story from its literary context, and this procedure has encouraged a proliferation of meanings which seem to have little to do with the original setting of the tale in the *Metamorphoses*. One way to control this seemingly endless variety of interpretation of this myth is to ground the interpretations more firmly in the context of the *Metamorphoses*. In the next section we shall see how recent scholarship has attempted to do precisely that.

The Literary Context of the Eros and Psyche Story

In her balanced study of Apuleius' *Metamorphoses*, Paula James has succinctly characterized the shift from the early allegorical treatments of the Eros and Psyche tale to the more recent studies which keep the literary context of the story in the forefront:

> The tale of Cupid and Psyche has, in the past, been treated as a temporary transportation of the reader, as well as Lucius and Charite, away from a dark and menacing world to the realms of "happy ever after." The myth has been retold on the understanding that it can stand alone, a story in and for itself. Current scholarship, however, concentrates upon the central role of the tale of Cupid and Psyche within the *Metamorphoses* and forges a number of links between Psyche's and Lucius' spiritual journey.[49]

While James recognizes that current scholarship is in agreement on a number of links between Psyche's and Lucius' spiritual journey, she cautions that these studies sometimes overemphasize one element, namely Psyche's and Lucius' curiosity, while ignoring other equally relevant motifs involved in the parallel.

This recent trend of interpretation is important not only because it represents a considerably different approach than the old allegorical interpretations but also because it emphasizes factors which are relevant to the psychological interpretations we shall consider later. Here I would like to review briefly this current literature which emphasizes the literary context of the Eros and Psyche tale.

The many scholars who have written about the parallels between Psyche and Lucius generally agree that Psyche's story is related to Lucius' life but they differ considerably on exactly how and to what degree. Carl Schlam points out that literary studies have demonstrated the often-disputed unity of Apuleius' novel precisely by highlighting themes common to both Lucius' and Psyche's adventures.[50] Similarly, Alex Scobie sees the parallel between Psyche and Lucius as central to the structure of the *Metamorphoses*: "... the nuclear tale of Cupid and Psyche ... not only refracts and recapitu-

lates Lucius' adventures up to the point at which the tale is introduced, but also looks forward to their happy conclusion."[51] Scobie
sees this recapitulation particularly in the misfortunes of Lucius. Just
as Psyche incurs the anger of Aphrodite, so Lucius must struggle
against cruel fortune.[52]

James Tatum stresses more than most commentators the summarizing role of the Eros and Psyche story:

> The elaborate series of explicit warnings that Cupid gives his
> wife in Book 5 resembles the rather subtler ones that crossed
> Lucius' path in Books 1-3. This part of the tale is a clear indication
> that we are going back over some of the same ground we covered
> in those earlier books, but at a more abstract and allegorical
> level.[53]

Tatum contends that when Psyche opens the beauty jar she is trying
to discover some kind of transcendental power, just as Lucius did in
Book 3. Tatum emphasizes that the Psyche tale mirrors what has
already happened to Lucius as well as key elements in his character,
namely, curiosity and guilelessness.[54] Moreover, Tatum highlights
the parallel between Psyche's torment by Aphrodite and Lucius' trials by unpredictable fortune. R. Van Der Paardt also stresses that the
Eros and Psyche tale cannot really be understood outside the context
of the frame narrative. He agrees with Scobie that this tale summarizes Lucius' experience and anticipates his future developments.[55]

Frances Norwood does not agree with those who say that the parallels between Psyche and Lucius help to unify the novel. Nevertheless, she does recognize that curiosity brought both of them to grief,
and she states: "Psyche is Lucius in Fairyland."[56] G.N. Sandy echoes
this view when he says that the Eros and Psyche story is a fairy-tale
version of Lucius' experience.[57] Like Norwood, Sandy focusses particularly on the way curiosity is the undoing of both Psyche and
Lucius, but he cautions against ignoring the differences which exist
between Lucius and Psyche.[58] For John Griffiths, too, curiosity plays
a large role in fusing the experiences of Psyche and Lucius.[59] According to Griffiths, Psyche's trials and dangers foreshadow Lucius'
experiences, and her tasks anticipate aspects of Lucius' initiation.[60]
Ronald Brown, on the other hand, underscores the *religious significance* of the parallel between Psyche and Lucius. He points out that
Eros warns Psyche against "sacrilegious curiosity" and contends
that this applies to both Psyche and Lucius, who dare to enter the
realm of the holy on their own initiative.[61] Contrary to those who
note a fundamental difference between the curiosity of Psyche and
Lucius, Brown insists that their curiosity is identical in its essence,
since both seek to pass beyond human limitations.[62]

Richard Hooper also calls attention to the religious implications of the Eros and Psyche myth and he highlights very well the relationship of this myth to the frame narrative: "The tale of Cupid and Psyche is not an allegory about love or a stylish myth inserted for relief from the bandits' cave: it is a miniature version of the whole novel, and a careful foreshadowing of its religious significance."[63] For Hooper, interpreting the Eros and Psyche myth as a miniature of Lucius' story clarifies certain elements in the myth which would otherwise be pointless. He sees Psyche's first three tasks as initiations paralleling Lucius' three initiations, and he notes that Psyche's journey to the underworld mirrors Lucius' descent to hell in the course of his initiation into the mysteries of Isis.[64]

Jan Trembley agrees with these views of the religious significance of the Eros and Psyche myth, and she interprets the tale as a portrait of human experience at a divine level. She argues that Psyche's story illustrates Lucius' symbolic death through religious initiation and his union with the divine as an initiate.[65] Furthermore, Psyche represents, in mythical terms, Lucius' credulity and sacrilegious curiosity about the supernatural. Trembley notes a significant parallel between Psyche's opening the box (*pyxis*) filled with divine beauty and Lucius' secretly viewing the witch with her box (*pyxis*) filled with magic ointment.[66]

The parallels between the Psyche tale and Lucius story also form the basis of Reinhold Merkelbach's complex interpretation. Like other commentators, he recognizes that Psyche and Lucius both suffer from curiosity and undergo a difficult period of wandering. But for Merkelbach, the key to understanding the Eros and Psyche tale is the symbolism of Lucius' initiation into the Isis mysteries.[67] In "Eros und Psyche" he gives a detailed account of how various elements in the Eros and Psyche tale are symbolic representations of Lucius' life and, especially, his initiation into the cult of Isis. Here I shall mention only a few of the many parallels Merkelbach draws.

First, Psyche's call (to marriage) is delivered through an oracle of the god, Apollo, while Lucius' call (to initiation) comes through a dream oracle of the goddess, Isis. According to Merkelbach, the lamp Psyche uses to illuminate the god, Eros, refers to the lamp as a holy object in the Isis cult, which is mentioned in the description of the Isis procession that Lucius experiences in Book 11 of the *Metamorphoses*.[68] Further, Merkelbach notes that Psyche first sees Eros at night, which anticipates Lucius' night-time initiation.

Psyche's sisters, furthermore, correspond to those who are not initiated into the Isis cult. Merkelbach understands Eros' command to tell the sisters nothing as a reference to the religious vow of secrecy, designed to keep the holy mysteries from outsiders.[69] When the sis-

ters seek to approach the god Eros without being invited, they fall to
their deaths. Merkelbach sees this as a clear reference to the priest's
warning in Book 11 that those who dare to be initiated without being
called by the goddess face certain death.[70]

Merkelbach explicitly links Psyche's final task, her journey to the
underworld, to Lucius' initiation. For him, the box of beauty ointment which Psyche must not open symbolizes the *cista mystica*,
which is spoken of in the description of the Isis procession in Book
11. Moreover, Merkelbach finds that Psyche's eagerness to open the
box, even though it will probably lead to her death, is like Lucius'
experience of initiation as a voluntary death (*voluntaria mors*). For
Merkelbach, the paradox of new life coming from death is involved
both in the taboo surrounding the box of beauty ointment in Psyche's story and in the *cista mystica* in the Isis mystery.[71]

Finally, Merkelbach sees Psyche's deification at the end of the Eros
and Psyche myth as a reference to the high point in Lucius' initiation, when he is decorated like the sun god. In the ritual, death and
rebirth are symbolized, and the initiate hopes that through the
power of the mysteries he will overcome physical death at the end of
his life. According to Merkelbach, this makes the initiate immortal
and godlike, which is exactly what Psyche's divination symbolizes.[72]

Carl Schlam focusses on three main parallels between the Eros and
Psyche tale and the frame narrative[73] : 1) Psyche's fall through curiosity is similar to Lucius' fall through lust and curiosity about magic;
2) Psyche's wanderings in search of Eros and her trials are like
Lucius' misfortunes as he passes from owner to owner in the body of
an ass; and 3) Psyche's redemption through Eros anticipates Lucius'
redemption by Isis. According to Schlam, these incidents in the Eros
and Psyche tale and the language used to describe them prefigure
the account of Lucius' initiation given in Book 11.

Schlam notes in particular the parallel between the way both Psyche and Lucius are saved by divine initiative.[74] Schlam maintains
that the parallel between Psyche and Lucius helps to bring out the
religious significance of the Eros and Psyche tale. Here Schlam
develops a point Franz Dornseiff made in 1938. Dornseiff noted a
close symbolic relationship between the Psyche story and Lucius'
experience, precisely in regard to the religious meaning of both
stories.[75] Dornseiff maintained that it was Apuleius' conscious intention to use the Eros and Psyche tale as a symbolic parallel for the
entire novel.

Schlam, like Merkelbach, interprets Psyche's last task, her descent
to the underworld, as a form of voluntary death, which is also seen
in Book 11 when Lucius undergoes the rites of initiation into the
mysteries of Isis. Schlam draws out the parallel:

These rites are interpreted as symbolizing the course of existence
of the initiate who passes through the misery of the world into a
new life under the protection of the *Fortuna videns* (Bk. 11, 15). She
extends a haven in this world and the promise of bliss in the here-
after. As Psyche is joined to Eros in marriage, so Lucius the *mystes*
takes on the role of *Osiris* joined to the goddess by sacred bonds.
The fruit of this union is joy.[76]

In Schlam's work there is no doubt about the importance of the parallels between Psyche and Lucius. We have already seen that
Merkelbach has emphasized more than anyone this initiatory meaning of the Psyche tale. Schlam disagrees with the way Merkelbach
has used the great variety of artistic representations to support his
interpretation of the Eros and Psyche tale as a refashioning of the
myth of Isis and a symbolic record of the process of initiation, but he
agrees that there are symbolic elements of initiation rites in the tale
and he views Psyche's symbolic initiation as a prefiguration of
Lucius' own initiation experience.

 W. Walsh is emphatic about the close relationship between Lucius
and Psyche. He also believes that significant parallels can be
observed between the trials of Psyche and Lucius' initiation into the
cult of Isis.[77] He cites the similarities Schlam discussed, namely:
1) the fall of both Psyche and Lucius through curiosity, 2) Psyche's
and Lucius' wanderings, 3) Psyche's and Lucius' redemption by
divine powers, and 4) Psyche's journey to the underworld as prefiguring Lucius' initiation. Walsh also adds that Psyche's child, Voluptas, represents Lucius' mystical joy as the consequence of his union
with the goddess Isis:

> After successfully performing these tasks, Psyche is united with
> Cupid in the company of the gods, and the fruit of their union is
> *voluptas*; this union reflects that special relationship of Lucius with
> Isis which after initiation is represented as apotheosis, and which
> brings Lucius *inexplicabilis voluptas*. In this sense Apuleius has
> made the histories of Lucius and of Psyche converge.[78]

Precisely in the context of Lucius' initiation, the figure Voluptas
takes on great importance in the Eros and Psyche tale.[79]

 Paula James calls attention to the general parallel themes of a similar fall through inquisitiveness, wandering and redemption, but also
adds some particulars not frequently cited. For example, she sees
Psyche's entrance into Eros' palace as a "replay in fantasy form" of
Lucius' arrival at his aunt's (Byrrhaena's) courtyard in Bk. 2, 5.[80]
James also notes that, like Lucius with Byrrhaena, Psyche fails to
heed Eros' prophetic warnings. But James also adds that there are

significant differences between the stories of Lucius and Psyche. In regard to the frequently mentioned theme of curiosity, she holds that Lucius' sustained desire for knowledge is not really akin to Psyche's momentary lapses with Eros and with Persephone's box.[81] For James, Psyche's curiosity, as a function of her *simplicitas*, is unlike Lucius' quest for magic and mystery.

Another commentator who argues for limits to the parallels between Psyche and Lucius is J. Penwill. While he recognizes that Psyche's tale generally mirrors Lucius' experience, he insists that this does not turn the Eros and Psyche story into a mere restatement of the *Metamorphoses'* main theme.[82] Like James, he does not see a close parallel between Psyche and Lucius in regard to their fall through curiosity.[83] He points out that after a disastrous experience with magic, Lucius is no longer interested in it, while Psyche continues to desire to see Eros despite the prohibition against doing so.[84] Another contrast Penwill notes is Psyche's and Lucius' experience of prayer. He points out that the Olympian goddesses refuse to help Psyche because they do not want to offend Aphrodite, while the Queen of Heaven mercifully comes to Lucius' rescue.[85]

Penwill takes exception to the view that Psyche's underworld journey mirrors Lucius' initiation. For Penwill, the difference lies in the effect of this underworld journey on Psyche and Lucius. He believes that Psyche has learned nothing through her journey because she is still motivated by a desire to please Eros, which according to Penwill, indicates the continuing dominance of irrational desire. Lucius, on the other hand, has learned to hold in check rash curiosity as shown by the care with which he keeps the secrets of his initiation.[86] Finally, Penwill finds a great difference between the "redemption" of Psyche and that of Lucius. In a striking passage he claims that Psyche is not redeemed at all:

> There is no sense of spiritual or mental development in Psyche: rather she goes downhill in both areas as she becomes more and more infatuated with Cupid. . . . Immortality for Psyche in a world controlled by Jupiter is thus contingent upon her being bound to Cupid. And when we compare the way in which Lucius' soul will achieve immortality *tenacibus castimoniis* ("with persevering chastity"), we realize that we are not dealing with a *redemption* but a *fall*.[87]

Penwill's Platonist interpretation may be unduly negative but it raises important questions about the relationship of the Eros and Psyche tale to Lucius' adventures.

This recent literature emphasizes the priority of the literary context for any interpretation of the Eros and Psyche myth. Some of the psychological interpretations we shall consider make an effort to observe the literary setting of the myth, but generally they tend to ignore precisely that which seems so prominent in recent advances in the literary understanding of the Eros and Psyche tale. Part of the reason for this lies in the traditional psychological approaches to myth. Psychoanalysts tend to look at myths as collective and even universal phenomena. Sigmund Freud sums up very well this approach when he speaks of myths as the dreams of early humanity.

> The study of constructions of folk-psychology is far from being complete, but it is extremely probable that myths, for instance, are distorted vestiges of the wishful phantasies of whole nations, the secular dreams of a youthful humanity.[88]

Both Otto Rank[89] and Carl Jung[90] refer to myths as "collective dreams," again emphasizing their general application and meaning. When psychoanalysts focus on a myth's universality, they are less likely to examine the specific context in which the story appears and, in fact, such a particular setting may seem to detract from the universal message of the myth. We may recall from our discussion at the start of this chapter that such definitions of myth as "collective dreams" reveal that in the psychological interpretation of myth there is an important link with dream interpretation. In the next chapter we shall explore this connection in greater detail before examining the psychological interpretations of the Eros and Psyche myth.

Notes

1 See E. Haight, *Apuleius and His Influence* (London, 1927).
2 S. Thompson, *The Folktale* (Berkeley, 1977), p. 99. Also see J. Wright ("Folk-Tale and Literary Technique in 'Cupid and Psyche,'" *Classical Quarterly* 21 [1971] 273-84) who shows which motifs are literary additions to the underlying elements of folk-tale material in "Eros and Psyche." D. Fehling diverges from the general view that there were at least oral versions of the Psyche tale pre-existing Apuleius' story.
3 *The Story of Cupid and Psyche* (London, 1910), p. li.
4 *Myths of the Greeks and Romans* (New York, 1962), p. 363.
5 *The Tale of Cupid and Psyche* (Lund, 1955), p. 377.
6 *The Folktale*, p. 99.
7 *Apuleius and Folklore* (London, 1983), p. 39.
8 *Studien zum Maerchentypus von Amor und Psyche* (Leipzig, 1922).
9 See J. Swahn, *The Tale of Cupid and Psyche* (Lund, 1955), pp. 398-403, and S. Thompson, *The Folktale* (Berkeley, 1977), pp. 99-100.
10 "Das Maerchen von Amor und Psyche bei Apuleius," in *AP*, pp. 87-158, and "Eros und Psyche in der aegyptisch-griechischen Kleinkunst," in *AP*, pp. 159-74.
11 *Die Griechisch-orientalische Romanliteratur in Religionsgeschichtlicher Beleuchtung* (Darmstadt, 1973), p. 192.

12 A detailed account of his approach is found in *Roman und Mysterium in der Antike* (Berlin, 1962).

13 Ibid., pp. 8-53.

14 In "Eros und Psyche" (*AP*, p. 395) Merkelbach states his complicated thesis concisely: "Der Psychemythos bringt die verschiedenen Aspekte der Goettin zur Darstellung, indem er sie in zwei Personen aufspaltet. Psyche, das ist die leidende Isis, deren mythische Schicksale der Myste nacherlebt. Venus, das ist Isistyche, die Herrin, die grausam scheint und den Menschen am Ende doch zur Seligkeit fuehrt, wenn er ihr treu gedient hat" ("The Psyche myth presents the different aspects of the goddess by splitting her into two persons. Psyche represents the suffering Isis, whose mythical destinies the initiate recapitulates. Venus represents Isis as Fate, the mistress who seems cruel, yet in the end leads a person to salvation if he/she has served her faithfully").

15 Although this may not be clearly Isis in this situation, there can be no doubt in relation to Lucius' future who the great goddess is. In the context of the *Metamorphoses* she is definitely Isis.

16 Carl Schlam evaluates Merkelbach's work this way: "Merkelbach draws upon a wide variety of artistic representations, but he uses them in a haphazard manner, without grounding his interpretation of individual monuments in their appropriate context of time and place" (*Cupid and Psyche: Apuleius and the Monuments* [University Park, PA, 1976], p. 44).

17 Ibid., p. 30.

18 Ibid., p. 40. Regarding the quest for the origins of the Eros and Psyche tale, also see G. Heinrici's "Zur Geschichte der Psyche: Eine religionsgeschichtliche Skizze," in *AP*, pp. 56-86. He relates the tale to the Isis mysteries, Platonic thinking and Gnosticism.

19 *Handbook of Greek Mythology* (London, 1953), p. 287.

20 Ibid., p. 287.

21 *Greek and Roman Folklore* (New York, 1927), pp. 99-100.

22 *The Story of Cupid and Psyche* (London, 1910), p. xlv.

23 *Myths of the Greeks and Romans* (New York, 1962), p. 363.

24 *Problems of the Feminine in Fairytales* (Irving, TX, 1979), pp. 1-2.

25 "Ich bevorzuge diese neutrale Bezeichnung [die Erzaehlung von Amor und Psyche] vor 'Mythos' und 'Maerchen,' obwohl beide Termini ihr auch unabhaengig von einer genetischen Beurteilung zukommen: 'Mythos' ist die Geschichte da sie mehr goettliche als menschliche Personen hat; als 'Maerchen' wird sie einem alten Weibe in den Mund gelegt" ("I prefer this neutral designation [the story of Amor and Psyche] to 'myth' or 'fairytale' although both terms could apply independently from a genetic point of view: myth as a story which has more divine than human persons; as a 'fairytale' it comes from the mouth of an old woman") (*Die Griechisch-orientalische Romanliteratur*, p. 191).

26 *The Uses of Enchantment: The Meaning and Importance of Fairy Tales* (New York, 1977), p. 294.

27 Ibid. p. 294.

28 "Sex and Sanctity: The Relationship of Male and Female in the 'Metamorphoses,'" in *AA*, p. 99.

29 "Apuleius' 'Cupid and Psyche' as a Platonic Myth," *Bucknell Review* 5 (1955): 38.

30 Ibid., p. 34.

31 "Amor und Psyche: Metamorphose eines Mythos bei C.S. Lewis," *Arcadia* 4 (1969): 287.

32 J. Griffiths' translation of Plutarch's *De Iside et Osiride* (Cambridge, Eng., 1970), p. 211. While some hold that allegorical interpretations imply that a myth is not true, Griffiths points out that this need not be the case. Griffiths argues that Plutarch seemed to believe in the historicity of the Osiris myth even while he valued allegorical interpretation. See J. Griffiths' introduction to Plutarch's *De Iside et Osiride*, pp. 100-101.

As an indication of Plutarch's importance for Apuleius, at the outset of the *Metamorphoses*, Lucius says that he has the distinction of being descended from Plutarch through his mother's family.

33 J. Griffiths points out that the original Greek sense of allegory implies a meaning other than the one which is immediately apparent ("Allegory in Greece and Egypt," *Journal of Egyptian Archaeology* 53 [1967]: 89).

34 In the oldest allegorical interpretations of the Eros and Psyche myth we shall see many examples of how this principle of resemblances is applied. For a specific instance of how metaphors operate symbolically through resemblances see my "Metaphorical Language," in *Flesh as Transformation Symbol in the Theology of Anselm of Canterbury* (Lewiston, NY, 1985), pp. 161-68.

35 *The Power of Myth* (New York, 1988), p. 31.

36 Ibid., p. 70.

37 Ibid., pp. 142-43.

38 *The Hero With a Thousand Faces* (New York, 1973), p. 4.

39 Ibid., p. 19.

40 See Hildebrand's review of the various allegorical interpretations of the Eros and Psyche tale in his edition of Apuleius' works: *Opera*, vol. 1 (Hildesheim, 1842), pp. xxviii-xxxviii.

41 See K. Dowden, "Psyche on the Rock," *Latomus* 41 (1982): 338. Here I am using L. Purser's translation of Fulgentius' text.

42 P. Walsh draws interesting conclusions about the meaning of the Eros and Psyche tale given Fulgentius' interpretative framework: "On the original interpretation, the finale would have demanded a reconciliation of the soul with lust and the soul's eternal marriage with desire! But much Christian typology is allusive rather than sustained, and Fulgentius presumably sees the close of the myth as representing man's reconciliation with God" (*The Roman Novel* [Cambridge, Eng., 1970], p. 219).

43 P. Grimal sees Fulgentius' allegorical interpretation as largely arbitrary and foreign to Apuleius' own understanding of the tale: "Mais l'exigèse de Fulgence ne persuade guère. L'ensemble de son interprétation fait une grande place aux idées chrétiennes, trop évidemment étrangères à Apulée, et l'on ne peut échapper à l'impression qu'elle est en grande partie arbitraire, imaginée peut-être par Fulgence lui-même" (*Apulei, Metamorphoses IV, 28-VI, 24: Le Conte d'Amour et Psyche* [Paris, 1963], p. 7).

44 K. Dowden, "Psyche on the Rock," p. 340.

45 Hildebrand, *Opera*, vol. 1, p. xxxvi.

46 Ibid., pp. xxxvii-xxxviii.

47 See Louis Purser's *The Story of Cupid and Psyche* (London, 1910), p. xliv.

48 Ann Ulanov and Jean Houston are two of the psychological commentators who have reflected on the multi-leveled nature of myth interpretation, and both emphasize that all great myths unfold on many levels which do not necessarily exclude each other. See Ulanov's *The Feminine in Jungian Psychology* (Evanston, IL, 1971), p. 215, and Houston's *The Search for the Beloved* (Los Angeles, 1987), p. 151. For Gisbert Kranz, this multi-meaning quality of myths makes them more valuable than simple allegories. See his "Amor und Psyche: Metamorphose eines Mythos bei C.S. Lewis," *Arcadia* 4 (1969): 287. Also see Carl Schlam, "Sex and Sanctity: The Relationship of Male and Female in the *Metamorphoses*," in *AA*, p. 99.

49 *Unity in Diversity* (Hildesheim, 1987), p. 120.

50 Antonie Wlosok's "Zur Einheit der Metamorphosen des Apuleius" (*Philologus* 113 (1969): 68-84), is a good example of this type of study.

51 "The Structure of Apuleius' *Metamorphoses*," in *AA*, p. 53.

52 Ibid., p. 53.

53 *Apuleius and "The Golden Ass"* (Ithaca, NY, 1979), p. 56.

54 Ibid., pp. 511-12.

55 "Technique in Apuleius' *Metamorphoses*," in *AA*, p. 81. William Nethercut also notes that the Eros and Psyche tale looks ahead to Lucius' future. See "Apuleius' Literary Art: Resonance and Depth in the *Metamorphoses*," *Classical Journal* 64 (1968): 118.

56 "The Magic Pilgrimage of Apuleius," *Phoenix* 10 (1956): 8.

57 "Knowledge and Curiosity in Apuleius' *Metamorphoses*," *Latomus* 3 (1972): 180.

58 "Book 11: Ballast or Anchor?" in *AA*, p. 129.

59 "Isis in the *Metamorphoses* of Apuleius," in *AA*, p. 149.

60 Ibid., p. 149.

61 "The Tales in the 'Metamorphoses' of Apuleius: A Study in Religious Consciousness" (Ph.D. thesis, Florida State University, 1977), p. 100.

62 Ibid., p. 101.

63 "The Structural Unity in the *Golden Ass*," *Latomus* 44 (1985): 399.

64 J. Beaujeu also calls attention to the parallel between Psyche's tasks and Lucius' initiation in "Sérieux et frivolité au 11e siècle de notre ère: Apulée," *Bulletin de l'Association Guillaume Budé* (1975): 89.

65 "The Beloved Self: Erotic and Religious Themes in Apuleius' *Metamorphoses* and the Greek Romance" (Ph.D. thesis, Princeton University, 1981), p. 84.

66 Ibid., p. 84.

67 "Eros und Psyche," in *AP*, p. 398.

68 Ibid., p. 400.

69 Ibid., p. 399.

70 Ibid., p. 401.

71 Merkelbach explains the paradox involved in the *cista mystica* symbolism in the following terms: "Aber die Oeffnung der cista mystica hat wieder einen doppelten Sinn: sie bezeichnet die Uebertretung des Gebotes und gleichzeitig die hoechste Weihe. Dies ist weniger paradox als es scheint. Das hoechste Sacrament ist verboten, denn es ist gefaehrlich, ja todbringend. Aber dem von Gott Gerufenen eroeffnet es ein neues Leben. Der Anblick der geheiligten Gegenstaende fuehrt die Kommunikation mit der Gottheit herbei. Indem er Toetet, macht er unsterblich." ("But opening the mystical vessel again has a double meaning: the transgression of the command becomes at the same time highest consecration. This is less of a paradox

than it seems. The highest sacrament is forbidden because it is dangerous, even lethal. But for one called by God, it inaugurates a new life. Seeing the sacred objects brings about communication with the divine. While it kills, it makes immortal.") Ibid., p. 404.

72 Ibid., p. 404.

73 *Cupid and Psyche: Apuleius and the Monuments* (University Park, PA, 1976), p. 3.

74 "Sex and Sanctity: The Relationship of Male and Female in the 'Metamorphoses,'" in *AA*, pp. 99-100.

75 Dornseiff expresses it this way, in "Lukios' und Apuleius' Metamorphosen," *Hermes* 73 (1938): 222-33: "Fall, Leiden, Umherirren und Muehsale, die ihnen durch die boese Macht auferlegt werden, und endliche Erloesung durch die hoechste Gottheit: das ist der im tiefsten Grunde religioese Inhalt beider Erzaehlungen" ("Fall, suffering, wandering and hardship are imposed by the evil force, but finally there is redemption by the highest divinity: this is the religious content, in the deepest sense, of both stories") (p. 223).

76 Schlam, "Sex and Sanctity," p. 35.

77 "Lucius Madaurensis," *Phoenix* 22: 146.

78 Ibid., p. 192.

79 To anticipate somewhat, we shall see that Voluptas is a figure that all of the Freudian interpreters ignore. Even where Bettelheim and Hoevels recognize the relevance of sexual initiation to the tale, they do not relate the result of that initiation, Voluptas, to the psychological state of the female initiate. In their interpretation, the tale is principally a symbolic record of a woman's initiation and not the story of a man's mystical union with a goddess.

80 *Unity in Diversity*, p. 128.

81 Ibid., p. 130.

82 "Slavish Pleasures and Profitless Curiosity: Fall and Redemption in Apuleius' Metamorphoses," *Ramus* 4 (1975): 50.

83 R. Heine also emphasizes that Psyche's curiosity is different from that of Lucius in *Untersuchungen zur Romanform des Apuleius von Madaura* (Goettingen, 1962), p. 136.

84 "Slavish Pleasures and Profitless Curiosity," p. 56.

85 Ibid., pp. 56-57.

86 Ibid., pp. 57-58.

87 Ibid., pp. 58-59. Penwill's view is very different from E. Haight's, who says that the Eros and Psyche tale seems to forecast Lucius' conversion, where he is worshipped as a god. See *Essays on Ancient Fiction* (New York, 1966), p. 193.

88 "Creative Writers and Daydreaming," *SE* IX, p. 152.

89 *Birth of the Hero*, p. 9.

90 *CW* 5, pp. 28-29.

2 Psychological Approaches to the Eros and Psyche Myth: Freudian Interpretations

Interpreting Myths and Dreams

From the perspective of dream interpretation we can gain a clearer understanding of what psychoanalysts are trying to do when they interpret myths. Just as they use dreams to shed light on the inner world of the individual person, so they study myths for clues about the psychological and spiritual life of entire cultures or even humanity as a whole. Both myths and dreams are viewed as symbolic stories which reveal these deep, unconscious dimensions of human experience.[1] The key to unlocking the meaning of both myths and dreams is the ability to identify similarities, and this was at least partially understood even in the ancient world.

According to Aristotle, the basic principle for understanding dreams is to notice similitudes or resemblances. In "Dream Divination" he says:

> He, however, is a judge of dreams according to the most consummate art, who is able to survey similitudes. . . . I say similitudes because phantasms occur in dreams similar to images in water . . . he is the best interpreter of dreams who can similarly discern the similitudes in these.[2]

Similitudes, like analogies, show correspondences between different things. In dreams we frequently experience a symbolic portrait of our existence, our inner life and our life in the external world. These images and stories frequently show what a person's life looks like from a symbolic point of view. For example, in dreams one's life may be "like climbing a mountain" or "like exploring the dark caverns below the earth." Such are the images dreams furnish to reveal another, deeper perspective on the meaning of life experience.

Psychotherapists and psychoanalysts who interpret myths have long recognized how closely dreams resemble myths. In fact ancient mythical themes often appear in the dreams of contemporary persons. Freud observes this in his *New Introductory Lectures*:

In the manifest content of dreams we very often find pictures and situations recalling familiar themes in fairy tales, legends and myths. The interpretation of such dreams thus throws a light on the original interests which created these themes, though we must at the same time not forget, of course, the change in meaning by which this material has been affected in the course of time. Our work of interpretation uncovers, so to say, the raw material, which must often enough be described as sexual in the widest sense, but has found the most varied application in later adaptations.[3]

Freud notes that mythical themes often appear in contemporary dreams and that interpreting such dreams can shed light on the nature of those mythical themes. According to Freud, the reason for this connection between myths and dreams lies in the common source of their symbolism, the unconscious.[4] Because of the similarities between the symbolic language of myth and dreams, Freud believed that many of the insights he had about the nature of dreams could be applied to understanding myths.

In Freud's dream interpretation, the goal is to get beneath the manifest content, the dream as it is remembered, in order to discover the latent content, those underlying dream thoughts which have been disguised in the dreamwork. Because Freud considers dreams to be the hidden fulfillment of repressed wishes, he supposes that unconsciously the dreamer censors forbidden wishes by distorting them. Consequently Freud believes that the characters and actions in a dream are merely the starting point for discovering what initially inspired a particular dream. The essential dream thoughts are converted into the manifest dream images and actions by means of the dreamwork mechanisms, the principal ones being condensation, displacement, and dramatic representation.

For Freud, *condensation* explains how the original dream thoughts are longer than the dream as remembered. The manifest dream omits some elements from the latent dream and condenses other elements into a single image.[5] With *displacement*, feelings, attitudes or meanings attached to an element in the latent dream change as this element enters the manifest dream.[6] Freud maintains that displacing the emotional charge or importance of a latent dream element distorts and disguises the underlying dream wish so that the ego does not have to face the latent dream wish in its original and unacceptable form. *Dramatic representation* consists in transforming thoughts, feelings and other inner experiences into visual images and sensory experiences.[7] This dreamwork process is the foundation of the subjective interpretation of dreams because it justifies treating dream elements as aspects of the dreamer's personality and, in Freud's view, many of these dream symbols reflect the dreamer's attitudes and feelings about various aspects of sexuality.[8] This sexual cast of symbols applies to myths as well as dreams since both originate in similar unconscious processes.

Freud's dream analysis reverses the dreamwork by moving from the manifest dream back toward the latent dream thoughts through a process of free association. The dreamer says whatever comes to mind in relation to each dream image or action and this chain of association leads wherever it will, no matter how far it might diverge from the manifest dream. These associated memories, images and feelings expand to form the psychological network that underlies the original manifest dream, and this web of associations is the frame of reference which the analyst uses to discover what aspect of the dreamer's life the dream is commenting upon.

Freud also considers the events of the day immediately preceding the dream in order to determine what latent dream thoughts are behind the manifest dream. He says that in every dream we can find a point of contact with experiences of the previous day (the "day's residues"), even though these recent impressions frequently escape waking memory.[9] The dreamer's present circumstances and life history offer further context within which dream symbols can be understood. In his analytical practice, Freud used the latent dream thoughts along with the patient's other communications in order to reconstruct forgotten childhood experiences, which he believed underlie the person's neurosis.

For Freud and his followers the close parallel between dreams and myths means that myths also 1) have a manifest and a latent content, 2) symbolize psychological states and events, and 3) frequently express sexual attitudes and feelings. In "Traum und Mythus, Eine Studie zur Voelkerpsychologie," an early statement on the relationship between dream and myth, Karl Abraham expands on the similarities between myths and dreams.[10] He points out that myths originate from the distant past of a people, what might be thought of as the childhood of a people, just as dreams go back to the childhood wishes of an individual.[11] Like dreams, where the dreamer only seldom understands the latent meaning behind the manifest dream, so people rarely understand the latent meaning behind myths.[12] For Abraham this inability to understand the original sense of the myth is due to mass repression (*Massenverdraengung*) in the same way that repression prevents the individual from penetrating manifest dream content.[13] Just as with elements in the manifest content of dreams, so elements of myths may be overdetermined (*ueberdeterminiert*), that is, a figure or symbol in the myth may refer to more than one element in its latent content or underlying meaning.

Abraham also sees wishfulfillment and various elements of dreamwork, such as secondary revision or displacement, as part of myths.[14] He summarizes these similarities by saying that the dream is the myth of the individual.[15] Like Freud, Abraham believed that the latent material of myths is of a sexual nature. For Abraham, the myth grows out of sexual fantasies; it does not express religious or philosophical ideas about the origins and nature of human existence and the cosmos. He says that just as children don't come into the world with an altruistic ethic, so early man had no religious or philosophical ideas.

For Otto Rank myths are the *dreams* of a whole people and this justifies using the techniques of dream analysis to interpret myths:

> The manifestation of the intimate relationship between dream and myth—not only in regard to the content but also as to the form and motor force of this and many other, more particularly pathological, psyche structures—entirely justifies the interpretation of the myth as a dream of the masses of the people, which I have recently shown elsewhere.[16]

Rank attributes the striking similarity between myths and dreams to their common origin in the human imagination.

Theodore Reik is another Freudian analyst who holds that the fantasies behind myths are similar to those motivating dream formation:

> Psychoanalysis explains the myth as the distorted relics of the wish fantasies of the people. . . . But the wish impulses which the myth, when interpreted, reveals as its basis, are similar to those which create the dream. They arise from the conflicts of the childish psyche.[17]

Reik goes on to specify the psychological dynamics of internal family life as the ambivalent attitude toward parents and siblings, libidinous impulses and ambitious tendencies, and these elements, he maintains, "are always found to be the essential content of mythical narratives."[18] Reik interprets Otto Rank's principle that the psychologist must believe in the psychic reality of myth to mean that he must believe that myths have a meaning, regardless how absurd they seem on the surface. The fundamental principle of interpreting both myths and dreams is to assume that they are meaningful despite the often bizarre appearance of the manifest content. So we must take myths seriously even though they may at first appear unintelligible.

For Reik, myths represent the psychological dynamics of the ancestors, "a picture of the secular repression of the age that gave it (the myth) birth."[19] By applying to myths the same techniques as dream interpretation Reik believes that we can perceive the hidden meaning which lies behind the gods, heroes and dragons. Reik speaks disparagingly of myth's mystical potential:

> But the myth itself proceeded on its way, gradually absorbing all the vital forces of religion and morality. What was once the elementary expression of the wildest instinctual force has become, in the course of countless generations, the vehicle of profound meaning and the ripest morality.[20]

He views the religious dimension of myths as a development of the personified powers of Nature into gods and demons; for him, myths do not put people in touch with divine or transcendent realities.

This Freudian line of myth interpretation, based largely on insights from dream interpretation, has had a rich history.[21] Of course, the psychoanalytic interpretation of myth has had its detractors, such as classicist H. Rose, who makes a sweeping negative judgment of this psychoanalytic enterprise:

> Hitherto, even allowing the truth of the main positions taken up by the psycho-analytic school with regard to the composition of the human mind, I have failed to find in its writings a single explanation of any myth, or any detail of any myth, which seemed even remotely possible or capable of accounting for the development of the story as we have it.[22]

This appears to be an extreme statement in light of all the psychoanalytic materials listed by N. Kiell and J. Glenn in their comprehensive survey of the literature. There is no indication in Rose's critique that he includes the Jungian attempts to understand myth, but I suspect that he would, due to certain basic similarities between Freud's and Jung's approach to myth.

Like Freud, Carl Jung emphasized the dreamlike character of myth and considered that the original myth-makers thought in the same way we dream. Jung cites with approval from Friedrich Nietzsche's *Human, All Too Human,*

> In sleep and in dreams we pass through the whole thought of earlier humanity. . . . What I mean is this: as man now reasons in dreams, so humanity also reasoned for many thousands of years when awake. . . . This atavistic element in man's nature still manifests itself in our dreams. . . . Dreams carry us back to remote conditions of human culture and give us a ready means of understanding them better.[23]

Jung also appreciates Freud's idea that myths are the "dreams of youthful humanity" as well as Rank's view of myth as the collective dream of a whole people.[24] However, Jung has serious doubts about Abraham's notion that myth originates from the "infantile" psychic life of the race for he considers myth to be the most mature product of humanity's youth.

In terms of Jung's own analytical psychology, he sees myths as projections from the deepest layers of the unconscious. For Jung, archetypal figures from the collective unconscious are projected into legends, fairy tales and myths in the same way constellations were once projected onto the stars. Even today such projections continue to occur in peoples' dreams, although they are not found in all dreams, but primarily in those dreams which people feel are particularly important and contain a general meaning.[25] Jung notes that in so-called primitive communities dreamers feel bound to announce these "big dreams" to the tribal assembly and even in ancient Rome such dreams were sometimes announced to the Senate. Jung finds it completely appropriate that people instinctively tell such mythological dreams because they express a collective human truth and do not belong exclusively to the individuals who dream them.[26]

Because Jung treats myths like dreams, I shall briefly consider his dream theory in order to understand his approach to myths. Jung does not believe that dreams intend to conceal, but rather to reveal a meaning.[27] According to Jung, the unusual characteristics of the manifest dream such as transformations, condensations, discontinuities and absurdities are simply features of symbolic language. Unlike Freud, who believed that these distorted thoughts of the manifest dream were designed to hide the real meaning of the dream, Jung valued the details of the manifest dream and tried to plumb the depths of each symbol therein.

Jung speaks of circumambulating (walking around) each manifest dream symbol to describe the way he carefully sifts through associations to each symbol.[28] The story given in the manifest dream, however fractured or absurd it may seem, is always the context for interpreting dream symbols. This context of the manifest dream guides the associations which the dreamer brings to dream symbols. Circumambulation, or directed association (rather than free association) to dream symbols continues to revolve around the way they operate in a particular dream story. If the dreamer is unable to come up with personal associations to the dream symbols, then the analyst may draw upon cultural and mythological associations, but these associations must be referred back to the specific context of the dream story and to the dreamer's life story.

Jung's attention to the dramatic structure of the dream report is another aspect of his concern with the manifest content. He carefully observes the actors, setting and plot development of the dream.[29] For Jung, the crucial point in any dream is the place where a major change in the action occurs, and he looks for the point of plot resolution as a clue to the meaning of the dream. Jung studies the dreamer's present circumstances to provide further context for interpreting dreams. In this regard Jung's method is like Freud's. The personal context of the dream helps to determine whether dream figures and symbols are to be understood at the subjective level of interpretation, as aspects of the dreamer's personality, or at the objective level, as referring to people or events in the external world.

Jung did not consider a dream interpretation to be complete until he discovered its compensatory function.[30] According to Jung, dreams compensate for the often one-sided attitudes of the waking mind, so he always wanted to know what new perspective a dream was adding to the dreamer's viewpoint. Dreams draw upon the broad network of the unconscious, which takes into account the experience and wisdom of the past as well as anticipations of the future, in order to relativize the often narrow here-and-now preoccupations of the dreamer's conscious mind.

Many of these points of dream interpretation apply to Jung's treatment of myth. The dramatic structure of the myth is important, as are the details about the actors, setting and plot development. Jung also states that myths, like dreams, usually compensate the conscious situation: "Thus we know that dreams generally compensate the conscious situation, or supply what is lacking to it. This very important principle of dream-interpretation also applies to myths."[31] But here it is not clear to which conscious situation he refers. Since he views myths as collective dreams, it is likely he means the conscious situation of an age or a whole people, though we must inquire further whether this refers to the popular self-understanding of a people or that of the rulers and historiographers. In regard to the Eros and Psyche myth this might refer to the Roman Empire of the second century CE or even to the ancient Greco-Roman world in general. A fundamental difference between myths and dreams is that with myths there is no dreamer to provide the personal context for interpreting the myth in the form of the dreamer's present circumstances and personal associations to the dream symbols. Actually, this is not entirely the case with the Eros and Psyche myth, because it is given a narrative context in the *Metamorphoses* which could make it the equivalent of Lucius' dream. Marie Louise von Franz has proposed this creative hypothesis, and in a future book I shall attempt to form my own interpretation of the Eros and Psyche tale around this hypothesis.

Franz Riklin

The first psychoanalyst to treat the Eros and Psyche story was Franz Riklin. At that time in his career Riklin's psychological orientation was Freudian and this can be observed throughout his book on fairy tales entitled *Wishfulfillment and Fairy Tales.*[32] For Riklin the central psychological characteristic of the Eros and Psyche tale is wishfulfillment. The "wish structure" of the story begins with the magical zephyr carrying Psyche off from the rocky mountain where she was left alone to wait for a terrible serpent who was to marry her. There is then a complete turnabout, as the expected marriage of death turns into a magnificent adventure in which Psyche becomes the queen of a beautiful castle. Riklin compares this dramatic turn of events to the dream or wish fantasy of a psychotic. Instead of the imminent death she feared, she finds a place where all her wishes are magically fulfilled. According to Riklin, this is exactly like the thought processes of some of his psychotic patients when they try to escape from difficult situations through dreams and fantasy.

Throughout his brief treatment of the Eros and Psyche tale Riklin calls attention to parallels between this story and certain hallucinatory phenomena he has observed in psychotic patients. For example, he finds the disembodied voices of the servants in Psyche's extraordinary castle like psychotic auditory hallucinations.[33] In both cases, voices are heard but no person is seen as the source of the sounds. That Psyche cannot see Eros in her dark bedroom at night also reminds Riklin of the hallucinatory perceptions (tactile hallucinations) of one of his patients who experienced a "connubial embrace" every night.[34] This patient, too, could feel, but could not see, a lover in the darkness.

Riklin even finds the talking tower which comes to Psyche's rescue like a "teleological hallucination," telling a psychotic what to do, and Psyche's tasks remind him of the dreams of mentally disturbed people. Aside from focusssing on pathological and wishfulfilling aspects of the Eros and Psyche story, Riklin emphasizes the sexual elements in fairy tales: "Fairy tales have a predilection to deal with various sexual motives. . . . These motives follow from the psychological sexual inclination, especially manifested in dreams, between father and daughter, son and mother (Oedipus saga!)."[35] Riklin does not develop the Oedipal elements in the Eros and Psyche tale as far as two other Freudian interpreters (Bettelheim and Hoevels) do, but he notes aspects of sexual initiation involved in the story. Riklin interprets Psyche's marriage of death as a vestige of virgin sacrifice and the light she uses to view Eros in bed as a symbol of discovering sexual secrets.

To gain greater clarity in understanding the psychological dynamics involved in Riklin's interpretation, it might be useful to view his reading of the myth in relation to Freud's picture of the "psychical personality." Freud offered a diagram of structural relations of the mental personality (see Diagram 1) in his *New Introductory Lectures on Psychoanalysis.*[36]

Diagram 1

EXTERNAL WORLD

Perception – Conscious (Pcpt–Cs)

SUPER EGO

Preconscious (Precs.)

EGO

Unconscious

Repressed

ID

Essentially this diagram shows that the ego is related to the external world through the perceptual system (pcpt-cs), that the id is unconscious, composed mainly of repressed material and relates to the external world through the ego (as the preconscious and conscious) and that the super ego merges into the id as a kind of instinctive conscience.

Now in Riklin's interpretation, Psyche herself would represent the vantage point of the ego, and in this particular case, the ego of a psychotic. Riklin characterizes her experiences in the course of the story as wishfulfillments which emanate from the unconscious. Instead of the psychotic's ego dealing with difficult situations in the external world, it escapes into the world of the unconscious. Riklin describes this mode of escape in Psyche's case as hallucinations which are projected onto the outer world. The magic castle itself might be considered as the overall context of projected unconscious contents by which the psychotic escapes a threatening reality. In this case, the wish to have every need taken care of is projected into the environment as the voices of servants in the magic castle. Freud's id can be seen as the source of this wish to be taken care of.[37] Diagram 2 shows how these dynamics might appear in relation to Freud's diagram.

Diagram 2

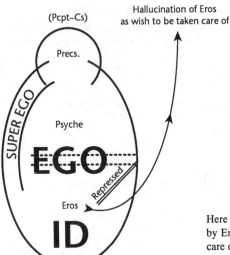

(Pcpt–Cs)

Hallucination of Eros
as wish to be taken care of

Precs.

SUPER EGO

Psyche

EGO

Repressed

Eros

ID

Here the unconscious contents (represented
by Eros loving Psyche in the dark and taking
care of her every need) are projected as hallucinatory phenomena.

The sexual impulses which dominate the id are at the basis of the psychotic's projection of the lover in the dark. For Psyche to be able to feel Eros in the darkness is, for Riklin, the mythical expression of this projection of the psychotic's deep unconscious, so that the patient actually experiences this as if it were happening in the external world. Riklin does not indicate whether he views the "psyche" symbolized in the Eros and Psyche myth as female or male. He does not specify if it makes a difference whether the lover embraced in the night by the psychotic patient is male or female, nor does he indicate the sex of the patient he has in mind for his example of this hallucinatory phenomenon. Given that in the myth the god projected into the outer world is Eros, a male, we might expect that Riklin's patient was a female.

One problem with Riklin's interpretation is that he treats the Eros and Psyche myth in total isolation from its literary context in the *Metamorphoses*. Combining Freud's theory about the prominence of wishful thinking in the unconscious with his own observations of psychotic patients, Riklin reads the Eros and Psyche story almost as if it were a case history of psychosis. Given the literary context of this myth in the *Metamorphoses*, it is difficult to see where he discovers the basis for this interpretation. Although Riklin does not explicitly refer to the origin of his particular ideas about the Eros and Psyche myth, it is remotely possible that he might have been influenced by reading the frame narrative of Lucius being changed into an ass as an example of a psychotic delusion. More likely, his interpretation is based on haphazard observations of some similarities between his patients and certain features of this myth. In any event, Riklin certainly does not take Apuleius' story of religious transformation as the basis for his reading of the Eros and Psyche myth. For Riklin, as for all of the Freudian interpreters, Voluptas, the daughter born to Psyche and Eros at the end of the tale, does not figure into the psychological interpretation.

Riklin interprets Psyche's marriage to a god as a typical "psychic, sexual wish structure" which occurs to psychotics and Christian mystics alike. In his book Riklin sees no possibility that the god Eros might refer to a real deity or, at least, to a divine aspect of the human being. Everything is lumped together for him: marriage to a god in mythology is like sexual wishfulfillment in psychosis which is like union with the divine in religious mysticism. He cites the mystic marriage of St. Catherine as an example of a Christian mystical "wish structure" as if it were merely another instance of the kind of psychotic hallucination symbolized in Psyche's marriage to Eros. This kind of automatic reduction of religious experience to pathological wishfulfillment ignores the vast difference in inner meaning between these two kinds of experience. The Christian mystic's ability to integrate the powerful impact of the mystical marriage into his or her overall world view would be a key factor in causing us to hesitate before equating such a transformative experience with serious pathology.[38] In the psychology of religion, William James would measure the value and validity of such a religious experience by the inner meaning it has for the individual and the consequences it has on all aspects of the person's life. As James pointed out long before Riklin disclosed his view of the mystic marriage, the "fruits," not the "roots," determine the validity and character of a religious experience. Judging from James' standard, even a person with a clinical psychosis could conceivably have a genuine religious experience. While Riklin shows considerable creativity in his hypothesis about a certain unmistakable element of wishfulfillment contained in the Eros and Psyche myth, he quickly associates that wish structure with severe psychopathology in such a way that the positive aspects of the myth are virtually ignored. Because he dismisses religious mysticism as a psychotic, sexual wish structure, he is also unable to appreciate the mystical potential of the Eros and Psyche myth.

J. Schroeder

Another of the early psychoanalytic interpretations of the Eros and Psyche tale is J. Schroeder's *Het Sprookje van Amor en Psyche in het licht der Psychoanalyse* (1917) which considers the Eros and Psyche myth as a variation on the motifs of Andromeda and Melusina.

Schroeder views Psyche's marriage of death as reminiscent of the Greek myth about Andromeda.[39] Just as Andromeda was tied to a rock awaiting a sea-monster sent by Neptune, so Psyche was left alone at the top of the hill waiting for the serpent spoken of in Apollo's oracle. Aphrodite's jealousy of Psyche also echoes Neptune's wrath against Andromeda's mother, who boasted that she was more beautiful than Juno. Schroeder sees the timeless psychological significance of this mythical marriage to a monster as a symbolic portrait of an adolescent girl's initial fear of the male's sex drive. At first the girl unconsciously pictures the unknown aspects of sexual love as something monstrous, but once her initial anxiety is overcome, she learns to see the would-be monster in a different light.[40]

Schroeder also focusses on the theme of the lover's disappearance in the Eros and Psyche story, which he calls the Melusina motif. Here he refers to the tale of the fairy princess Melusina, from whom the kings of Albania are said to be descended. As a punishment for having shut her father in a mountain, Melusina was changed into a snake from the waist down every Saturday and she could be released from this punishment only if she married a man who never saw her in serpent form. She found such a man, but one day when his curiosity was aroused by her unusual ways, he looked at her while she was bathing and consequently she fled in her serpent form. In Schroeder's view, Melusina's situation is very much like the crucial lamp scene where Psyche breaks the taboo against seeing the god Eros, thereby causing him to depart and thus ending her paradise of love with him. When Eros (a god) disappears as a result of Psyche (a mortal) looking at him, this is directly parallel to the way Melusina (a fairy) disappears when her husband (a mortal) looks at her.

Besides amplifying the traditional motifs of the marriage to a monster and the disappearance of the lover, in order to illuminate the Eros and Psyche myth, Schroeder builds on Ludwig Laistner's hypothesis that basic folk-tale motifs originate in dreams.[41] In Das Raetsel der Sphinx, Laistner concentrates primarily on the nightmare motifs found in folk stories. Schroeder applies Laistner's theory to the Eros and Psyche tale. For Schroeder, both the Eros and Psyche tale and the Melusina story are nightmares insofar as the lover disappears when a taboo is broken. The sudden, shocking sense of loss is at the heart of these nightmares. Unfortunately, Schroeder merely broaches the subject of the nightmare and dream aspects of the Eros and Psyche story but does not develop them or go into detail about their psychological significance.

As with Riklin, Schroeder does not seek to place his commentary on the Eros and Psyche myth in the context of Apuleius' *Metamorphoses*. Clearly he is concerned about the *universal significance* of the myth, as can be seen in his attempt to draw parallels between it and important motifs in mythology and folklore. In Schroeder's interpretation of the Eros and Psyche story as an erotic dream he takes the point of view that it deals with a girl's anxiety, and this could conceivably refer to Charite in the context of the *Metamorphoses*. Charite, just as she was preparing for her wedding, was kidnapped by bandits who then held her for ransom. She had just fallen asleep from weariness and depression in the bandits' cave when she dreamed the whole kidnap scene again, only in her dream her bridegroom follows the bandits and is killed by one of them. When Charite wakes from this nightmare she is hysterical, and in an effort to comfort her, an old woman who works for the bandits tells her the story of Eros and Psyche. So it is conceivable that this tale reflects Charite's own situation, and from Schroeder's perspective on the myth's origin from a common nightmare motif, it might even appear that he is attempting to ground his interpretation in the literary context of Apuleius' novel. But surprisingly, he does not connect the typical nightmare motif of the disappearance of the lost lover to Charite's nightmare in the frame narrative, even though it is immediately juxtaposed with the old woman's telling of the Eros and Psyche tale. Precisely the point that he is making about the nightmare motif of the lost lover is exemplified in the story which Apuleius' uses to introduce this myth. But because Schroeder is more interested in the underlying psychological meaning of the myth in relation to a girl's sexual anxiety, he ignores this immediate literary context and goes on to the more general mythical parallels and the way they shed light on female sexual attitudes.

Again using Freud's diagram of the psychical personality, Diagram 3 pictures Schroeder's interpretation of the psychological dynamics of the Eros and Psyche myth. Schroeder sees the marriage-to-a-monster theme as dealing primarily with a girl's sexual anxieties. In terms of Freud's revised view of anxiety, there are potentially three aspects to Schroeder's interpretation.[42] In Schroeder's view the girl's anxiety is symbolized in Psyche's story as the fear of being married to a monster. In the first part of the myth this is taken literally as a result of the oracle of Apollo. This is the aspect of the myth Schroeder focusses on when he emphasizes its mythological parallel with Andromeda. The girl fears the as-yet-unknown lover as a monster, and for Schroeder, this fear is tied to a girl's apprehensions about the male's differentness, especially as this is symbolized by the penis. This situation has some aspects of realis-

Diagram 3

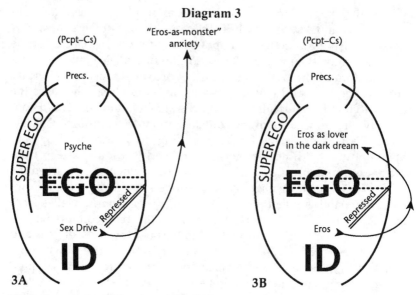

These diagrams show the story as (A) a girl's (Psyche's) anxiety fantasy where repressed aspects of her sex drive are projected onto a male (Eros) who appears as a monster, and (B) a girl's (Psyche's) dream where she projects fulfillment of id wishes in a dream and then her phantom lover (Eros) disappears.

tic anxiety in that the girl's fear is based on a potentially real situation which might involve pain in losing her virginity. Also her fear might depend on the particular man who is to be her husband. In some cases experiencing the husband as a monster is undoubtedly realistic anxiety. But in the Eros and Psyche story, the anxiety proves to be closer to neurotic anxiety. In neurotic anxiety repressed aspects of a woman's sexual drive may be projected onto the male as something fearful. Here Eros, in the tale, would appear as an aspect of the id which is both repressed and projected onto a man or men in the external world.

Insofar as Schroeder sees the Eros and Psyche tale as an erotic dream, or rather, an erotic nightmare, Eros as a woman's lover in the night is very much an expression of her own sexual drive. Here Schroeder has in mind not the marriage-of-death scene, but rather the phantom-lover-in-the-magical-castle scene. Freud's definition of dream as the "hidden fulfillment of a repressed wish" sheds light on Schroeder's understanding of this myth as a dream, since the wishful element is so strong in the Eros and Psyche myth. We have already seen how Riklin emphasizes this wishful element in the magic castle, although he relates it to pathological processes in the unconscious rather than to ordinary dream formation.

For Schroeder, however, the Eros and Psyche myth is more connected to normal than abnormal unconscious activity. The substance of this myth as a dream wish is the lover who appears in the night. Eros symbolically expresses certain id impulses in a woman, her unconscious wish for a lover. The nightmarish aspect of the dream is tied to the taboo against seeing the lover and the disappearance of the lover as a result of her breaking the taboo. Whether Freud's theory of the dream censor has something to do with this taboo or with triggering the nightmarish disappearance of the lover due to mounting sexual anxiety, Schroeder does not speculate. The Eros and Psyche myth as nightmare may also express a certain degree of moral anxiety (symbolized by the taboo as pressure coming from the woman's super ego) but Schroeder does not explicitly refer to this aspect of a woman's anxiety. He only calls attention to the general way in which the Eros and Psyche myth appears to be like a nightmare. Schroeder effectively highlights the nightmare aspect of this myth and calls attention to parallels in the Andromeda and Melusina stories, but like Riklin he neglects the literary context of this story in Apuleius' *Metamorphoses*. He also ignores the psychological symbolism involved in Aphrodite, Psyche's sisters, Voluptas and Psyche's tasks.

Jacques Barchilon

Jacques Barchilon treats the Eros and Psyche tale as a version of the Beauty and the Beast story, which means he focusses primarily on the fear that Eros is a beast or monster in disguise. In our look at Schroeder's ideas about the marriage-to-a-monster motif, we saw that this aspect of the tale comes to the fore both in the marriage-of-death sequence, where a serpent husband is to take Psyche, and in the part of the story where Psyche's sisters portray Eros as a monster and devouring serpent. In "Beauty and the Beast: From Myth to Fairy Tale," (1959) Barchilon interprets the "taboo against seeing the husband" as the struggle of an adolescent who passes from an innocent state of mind to a confused state primarily because of her struggle with the matter of sexual love.[43]

When Psyche's sisters elaborate on their fantasies about the monstrous aspect of Psyche's husband, Barchilon sees this as an attempt to disguise, yet at the same time emphasize, the sexual dimension of Psyche's relationship to Eros.[44] According to Barchilon, this whole sequence deals with a traditional attitude which considers sex as beastlike in order to reinforce the taboo against expressing or even acknowledging infantile sexuality.[45]

The adolescent wrestles within herself to overcome this negative childhood attitude toward sex (here represented by Psyche's sisters) so that mature sexuality can eventually be accepted as a normal part of life. For Barchilon, the fact that in Apuleius' novel the Eros and Psyche story is told to comfort a young bride who has been kidnapped further supports his view that the tale is really about the adolescent crisis of a young woman struggling to develop a healthy attitude toward sexual love. Here Barchilon differs markedly from Riklin's view that this story primarily illustrates wishfulfillment and pathological processes, but he is very close to Schroeder's focus on the marriage-to-a-monster motif.

Barchilon also points out how aspects of the Oedipal drama are portrayed in the Eros and Psyche story. He interprets both characters, Eros and Psyche, as children trying to deal with conscious and unconscious attitudes toward their parents. In Barchilon's view, Eros' betrayal of his mother shows how a son's original attachment to his mother must be severed in order for him to love a woman. This is particularly important for Eros, because his mother is portrayed as incestuously attached to him when she kisses him fervently. This viewpoint sheds further light on Aphrodite's attempts to hang on to her son, Eros, as well as her growing hostility toward Psyche, as the rival who is pulling her son away from her.

In considering the mother-son relationship, Barchilon even adopts the viewpoint that the lover-in-the-dark motif in the first part of the Eros and Psyche myth is Eros' attempt to solve his dilemma of how to keep his mother happy and still have a lover on the side.[46] Barchilon interprets the lover-in-the-dark situation as Eros' attempt to hide Psyche from his mother. Here he does not understand this as a part of the "looking taboo" motif (a view which he did adopt earlier when he examined the story from Psyche's standpoint), but rather as an aspect of Eros' relationship with his mother. From this point of view, he interprets Psyche's tasks, which keep her separated from her lover, as Aphrodite's way of punishing her son as well as Psyche.

By adopting this perspective, Barchilon tries to understand the myth from Eros' point of view. This would make Eros the ego and Psyche the object of his sexual desires or id. He tries to satisfy his sexual needs, as Barchilon puts it, to fulfill a dream, while at the same time satisfying the demands of his conscience, or super ego, which is influenced by his mother, Aphrodite. If we attempt to diagram the psychological dynamics of this situation using Freud's picture of the psyche, we find that it might look like Diagram 4.

When Barchilon says that Eros keeps Psyche hidden in the magic castle, away from everyone, to fulfill a dream, this might appear as Eros' projection of his id impulses onto the dream screen during sleep. This would appear to be a variation on the nightmare of the disappearance of the lover which Schroeder described in his work,

Diagram 4

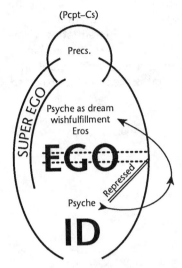

(Pcpt–Cs)

Precs.

SUPER EGO

Psyche as dream
wishfulfillment
Eros

EGO

Repressed

Psyche

ID

This diagram shows Eros as the subject (ego) and Psyche in the magic castle is a projection of his sexual impulses in a dream.

only here the nightmare ends with Eros getting burnt by the oil of Psyche's lamp and having to fly away. It is Aphrodite, as an influence on Eros' super ego, who forces Eros to dream his wishfulfillment rather than to act it out in reality. In Barchilon's speculation about the mother-son relation, Eros is not yet ready to act out his wish because it would force him to confront his mother consciously and sever his excessively close bond to her.

Now from the vantage point of Psyche, Barchilon argues that she must deal with her fears about "the beast that is her father" when Eros ravishes her.[47] Although there is little in the Eros and Psyche story itself which indicates that Psyche experiences her father as a beast and that this is a source of her sexual anxiety about her marriage to Eros, Barchilon draws on aspects of the Oedipal drama which derive from psychoanalytic theory rather than what is given in Apuleius' text. Barchilon presents the psychoanalytic reasoning this way:

> But we know that the Beast is a double symbol. It is at the same time the stern father she may unconsciously fear because she is in love with him (as she should not be) and the kind father, whence the gentleness of the Beast. The monster contains both images; it is the father provider after she has left her real father, and it is the father lover whom she fears in her unconscious and who does have a terrible appearance (as he would be symbolized if she dreamed of making love to her father).[48]

Barchilon, like Riklin, does not expand upon these Oedipal elements in the Eros and Psyche story, so we are left with only hints about the psychological dynamics of the tale as it would be understood from Psyche's point of view. If we were to diagram this situation (Diagram 5, using Freud's picture of the psyche), it would be similar to Schroeder's view of the myth as a portrait of a woman's sexual anxieties. There we saw that the woman's sexual drive may be projected onto the male as something fearful.

Diagram 5

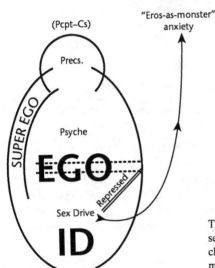

This diagram illustrates a woman's (Psyche) sexual anxiety. Repressed aspects of Psyche's own sexual drive are projected onto a male (Eros) who then appears as a monster.

Barchilon's explanation helps to clarify this situation. He sees that society fosters, or at least supports, a taboo or an attitude that sex is dangerous and beastlike in order to keep the child's sexual drive in check. Given this attitude, the child's ego cannot yet integrate her own sexual impulses, and one of the most common ego defences is to project unconscious and unacceptable tendencies onto someone in the external world. According to Barchilon, the child projects this fearful, beastlike aspect of sexuality onto both her father and her future husband.

As I mentioned in relation to Schroeder's interpretation of the myth as a portrait of a woman's sexual anxiety, these dynamics of ego defence may be more or less pronounced, depending on the degree to which this anxiety is neurotic or realistic.[49] In any event, projection is a normal psychological mechanism (ego defence) and, to some degree, it appears that, like Schroeder, Barchilon has presented a plausible version of the psychological dynamics at work in this myth. But, as with Riklin and Schroeder, Barchilon does not attend to the literary context of the Eros and Psyche myth, and he also neglects the psychological meaning of Pyche's tasks and Voluptas.

Bruno Bettelheim

In *The Uses of Enchantment* (1975) Freudian analyst Bruno Bettelheim interprets "Eros and Psyche" as a story about the development of mature consciousness, the difficulty of joining wisdom and sexuality, and the problem of sexual anxiety. He also sees some aspects of Oedipal love involved in this story, especially Aphrodite's possessive jealousy of her son, but Bettelheim does not emphasize this. Overall, his interpretation is very optimistic about the psychological potential of human development as it is presented in the Eros and Psyche tale.

When Psyche breaks the taboo by using the lamp to see Eros in the darkness, Bettelheim understands this as an attempt to expand her consciousness before she is ready for it:

> The story warns that trying to reach for consciousness before one is mature enough for it or through short-cuts has far reaching consequences; consciousness cannot be gained in one fell swoop. In desiring mature consciousness, one puts one's life on the line, as Psyche does when she tries to kill herself in desperation. The incredible hardships Psyche has to endure suggest the difficulties man [*sic*] encounters when the highest psychic qualities (Psyche) are to be wedded to sexuality (Eros).[50]

Here Bettelheim emphasizes the dangers involved in developing consciousness. Psyche's repeated decisions to kill herself in order to end her despair at the prospect of completing her seemingly impossible tasks symbolically express the depression which frequently accompanies psychological development. For Bettelheim, a primary aspect of this development is the integration of sexuality with the highest aspirations of consciousness. He insists that nothing less than a spiritual rebirth is required to bring together these seemingly opposite aspects of the human being. The troubled relationship between Eros and Psyche symbolizes the difficulty involved in this integrative process, and Psyche's journey to the underworld dramatically portrays the powerful experience of rebirth which precedes and helps to bring about this hard-won integration.

There are valuable insights in this line of interpretation, but it would have been useful for Bettelheim to explain in greater detail how he arrived at certain aspects of his commentary. For example, he does not explain where in the text we might find suggestions that Psyche represents the "highest psychic qualities," or that Eros is simply sexuality. We might imagine from the meaning of the Greek word "psyche" that she represents the soul or the mind, but not necessarily the highest psychic qualities. And what "highest qualities" does he have in mind? Wisdom? A highly developed intellect? A powerful intuition? A decisive or strong will? In regard to Eros, we may grant Bettelheim that there is clearly an association with erotic love, but the word "eros" also has the more general meaning of "connectedness" which Jungian analysts have stressed so much. The point is not that Bettelheim is necessarily wrong, but that he does not provide textual support for his interpretation.

Bettelheim, like the other psychological interpreters we have seen thus far, does not attend to the specific literary context of the myth, but is more concerned with a "universal" meaning which can be drawn from it. He considers the Eros and Psyche story as merely one example of the general animal-husband theme in fairy tales. This emphasis on universal motifs is reminiscent of Schroeder's search for parallels in the Andromeda and Melusina stories and it results in a similar neglect of literary context. Bettelheim views the animal-husband in these tales as a symbol of a girl's sexual anxieties:

> To begin with, the prediction that Psyche will be carried off by a horrible snake gives visual expression to the inexperienced girl's formless sexual anxieties. The funeral procession which leads Psyche to her destiny suggests the death of maidenhood, a loss not easily accepted. The readiness with which Psyche permits herself to be persuaded to kill Eros, with whom she cohabits, indicates the strong negative feelings which a young girl may harbor against him who has robbed her of her virginity.[51]

According to Bettelheim, the value of the animal-husband tales, including the Eros and Psyche story, is that they assure children that their fear of sex as something beastly is not unique to them[52] and that sexual anxiety, which is often implanted by others, frequently turns out to be unfounded:

> Stories about the animal-husband assure children that their fear of sex as something dangerous and beastly is by no means unique to them; many people have felt the same way. But as the story characters discover that despite such anxiety their sexual partner is not an ugly creature but a lovely person, so will the child. On a preconscious level these tales convey to the child that much of his anxiety is implanted in him by what he has been told; and that matters may be quite different when one experiences them directly, from the way one sees them from the outside.[53]

So when Psyche discovers that her lover is not the monster she feared but a magnificent god, this reassures people on a subconscious level that sex is not beastly but potentially beautiful.[54] In this reasoning Bettelheim goes a step beyond Schroeder and Barchilon, who more or less use the Eros and Psyche myth to illustrate the dynamics of projection as a girl's way of dealing with her sexual anxieties. Bettelheim stresses more than these other two commentators the role of society in generating sexual anxiety in children and the positive unconscious role which the Eros and Psyche myth and other animal-husband tales have in offsetting such anxiety.

Although Bettelheim focusses primarily on Psyche's breaking of Eros' taboo as a symbol of her premature grasping for consciousness, he also attempts to discover the meaning of this taboo in relation to Eros. Bettelheim sees Eros' taboo as an attempt to keep his sex life separated from everything else he does when he is not with Psyche, but Psyche refuses this isolation of the sexual aspects from the rest of life. This appears close to Barchilon's interpretation, which claimed that Eros sought to satisfy his need for a lover while still keeping his mother from knowing about the relationship. In both Barchilon's and Bettelheim's interpretations, Eros' taboo can be seen as an attempt to benefit himself, to keep his situation from being consciously examined, and to avoid facing the conflict necessary to solve the problematic situation. But Bettelheim also recognizes the positive dimension of Eros' striving as an important move to gain independence from his possessive mother. It is by going his own way, defying his mother, and being involved with Psyche, that he gradually reaches a higher state of consciousness.[55] Just as with Barchilon's dual perspective on Eros' taboo, it is not clear from Bettelheim's presentation exactly how these two interpretations of the taboo sequence fit together, the one being from Psyche's viewpoint and the other from Eros' viewpoint. It would appear that they are complementary perspectives and that they may both be valid psychological interpretations.

While Bettelheim's interpretation is close to Schroeder's and Barchilon's notion that this tale deals with an adolescent girl's sexual anxieties, it appears to be far from Riklin, who considers the Eros and Psyche story to closely parallel the hallucinatory wishfulfillments of psychotics. In contrast to Riklin's emphasis on the pathological, Bettelheim interprets the tale as a symbolic portrait of the fullest possible human development: "Not physical man, [sic] but spiritual man must be reborn to become ready for the marriage of sexuality with wisdom ... wedding of the two aspects of man requires a rebirth."[56] This emphasis on the spiritual implications of the Eros and Psyche tale resembles more the Jungian interpretations we shall examine in the next section than the other Freudian approaches to this tale.

Bettelheim's interpretation of the Eros and Psyche myth using Freud's diagram of the psyche is shown in Diagram 6.

Diagram 6

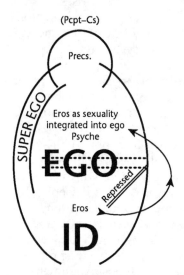

In this diagram the marriage of Eros and Psyche symbolizes the integration of sexuality (Eros as part of the id) with the ego (Psyche).

For Bettelheim, Psyche primarily symbolizes the ego, and particularly the developed, conscious aspects of the ego. This follows from his view that the myth is about the development of consciousness. It is not entirely clear whether Bettelheim restricts this description of development to one gender, but there is reason to believe that he does relate the Eros and Psyche myth primarily to the female's perspective:

> Despite all warnings about the dire consequences if she tries to find out, woman is not satisfied with remaining ignorant about sex and life. Comfortable as an existence in relative naivete may be, it is an empty life which must not be accepted. Notwithstanding all the hardships woman has to suffer to be reborn to full consciousness and humanity, the stories leave no doubt that this is what she must do.[57]

Here Bettelheim seems to emphasize the *female's* path of development, but he broadens his focus when he goes on to indicate how the female's development is usually inextricably bound up with a corresponding development in the male:

Once woman has overcome her view of sex as something beastly, she is not satisfied with being kept merely as a sex object or relegated to a life of leisure and relative ignorance. For the happiness of both partners they must have a full life in the world, and with each other as equals. That, these stories convey, is most difficult to achieve for both, but it cannot be avoided if they wish to find happiness in life, and with each other.[58]

He does not indicate whether he believes there are specific differences between men and women in the course of psychological development, but there is little in his interpretation of this myth to suggest such a difference. Eros would be seen as part of the id, especially the sex drive. In the diagram, the wedding of Psyche and Eros symbolizes the integration of sexual impulses by the ego. For the ego, this acceptance of the sexual nature of the human being requires honesty and humility, as psychological wholeness requires all aspects of the person to be acknowledged and accepted, including the so-called "lower" or animal functions of the body.

When Bettelheim discusses the relation between sexual anxieties and psychological development portrayed in the Eros and Psyche myth, he emphasizes the valuable role this myth can play in reconciling these widely diverse aspects of the psyche. The myth is able to overcome the apparent opposition between wisdom and sexuality because it is itself a union of opposites as a story of bringing together the divine and the human.

In psychoanalytic perspective, the id is more likely to be a source of anxiety before it is integrated. So long as sex remains unknown, "buried in the unconscious," and unintegrated, it seems dangerous and taboo. This is particularly the case for children. Bettelheim believes that the message of the Eros and Psyche myth reaches the individual at a deep level, possibly at the level where sexual anxieties arise. By showing that the monster is actually divine (Eros as a god), the myth supports the ego's attempt to face and assimilate sexuality. Thus the myth helps to overcome a person's initial anxiety and offers hope that the id is not what it at first seems to be, but that once it is confronted and accepted by the ego, it is transformed into something that benefits and enlarges consciousness. Like the other Freudian interpreters, Bettelheim ignores the symbolism of the birth of Voluptas and he ignores the literary context of the myth in Apuleius' *Metamorphoses*.

Fritz Hoevels

The most thorough Freudian treatment of the Eros and Psyche tale is contained in Fritz Hoevels' *Maerchen und Magie in den Metamorphosen*

des Apuleius von Madaura (1979). Going well beyond the brief refer-
ences to Oedipal elements in the works of Barchilon and Bettelheim,
Hoevels sees this story as a dramatic portrait of the feminine
Oedipus complex. He focusses on the elements of sibling rivalry,
transference, sexual curiosity and mother fixation in the Eros and
Psyche story.

Hoevels admits that Apuleius' story does not emphasize the
aspect of sibling rivalry as much as some tales which contain three
brothers or sisters, nevertheless he argues that sibling rivalry and
death wishes play an important role in this tale. Hoevels sees the
psychological mechanism of projection at work in the way Psyche
experiences her own evil wishes as the malevolence of her sisters
plotting against her and thus she feels justified in the removal of
these sisters from the picture.[59] He considers the removal of the sisters as Psyche's fantasized Oedipal wishfulfillment, but this is all
presented in such a way that Psyche appears to be completely innocent and the sisters seem responsible for their own undoing.[60]

He interprets Aphrodite's hatred of Psyche in the same way as the
sisters' hatred, namely as the projection of Psyche's own Oedipal
hostility. There definitely are grounds for viewing Aphrodite as Psyche's rival for Eros, given the incestuous relationship between Aphrodite and Eros described in Apuleius' tale. According to Hoevels,
Psyche's relationship to Aphrodite and Eros actually portrays her
Oedipal fantasy about her own parents. In the fantasy's typical form
the mother is feared and removed while the father is idealized and
made young again.[61] There is nothing in the Psyche tale itself that
indicates that she was involved in an Oedipal struggle with her parents, but here Hoevels presents his view of Psyche's fantasies quite
apart from any textual grounding in the *Metamorphoses*.

Even though Psyche's death wishes are unconscious, they still
have consequences. Hoevels's understands Psyche's sorrowful
search for the lost Eros and her seemingly impossible tasks as punishment for her death wishes toward her sisters and Aphrodite. In
Hoevels' view, when Psyche undergoes her difficult search and
tasks, she is appeasing her own unconscious guilt feelings resulting
from harbouring such morally reprehensible wishes.[62]

Hoevels sees an inner identity between Psyche's sisters, who wish
to have Eros for themselves, and Aphrodite, who has strong Oedipal
ties to Eros. Hoevels believes that the part of the story where Aphrodite wants Psyche's death is another instance of Psyche's projection
of her own Oedipal wishes for Aphrodite's death, or at least,
removal. Here, again, the psychological projection of Psyche's
unconscious death wishes is an important key to Hoevels' reading of
the tale. With some effort he strives to show that Eros is actually a

father substitute for Psyche so that the Oedipal dynamics of their situation are more evident. Hoevels states that the way Eros was described as a great snake resembles how children think of their father's penis, and the disgust Psyche experienced for the monster was actually a reaction-formation to cope with her infantile incest wishes for her father.[63] Along this same line of thought Hoevels also suggests that Eros' ravishment of Psyche was actually Psyche's projection of her own unconscious incest wishes. For Hoevels, Psyche's marriage of death calls to mind the child's and the neurotic's expectation that their father's sexual advances would bring death, should their repressed incest wishes ever be realized.[64]

Hoevels interprets the prohibition against seeing Eros in this Oedipal context as part of an initiation and defloration ritual. For him this taboo deals with the prohibition against seeing the father naked, and especially against seeing the father's penis. According to Hoevels, this taboo is ultimately designed to protect the man because if a man does deflower a maiden, he becomes the object of her wrath. Psyche's plan to chop off the head of the dragon symbolizes her wish to castrate the man who sexually initiated her.[65] For Hoevels, the prohibition against curiosity, especially as it implies these sexual meanings[66] is at the heart of Apuleius' novel and the lamp scene with its focus on the taboo against seeing Psyche's lover is the crucial point of the Eros and Psyche tale.

Hoevels believes that the unconscious meaning of this tale, especially as it regards sexual curiosity, corresponds to Apuleius' own unconscious situation; this unconscious agreement was the principle cause of Apuleius' selecting the Eros and Psyche story for inclusion in the *Metamorphoses*.[67] He notes that sexual voyeurism, as symbolized in the lamp scene, is a prime example of forbidden curiosity which plays so prominent a role in Apuleius' novel.[68] Hoevels links this sexual voyeurism to the dominant role of magic in the *Metamorphoses* when he cites the scene where Lucius first makes his acquaintance with magic by watching a naked old witch transform herself into a bird.

Throughout the *Metamorphoses* Lucius' driving curiosity reflects Apuleius' own searching nature,[69] according to Hoevels, and nowhere is this more evident than in Lucius' interest in the mysteries of Isis. From a psychoanalytic perspective Hoevels sees repressed infantile curiosity at the heart of both the mystery cults and the Eros and Psyche tale, and exactly this curiosity is the mainspring of Lucius' (or Apuleius') own motivation.[70] Hoevels believes there is a connection between the infantile fixation on sexual curiosity in the initiation rites of the mystery cults and in Lucius' obsessive need to be initiated into religious mysteries on three different occasions.[71]

In regard to Eros, Hoevels calls attention to elements of the male Oedipus complex. When he assumes for a moment that the Eros and Psyche story might be a man's fantasy, Hoevels finds that psychological transference is strongly at work. Since Psyche represents a newer and younger version of Aphrodite, Hoevels sees Eros' attachment to Psyche as a projection or transference of his mother-image onto Psyche."[72]

Again using Freud's diagram of the psyche, we can view Hoevels' main interpretation that the Eros and Psyche myth symbolizes the feminine Oedipus complex as it is shown in Diagram 7. Psyche represents the female ego or the subject of the Oedipal fantasy. The sisters would refer to a woman's sibling rivals in the external world. For Hoevels, Aphrodite symbolizes the woman's mother in the first instance, and then also an aspect of her super ego. Hoevels describes Psyche's death wishes against Aphrodite and the sisters, and from this perspective, the Eros and Psyche story appears to represent a woman's aggressive id impulses acted out in fantasy (Diagram 7, A). Because these impulses are not recognized, but rather projected, they are seen in the story from Psyche's point of view as the evil motives and intentions of Aphrodite and the sisters. Aphrodite plays the role of a harsh super ego figure (which she would be as an internalized parent imago) who punishes Psyche for her unconscious death wishes (Diagram 7, C). Since the super ego operates largely in the unconscious (like the id), it knows directly about the id wishes and can generate guilt feelings in the ego, even though the ego may be unaware of the death wishes themselves. In Hoevels' view, Psyche's tasks only *seem* to her to be forced upon her from the outside (by Aphrodite) but actually they are motivated by an unconscious desire to appease the guilt due to her death wishes.

According to Hoevels, in Psyche's fantasy, she is torn between forbidden incestuous desires towards Eros and disgust at the thought of him as a monster. Hoevels describes Psyche's disgust as a reaction formation, i.e., an ego defence which distorts the actual psychological dynamics of her relationship to Eros (Diagram 7, D). Her disgust hides her incestuous longing. Hoevels considers Psyche's reaction to be symbolic of a woman's anxiety which results from guilt."[73] When we remember that Aphrodite symbolizes Psyche's super ego and that she was responsible for the near-impossible tasks which pushed Psyche into the pit of despair and to the verge of suicide, we can understand Psyche's awareness of the danger stemming from her super ego (Diagram 7, C). According to Hoevels' interpretation, just as Aphrodite punished Psyche for her death wishes, so she also threatens her as the mother symbol and Oedipal rival of Psyche's father-lover (Eros). Hoevels believes that Psyche's Oedipal anxiety is also symbolized by the marriage-of-death scene where Psyche's

Diagram 7

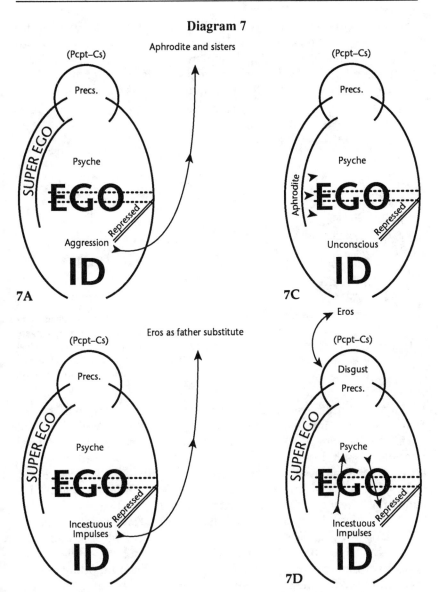

This diagram shows various aspects of the female Oedipus complex: (A) a woman's (Psyche's) aggressive impulses against her sisters and Aphrodite are experienced in fantasy; (B) a woman's incestuous impulses are projected onto a male (Eros) as a father substitute; (C) Aphrodite as a super ego figure punishes the ego (Psyche); and (D) a woman's disgust at the male as monster (Eros) is a reaction formation against her own incestuous longing for the male as a father substitute.

expectation of the monster (i.e., father or penis)[74] is an ominous, cata-
strophic expectation of what might happen (death) if the father-mon-
ster actually made love to his daughter.

Diagram 8 indicates Hoevels' secondary interpretation of the Eros
and Psyche story as symbolic of the male Oedipus complex.

Diagram 8

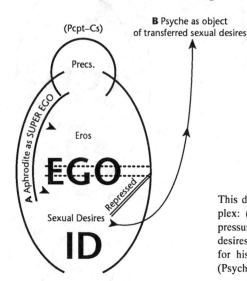

This diagram shows the male Oedipus complex: (A) Aphrodite as a super ego figure
pressures her son (Eros) against his Oedipal
desires and (B) a son's (Eros') sexual desires
for his mother are transferred to a woman
(Psyche).

Here Aphrodite as Eros' mother represents at least part of his
super ego (as internalized parent) and the object of his Oedipal
desires (Diagram 8, A). Since Eros cannot fully carry out his sexual
impulses with his mother,[75] he redirects these blocked impulses
towards Psyche as a younger version of Aphrodite (Diagram 8, B).
Hoevels speaks of this as a transference, where the boy's attitudes
and attachment to his mother are transferred to his lover.

When Hoevels attempts to link the Eros and Psyche tale to
Apuleius' *Metamorphoses*, he focusses on the element of sexual curiosity which he believes is a major characteristic of both Apuleius and
the novel's main character, Lucius. In Freud's diagram of the psyche
we might picture the ego as Apuleius' or Lucius' ego and the sexual
curiosity would be a repressed id impulse (see Diagram 9).

When these id impulses are repressed, they work "underground"
in the unconscious and seek some suitable outlet. Hoevels believes
that this repressed sexual curiosity finds obsessive expression in
Lucius' repeated initiations into the mystery religions as described in
Apuleius' *Metamorphoses* (Diagram 9).

Repressed infantile sexual curiosity not only generates compulsive
phenomena, which Hoevels finds in Lucius' repeated initiations into

Diagram 9

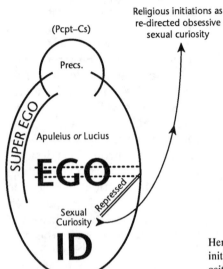

Religious initiations as re-directed obsessive sexual curiosity

(Pcpt–Cs)

Precs.

SUPER EGO

Apuleius *or* Lucius

EGO

Repressed

Sexual Curiosity

ID

Here Apuleius' or Lucius' repeated religious initiations are seen as redirected sexual curiosity.

religious mysteries and in his hair fetish[76] but also undergirds the "drive to know," as Freud emphasized. Hoevels believes that all these elements, sexuality, knowledge, and power (magic) blend together in the unconscious, so there is a thread of continuity in Lucius' preoccupations with magic, sex and religion. Hoevels characterizes the psychological relationship of these preoccupations as follows: Magical thought, as a stage in the development of human thinking in the individual and in the race, is originally in the domain of the id and the pleasure principle. It is characterized by what Freud called "omnipotence of thought," where a person does not yet distinguish sufficiently between the inner and outer worlds and where thoughts and wishes are believed to influence external reality directly. Magic becomes religion when this primitive form of thought is subordinated to the super ego instead of becoming modified by the reality principle and placed in the service of the ego.[77] Whereas magic is tied to the individual's autonomy by way of wish and fantasy, religion commits the person to heteronomy by subordination to the gods and the super ego.[78] From this perspective, religion is close to, yet opposes, magic. For Hoevels, this helps to explain why on the one hand Lucius is so intrigued by magic and curiosity while on the other hand, these interests are cast in an unfavourable light and Lucius turns to religion to be saved from the unfortunate consequences of magic and curiosity.

Hoevels' interpretation offers a valuable perspective on the Eros and Psyche tale in that it views the story critically, primarily as Psyche's Oedipal fantasies. This point of view casts a new light on the rivalry between Psyche and her sisters, as well as on the antagonism between Psyche and Aphrodite. From the psychoanalytic vantage point, Psyche no longer appears to be the innocent bystander, and she must take responsibility for her Oedipal fantasy. In this view, Psyche's death wishes set the stage for the main action of the tale, since they determine the destiny of her sisters as well as the meaning of the tasks she must perform. Hoevels' analysis of the projection mechanism also reorients the marriage-of-death and lamp sequences as they now become a product of Psyche's own unconscious desires.

These interpretations offer a fresh look at the story, even though they do not shed a great deal of light on the relation of Psyche to Lucius in the *Metamorphoses*. Yet Hoevels is the only Freudian interpreter of this myth who seriously attempts to relate the Eros and Psyche story to its literary context. Unfortunately, he limits this connection primarily to the sexual curiosity which affects both Psyche and Lucius. When Hoevels ties Psyche's repressed sexual curiosity to the curiosity which attracts Lucius to magic, this offers an intriguing lead regarding the psychological importance of the Eros and Psyche story in the *Metamorphoses*. Yet Hoevels does little with Psyche's tasks (except as guilt due to death wishes) or with the deification of Psyche at the end of the tale. Both of these aspects of the story take on a more central position in the Jungian interpretations which follow.

To summarize this chapter, the Freudian interpretations focus on the way the Eros and Psyche myth symbolizes certain phenomena described in Freud's theory of the unconscious. These phenomena include psychotic wishfulfillment (Riklin), an erotic dream or nightmare (Schroeder), a girl's sexual anxieties (Schroeder, Barchilon, Bettelheim, and Hoevels), a girl's sexual curiosity (Hoevels), the development of consciousness and the integration of sexuality with wisdom (Bettelheim), and a girl's Oedipal fantasies (Hoevels). Given the central place of the sexual theory in Freud's thought, it is not surprising to find four of the five Freudian interpreters concentrating on the way this myth expresses the timeless problem of a woman's sexual anxieties, especially girls who are entering puberty. The scenes from the myth which are central to this interpretation are the marriage-of-death and the monster-lover sequences. However, these interpretations neglect Psyche's tests and deification, or the resolution of the story. With one exception (Hoevels), the Freudians ignore the literary context of the myth as they attempt to understand the psychological dynamics of the story.

Notes

1 Even in the Freudian perspective where repression is assumed to be at work in the formation of myths and dreams, these symbolic stories contain the clues which allow the analyst to arrive at underlying psychological dynamics.

2 Translated by Thomas Taylor in *The New World of Dreams* (New York, 1974), p. 171.

3 *SE* XXII, p. 25.

4 *Introductory Lectures, SE* XV, p. 166.

5 Ibid., p. 171.

6 Ibid., pp. 208-209.

7 Ibid., p. 175.

8 In his *Introductory Lectures on Psychoanalysis*, Freud gives many examples of this kind of sexual interpretation. The male organ may be represented by reptiles, fish, snakes, hats, overcoats, water-taps, fountains, hanging lamps, pencils, pen-holders, nail-files, hammers, balloons, airplanes, sticks, umbrellas, trees, knives, spears, rifles and pistols. The female genitals (including breasts and pubic hair) may be represented by pits, cavities, vessels, bottles, boxes, trunks, cases, chests, pockets, cupboards, stoves, doors, gates, snails, mussels, the mouth, churches, chapels, apples, peaches, woods, bushes and jewel-cases. For Freud, all of these visual images could represent the dreamer's attitude and feelings about sex. Ibid., pp. 154-57.

9 *The Interpretation of Dreams, SE* IV, p. 165.

10 See *Psychoanalytische Studien* (Frankfurt am Main, 1971), pp. 161-323.

11 Ibid., p. 290.

12 Ibid., p 288.

13 Ibid., p. 291.

14 Jean Defradas adds to this list of similarities between dream and myth, pointing to metamorphoses, lack of logical connections and condensations. See his "Études psychanalytiques sur la mythologie grecque," *IL* 10 (1958): 159-60.

15 Ibid., p. 321.

16 *The Myth of the Birth of the Hero: A Psychological Interpretation of Mythology* (New York, 1964), p. 9.

17 *Dogma and Compulsion: Psychoanalytic Studies of Religion and Myths* (Westport, CT, 1973), p. 283.

18 Ibid., p. 283.

19 Ibid., p. 284.

20 Ibid., p. 286.

21 See Kiell's *Psychoanalysis, Psychology and Literature: A Bibliography* (Madison, WI, 1963), and J. Glenn's "Psychoanalytic Writings on Greek and Latin Authors, 1911-1960," *Classical World* 66 (1972): 129-45.

22 *Handbook of Greek Mythology* (London, 1953), p. 10.

23 Cited by Jung in *Symbols of Transformation, CW* 5, p. 23.

24 Ibid., p. 24.

25 *The Tavistock Lectures, CW* 18, p. 111.

26 Ibid., p. 111.

27 In *Dreams in the Psychology of Religion* I have discussed differences between Freud's and Jung's theories of dream interpretation.

28 *Symbols and the Interpretation of Dreams*, CW 18, pp. 190-91.

29 *On the Nature of Dreams*, CW 8, pp. 294-95.

30 *General Aspects of Dream Psychology*, CW 8, pp. 250-55.

31 CW 5, p. 390.

32 For many examples of Riklin's Freudian perspective see *Wishfulfillment and Fairy Tales*, trans. W. White (New York, 1915). The German version originally appeared as *Wunscherfuellung und Symbolik im Maerchen* (Wien, 1908).

33 Ibid., p. 80.

34 Ibid., p. 45.

35 Ibid., p. 65. Parentheses are in the text.

36 From *The Dissection of the Psychical Personality*, SE XXII, p. 78.

37 This situation seems related to Freud's view of God as a projection of the infantile wish to be taken care of, which leads Freud to view religious ideas of God in their most extreme form as delusional ideas. See Freud's *Future of an Illusion*, SE XXI, p. 81. Riklin does not explicitly relate Psyche's hallucinated voices to this aspect of Freud's psychology of religion, but given Riklin's dismissal of mysticism as a "psychic, sexual wish structure" he appears to be very close to Freud on this point.

38 See Kenneth Wapnick's excellent discussion of the similarities and differences between mysticism and psychosis in "Mysticism and Schizophrenia," *Journal of Transpersonal Psychology* 1, 2 (Fall 1969): 49-67.

39 *Het Sprookje van Amor en Psyche in het licht der Psychoanalyse* (Baarn, Netherlands, 1917), pp. 27-28.

40 Ibid., p. 27.

41 Ibid., p. 28.

42 In Freud's early view, anxiety is transformed sexual energy. See "On the Grounds for Detaching a Particular Syndrome From Neurasthenia Under the Description 'Anxiety Neurosis,'" (1895) SE III, pp. 90-117. Later he distinguished three types of anxiety: realistic, neurotic and moral anxiety. Realistic anxiety is a reaction to a danger in the external world; neurotic anxiety is a reaction to strong passions in the id; and moral anxiety is a response to pressure from a strict super ego. See *New Introductory Lectures on Psychoanalysis* (1933), SE XXII, pp. 77-79.

43 *Psychoanalysis and the Psychoanalytic Review* 46, 4 (1959): 20.

44 Ibid., p. 21.

45 Ibid., p. 27.

46 Ibid., p. 20.

47 Ibid., p. 29.

48 Ibid., p. 27.

49 By realistic anxiety I refer to the situation where the father or husband are a real threat and source of danger.

50 *The Uses of Enchantment* (New York, 1977), p. 293.

51 Ibid., p. 253.

52 Ibid., pp. 297-98.

53 Ibid., pp. 297-98.

54 Ibid., p. 298.

55 Ibid., p. 294.

56 Ibid., p. 293.

57 Ibid., p. 295.

58 Ibid., p. 295.

59 *Maerchen und Magie in den Metamorphosen des Apuleius von Madaura* (Amsterdam, 1979), p. 254.

60 Ibid., p. 255: "Psyches aggressive Tatkraft, die sie ausschliesslich gegenueber ihren Schwestern an den Tag legt, ist Dementi der spaeteren Tuenche und Original in einem Begreifen wir das Maerchen als entstellte und phantastische oedipale Wunscherfuellung, dann loesen sich alle Widersprueche" ("Psyche's aggressive energy, which she exhibits exclusively in relation to her sisters, is a denial of the later whitewash and it is original if we are to understand the fairytale as the distorted and fanciful Oedipal wishfulfillment which resolves all contradictions").

61 Ibid, p. 261: "Die verliebte Sprache der Venus im ersten Gespraech mit Amor (IV, 31, 1sq.) tut ein Uebriges, um ihn als ihren insgeheimen Sexualpartner zu kennzeichnen, d.h. als Objekt gemeinsamer Eifersucht von Psyche und Venus. Uebertragen wir diesen Tatbestand in psychoanalytische Terminologie, so heisst das, dass die Erfinderinnen des Volksmaerchens, repraesentiert durch Psyche, sich in Prinz und Hexe ihr Elternpaar phantasierten, wobei die Mutter herabgesetzt (Haesslichkeit), gefuerchtet, ausgetochen und meistens auch noch getoetet, der Vater verjuengt, idealisiert und entschuldigt wurde" ("The amorous language of Aphrodite in the first conversation with Eros further characterizes him as her secret sexual partner, that is, as the object of the joint jealousy of Psyche and Aphrodite. If we translate this situation into psychoanalytic terminology, it means that the inventor of the fairytale, represented by Psyche, fantasized her parents as prince and witch, whereby the mother is degraded [as ugly], feared, devalued and usually also killed, while the father is rejuvenated, idealized and excused").

62 Ibid., p. 263: "Wir koennen jetzt den Sinn dieser Leiden erschliessen: der Tod der Helden stellt die Talionstrafe fuer ihren (gewuenschten) Muttermord bzw. den (vollzogenen) Schwesternmord dar. Ebenso sind ihre sonstigen Leiden nicht nur als boshafte (projizierte) Nachstellungen der ('Schwieger'-)Mutter zu verstehen, sondern auch als Mittel zur Beschwichtigung des eigenen unbewussten Schuldgefuehls" ("Now we can understand the meaning of this suffering: the death of the hero represents the *lex talionis* punishment for the wished-for murder of her mother, or rather, the actual murder of her sisters. So also are her other sufferings to be understood not only as malicious (projected) persecution of the mother-in-law, but also as the means to appease her own unconscious guilt-feelings").

63 Ibid., p. 258.

64 Ibid., p. 259.

65 Ibid., p. 268: "So besitzt das Tabu, den Maerchenprinzen nackt zu sehen, genauer: seinen Penis zu sehen, einen klaren Sinn. Es soll ihn vor Kastration(swuenschen) der Frau schuetzen, die sich unbewusst aus der Defloration ergeben" ("Thus, the taboo against seeing the fairytale prince naked, or more precisely, against seeing his penis, possesses a clear meaning. It should protect him from the woman's castration wishes which arise unconsciously from having been deflowered").

66 Ibid., p. 276. Hoevels holds that the object of the forbidden curiosity is sexuality: "Gegenstand der verbotenen Neugier ist also die Sexualitaet, genauer: die Genitalien und ihr Gebrauch" ("The object of the forbidden curiosity is sexuality, or, to be more exact, the genitals and their use.")

67 Ibid., p. 269: "Wir erinnern uns daran, dass nach dem uebereinstimmenden Befund aller neueren Interpreten das Neugierverbot den ganzen Eselsroman dominiert und die Aufnahme der Psyche-einlage begruendete. Die Lampenszene war dementsprechend auch fuer Apuleius der bedeutsamste Punkt der Erzaehlung und gab den Ausschlag fuer die Wahl des Maerchens. Es waere nicht verwunderlich, wenn ihr unbewusster Gehalt auch mit dem Unbewussten des Autors korrespondieren wuerde und in ihm ein Echo hervorgerufen haette" ("Remember that, according to the unanimous findings of all the latest interpreters, the curiosity taboo dominates the entire Metamorphoses and provides the basis for the Psyche story. Accordingly, the scene with the lamp was also crucial for Apuleius and provided the stimulus for the choice of this fairytale. It would not be astonishing if its unconscious content would also correspond with the author's unconscious and would have called forth an echo in him").

68 Ibid., p. 270.

69 Hoevels states that Apuleius "himself was one of the most inquisitive men of his time": "selbst einer der neugierigsten Menschen seines Zeitalters war." Ibid., p. 272.

70 Ibid., p. 273.

71 Ibid., p. 277: "Gerade Apuleius, der unermuedliche Myste, ist ein gutes Studienobjekt dieses Wiederholungszwanges, der durch seine unerledigt fortbestehende, infantil fixierte Sexual-neugier immer neue Initiationen erzwang; die beiden Wiederholungen der Isisweihe am Schluss des 11. Buches, von denen mindestens die letzte aeusserst schwach motiviert ist, geben uns ein gutes Beispiel fuer die Wirksamkeit des Zwangsmoments" ("Precisely Apuleius, the tireless mystic, is a good example of this repetition-compulsion in that his unresolved, continuing, infantile sexual fixation and curiosity always demanded new initiations. Both repetitions of the Isis consecration at the end of Book XI [of which at least the last one was very weakly motivated] give us a good example of the efficacy of the compulsion element").

72 Ibid., pp. 262-63: "Diese Aehnlichkeit [zwischen Psyche und Venus] laesst sich als Ergebnis einer maennlichen Phantasie verstehen, die mit der Uebertragung der [jungen, schoenen] Mutterimago auf ein anderes Objekt diesem alle Eigenschaften der Mutter mitzuschreibt und sich dadurch gleichzeitig vom gealterten Original, das der Imago immer unaehnlicher geworden ist, loesen kann" ("This similarity [between Psyche and Aphrodite] can be understood as the result of a male fantasy which transfers the [young and beautiful] mother imago onto another object together with all the maternal characteristics, thereby simultaneously permitting the severance from the aged original which has become progressively dissimilar to the imago").

73 This refers to Freud's moral anxiety as a sense of danger coming from the super ego.

74 In this regard Freud speaks of equivalent or interchangeable elements in the unconscious. See SE XVII, pp. 128-29.

75 In Apuleius' version of the story, their embraces and kisses might make us wonder how far short of incest they stop.

76 *Maerchen und Magie*, p. 285.

77 Ibid., p. 280: "Vielmehr wird das primitive Denken, das dem Es bzw. dem Lust-
prinzip verhaftet ist, nicht einfach dem Ich uebertragen und dadurch dem Reali-
taetsprinzip unterstellt, sondern vielmehr unter den Bedingungen der Familie ohne
Aenderung seiner alten Charakteristiken dem Ueber-Ich unterstellt. Die Magie ist
dadurch zur Religion geworden; Religion ist gewissermassen delegierte Magie"
("Primitive thinking, which is governed by the id, or rather, the pleasure principle,
is not simply carried over to the ego and thereby placed under the control of the
reality principle, but rather placed under the control of the super ego, subject to the
conditions of the family without changing its old characteristics. Magic thereby
becomes religion and religion is, in effect, delegated magic").

78 Ibid., p. 280.

3 Psychological Approaches to the Eros and Psyche Myth: Jungian Interpretations

Erich Neumann

In this chapter we shall examine the Jungian interpretations of the Eros and Psyche myth. Erich Neumann's well known study *Amor and Psyche* (1956) has greatly influenced the way Jungians interpret the story. Because Neumann's work is foundational to the Jungian interpretation of this myth, we shall consider his view first and in some detail.

The overall presupposition of Neumann's interpretation is that this story represents a mythical expression of the psychic development of the feminine. This perspective is similar to the Freudian focus on the feminine which shows how the myth symbolizes a woman's sexual anxieties, but it is foreign to those recent studies which stress the literary context of the myth. As we saw in Chapter 1, there is agreement in the recent literature that "Eros and Psyche" is a tale within a tale which summarizes and symbolizes the central motif of Lucius' psychological and spiritual transformation.[1] In such a case we would expect that the story of Psyche symbolizes the essential transformation of a man's psyche. But Neumann tends to ignore this immediate literary context and interpret the tale not as parallel to and recapitulating the transformation of the narrator, Lucius, but as descriptive of the way women develop psychologically.[2]

Neumann's interpretation of the Eros and Psyche myth is influenced by his view of the development of human consciousness which he describes in his major work, *The Origins and History of Consciousness*. There he traces the stages of human consciousness beginning with the self-contained *uroboros* (the symbol of the primal dragon that bites its own tail), where there is not yet individual consciousness differentiated from the environment or from the original unconscious matrix. Neumann sees the uroboric state expressed in creation myths, especially the myth of the Great Mother. Aphrodite (Venus) is one of the primary mythical figures representing the Great Mother and she is also at the starting point of the Eros and Psyche tale. Neumann sees Aphrodite as a symbol of the seductive inertia of nature and the collective unconscious. She is the original, conservative, maternal source of life and her beauty serves the purpose of fertility.

Neumann contrasts Aphrodite with Psyche who, from the very beginning of the tale, is in conflict with the Great Mother. Aphrodite is jealous of Psyche's human beauty and the fact that human beings worship her as a goddess, and even Aphrodite's divine son, Eros, desires her. In one respect Neumann sees Eros as an extension of the Great Mother archetype, since Psyche's entire story involves a conscious separation not only from the Mother but also from Eros as the Great Mother's son. For Neumann the whole process of Psyche's development represents 1) a differentiation of consciousness out of an original unconscious unity, and 2) a monumental step in human history where women become responsible for their own decision-making so that their experiences are no longer merely a function of the arbitrary will of the gods or the work of transpersonal forces:

> Psyche's act ends the mythical age in the archetypal world, the age in which the relation between the sexes depended only on the superior power of the gods, who held [sic] men at their mercy. Now begins the age of human love, in which the human psyche consciously takes the fateful decision on itself. And this brings us to the background of our myth, namely the conflict between Psyche, the "new Aphrodite" and Aphrodite as the Great Mother.[3]

Psyche's act refers to her rebellious act of disobeying Eros' command that she remain with him in the paradisiacal embrace of darkness and not know his identity. Neumann interprets Eros' command as an extension of Psyche's original unconscious state of unity with the Great Mother archetype. With Psyche's heroic act, suffering, guilt and loneliness enter the world of female consciousness.

According to Neumann, Psyche's act resembles the heroic male who so frequently in myth must overcome the dragon monster in his quest for conscious development. Neumann sees her existence in the dark paradise of Eros, pleasurable as this is, as a variant of the mythical male hero's engulfment by the whale, dragon or monster.[4] In the traditional night sea journey, the male solar hero kindles a fire in the belly of the whale and cuts himself out of the darkness. Neumann notes that Psyche too uses a light and a knife to perform her parallel tasks. She does not kill the monster, though she is prepared to do exactly that. For the sake of greater knowledge Psyche drives Eros and herself from their paradise of uroboric unconsciousness, but the knowledge she acquires is for the sake of establishing a conscious relationship with him. For Neumann, the fundamental difference between Psyche as a female heroine and the male solar hero is that her deed turns into an act of love. In fact the rest of the story of her development is to overcome through suffering and struggle the separation caused by her deed. This crucial difference prompts Neumann to interpret the Psyche story as a mythical portrait of woman's development.

Neumann interprets the "marriage of death" which Aphrodite has arranged for Psyche as a mythical vestige of matriarchal psychology in which marriage is seen from the woman's perspective as rape of the virgin. He points out that this was a central aspect of feminine mysteries wherein the maiden was ritually sacrificed to a monster or dragon. According to Neumann this viewpoint grows out of the primordial relationship of identity between mother and daughter, and consequently, the approach of the male in marriage is considered to be a painful separation from the mother.

The jealous sisters represent, for Neumann, a man-hating matriarchal stratum in Psyche's soul. Here there is no hint of the sisters as symbols of sibling rivalry, a theme so prominent in Hoevels' analysis. Neumann, rather, speaks of them as aspects of Psyche's shadow[5] which manifest the beginning of a higher form of feminine consciousness.[6] The sisters appear very negative in the story, but from Neumann's perspective, they contribute to Psyche's overall development by pushing her to confront Eros. While the sisters do not yet represent a higher consciousness, they are its precursor. Although for the wrong reasons, the sisters raise important objections to the matriarchal situation of Psyche's blind servitude, which Neumann considers appropriately described as being devoured by a monster. The sisters not only represent aspects of the matriarchy, they push Psyche beyond this state of development:

> The basic law of the matriarchate forbids individual relations with the man and acknowledges the male only as an anonymous power, representing the godhead. For Psyche this anonymity is fulfilled, but at the same time she has incurred the profound, ineradicable disgrace of succumbing to this manhood, of falling into its power. From the standpoint of the matriarchate there is only one answer to this disgrace: to kill and castrate the masculine, and that is what the sisters demand of Psyche. But they not only embody regression; a higher feminine principle is also at work, as is made plain by the symbolism with which the myth literally "illuminates" Psyche's unconscious situation.[7]

In order to understand the positive meaning and function of the sisters, Neumann advises the reader to disregard the way they are presented in Apuleius' story as jealously plotting against Psyche.

The sisters represent an underlying, largely unconscious strength that appears to contradict Psyche's softness and conscious willingness to remain in the dark paradise of sensuality.

But it is precisely Neumann's readiness to ignore the particular context of the story, "to wholly disregard the surface intrigue,"[8] which makes his interpretation suspect at certain points. This appears to be part of what P. Katz criticizes in Neumann's interpretation when she writes: "The symbolic and psychological significance of the myth here rests upon subjective criteria giving a dimension or meaning to the myth that seems to me to go beyond its fundamental context."[9] The subjective criteria to which Katz refers would include Neumann's assumptions about the development of consciousness in the human race, in the individual person and in woman in particular.

In picturing the psychological dynamics represented by Neumann's interpretation, Psyche seems to represent, in the first instance, the conscious mind of the female or the conscious functions of the female ego. Neumann contrasts the psyche as ego with the gods, who are archetypes of the unconscious: "The human psyche is an active ego which dares to oppose transpersonal forces—and successfully so. The consequence of this enhanced position of the human, here the feminine, personality is to enfeeble what was formerly all-powerful."[10] In this case the psyche is seen as ego consciousness in relation to Eros, Aphrodite and the gods.[11] But later in his commentary he speaks of Psyche as an aspect of the unconscious. In the following statement he seems to be aware of some ambiguity in his interpretation when he speaks of the *Psyche-archetype*:

> Here it will not be possible to describe the psychological difference between the "Psyche-archetype" and that of the anima in man, or of the feminine self in woman. A few indications may suffice. It is no accident that we speak of the "soul" of man as well as woman; and it is no accident that analytical psychology defines the totality of consciousness and the unconscious as the "psyche." This psyche as the whole personality must be characterized in man as well as woman as feminine, because it experiences that which transcends the psyche as numinous, as "outside" and "totally different." For this reason, the mandala figure, which appears in man and woman as the totality of the psyche, is feminine in its symbolism as circle and round, or uroboric as that which contains the opposites.[12]

Here Neumann doesn't clear up the ambiguous meanings of Psyche and "feminine," and he even adds to the confusion with his view that consciousness in both men and women is masculine, while the

unconscious in both is feminine. Neumann's perspective is contro-
versial even among Jungians. In traditional Jungian thought the total
psyche of both men and women is conceived of as a relationship
between the conscious and unconscious mind. Jung has posited that
the unconscious of each man and woman is personified by symbols
or figures of the opposite sex, so a man's unconscious is personified
by female figures, while a woman's unconscious is personified by
male figures. The classical statement of Neumann's unusual view is
found in *The Origins and History of Consciousness*:

> But one thing, paradoxical though it may seem, can be established
> at once as a basic law: even in woman, *consciousness has a masculine
> character* [italics added]. The correlation "consciousness-light-day"
> and "unconsciousness-darkness-night" holds true regardless of
> sex and is not altered by the fact that the spirit-instinct polarity is
> organized on a different basis in men and women. Consciousness,
> as such, is masculine even in women, just as the unconscious is
> feminine in men.[13]

From this perspective Neumann interprets Psyche's development as
a growth toward the masculine, by which he means consciousness.

Diagram 10

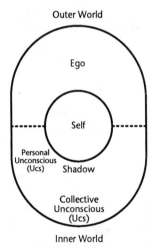

Outer World

Ego

Self

Personal
Unconscious
(Ucs)   Shadow

Collective
Unconscious
(Ucs)

Inner World

This diagram shows that the functions of the
ego orient the individual in the external
world; that the self archetype is at the core of
the personality; that a personal unconscious
composed of neglected and repressed material acquired in the individual's lifetime lies
closer to the ego than a deeper layer of the
unconscious, the collective unconscious,
which is the common heritage of all humanity; and that the shadow is mainly the underdeveloped aspects of the personality in the
personal unconscious but it also is an archetype representing evil in the collective unconscious.

To understand more clearly the various aspects of Neumann's
interpretation, it might be useful to use a diagram similar to the one
used in the last chapter. Jung himself did not offer a diagram of the
structure of the psyche, but one of his close associates, Jolande
Jacobi, did offer an approximate diagram of the Jungian perspective
(Diagram 10).[14] Following Jacobi's diagram, Neumann's interpreta-

tion is shown in Diagram 11. Eros is difficult to understand in relation to the psychological dynamics described in Jungian thought. On
the one hand he is an aspect of or an extension of Aphrodite. This
connection is underscored when he is portrayed as the son who is
still under his mother's domain and who returns to her when he is
wounded by the oil of Psyche's lamp. The sensuous kiss Aphrodite
gives Eros also highlights this incestuous bond between them and
shows their close alliance in psychological role. When Neumann
speaks of Eros as a god, the son of Aphrodite, he represents him as a
person apart from Psyche. At other times Neumann speaks of Eros
as relatedness—a quality Jung used to characterize female consciousness. Neumann writes: "It is characteristic of the 'labors of Psyche'
that the component of relatedness, that is, the Eros-component, is
increasingly accompanied by a masculine spiritual element, which is
at first unconscious but gradually develops into a conscious attitude."[15] In this case Eros is considered as a part of Psyche, though
we may wonder whether this is an aspect of her conscious or unconscious mind. Jung, and Neumann after him, have described Eros as a
predominant characteristic of the female (whereas *Logos* is the term
Jung employs to describe what he sees as the main characteristic of
the male.) So we have a male figure in the story who represents a
primarily "feminine" characteristic. When Neumann uses the Greek
name "Eros" to refer to Cupid, we cannot always be certain whether
he is speaking about the god or the feminine relational aspect of the
human personality.

Diagram 11

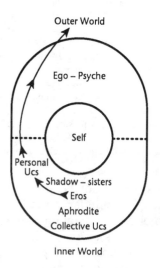

This diagram shows the development of a
woman's consciousness. Eros, as the capacity
for personal relationship, becomes differentiated from the unconscious and available to
the ego (Psyche) as a capacity to relate to
other people. Aphrodite represents the unconscious in its most primitive and undeveloped
form. The sisters symbolize shadow aspects
of Psyche's unconscious.

Neumann also refers to Eros as the "paternal *uroboros*"[16] when he describes Psyche's development as an individual struggling to free herself from matriarchal powers. When he refers to Eros as "the archetype of relatedness" it appears as though he considers Eros as a content of Psyche's unconscious, inasmuch as the collective unconscious is a part of all persons. But he then makes reference to the "Psyche-Eros constellation" as "the archetype of the relation between man and woman" and says it also reflects the "interrelation of contents in the collective unconscious."[17] In the latter description Neumann returns to the idea of both Eros and Psyche as elements in the collective unconscious and their relationship therein as a personification of the state of the unconscious where polar opposites are not yet differentiated, the condition also symbolized by the Great Mother and the Aphrodite-Eros constellation. From the Jungian perspective all of these symbols might be mixed in a "contamination of unconscious contents" where various symbols of the unconscious merge and it is no longer possible to distinguish clearly between the various contents.[18]

Neumann sees Psyche as originally bound to Eros in a paradise of uroboric unconsciousness, and when she sees Eros in the light, this original unconscious tie is dissolved. For Neumann this change represents a shift from the principle of fascinating attraction and the fertility of the species to a genuine love principle of personal development and encounter. For Neumann the link between individuation and love as encounter is one of the central psychological insights of this myth: "With Psyche, then, there appears a new love principle, in which the encounter between feminine and masculine is revealed as the basis of individuation."[19] Individuation is accomplished through a conscious encounter with the unconscious, which is symbolized by contrasexual symbols: the male achieves individuation by confronting his unconscious, personified as a feminine anima and the female meets her unconscious personified by male figures. This process is usually understood intrapsychically, but it is generally influenced by encounters with persons of the opposite sex in the external world. In this view, a loving encounter is often the occasion for an intensification of the individuation process.

From this traditional Jungian perspective Eros can be seen as either Psyche's inner masculine side or as a figure who transcends (is outside of) her own mind—either as a person in the external world or as a god in a transcendent reality. It almost appears as though Neumann is speaking of Eros both as a god and as a potentially human person when he says: "Aphrodite's son-beloved must become a human lover, Eros must be saved from the transpersonal sphere of the Great Mother and brought into the personal sphere of the human Psyche."[20] But then it is difficult to imagine that Neumann is actually speaking of Eros as a god here, since it would hardly make sense to think of saving a god from the transpersonal sphere as that is his appropriate mode or place of reality. One way to resolve this apparent contradiction would be to say that Neumann considers a god to be an unconscious content needing to be integrated. Yet that does not seem entirely satisfactory either, since Neumann treats Eros here as a man caught up in the transpersonal sphere or "identified with an archetype," to use the Jungian diagnostic vocabulary. If such were the case, it would make sense to see Psyche as saving him from the domination of the unconscious as represented by the Great Mother, Aphrodite. Yet the ambiguity remains, for Eros is still portrayed as the actual son of Aphrodite and not simply as a man caught up in the Great Mother archetype.

To some extent, Neumann attempts to explain this ambiguity by what he calls "secondary personalization." By this term he means that psychological contents which are primarily transpersonal and originally appeared in transpersonal form (as deities) are eventually taken to be personal.[21] In other words, psychological contents which were originally projected onto the gods are now experienced as aspects of the human psyche. Neumann considers this a normal process of development and not dangerous so long as the psyche itself is regarded as a "numinous world of transpersonal happenings." Here Neumann brings the realm of the gods into the human mind but not in such a way as to remove the divine aura from these highly charged contents.[22]

Neumann maintains that secondary personalization sheds light, not only on the formation of myths and fairy tales, but also on the course of personal development. Secondary personalization causes the child to project onto the parents much material which is really transpersonal and has nothing to do with the actual parents,[23] allowing the child to deal with that material in a concrete way. It may also be very surprising to parents to find themselves perceived by their child as divine or demonic characters. This constitutes a kind of reduction of archetypal material to personal material.

Neumann sees this process as parallel to the historical development of ego consciousness out of humanity's originally unconscious state. This is part of the progressive assimilation of unconscious contents that builds up the personality and helps separate the individual from the collective—a process that occurs in the development of both the human race and the individual human being. Neumann sees secondary personalization at work in the development of human history in what he calls the "psychization" of the world.[24] In this process of "psychization" we are dealing, not only with the reduction of the deep layers of the psyche to personal elements in myths and fairy tales, but also with the potential reduction of transcendent religious phenomena to forces within the psyche. I do not wish to deal with the question of psychological reductionism in Neumann and other depth psychologists here, but only to comment on "secondary personalization" as a reduction of archetypal processes to personal details in myths and fairy tales.

Gradually the processes which Neumann sees as essentially psychological are increasingly translated into stories where the deep archetypal dynamics become hidden in the stories of myths, fairy tales and the early romances. This is why we are likely to miss the psychological dimension of these stories and why Neumann advises us not to be side-tracked by the secondary personalizations involved in the specific details of the intrigues of Eros, the sisters, Aphrodite and Psyche. But it is difficult to know when we are dealing with the misleading elements of secondary personalization and when we are plumbing the psychological depths of the story. Neumann does not furnish a hermeneutical guide for making these judgments so we are frequently left wondering why he values some of the details of the story while others are discounted as secondary personalizations. When we examine Neumann's interpretation we are tempted to conclude that some details are important because they fit into his theoretical presuppositions about the overall meaning of the story, while other details do not fit and are therefore relegated to secondary personalizations.

When it comes to interpreting the seemingly strange tasks Psyche must perform, Neumann sees the details as crucial to deciphering the meaning of the story. While none of the Freudians go into a thorough analysis of the symbols involved in Psyche's tasks, the Jungians take great pains to draw out from these tasks the last shred of symbolic meaning. First Psyche must sort out a seemingly impossible mixture of grains. Neumann says the mound of seeds symbolizes an "uroboric mixture of the masculine," i.e., masculine promiscuity, and the ants who assist her represent chthonian powers associated with the vegetative nervous system:

> Psyche counters Aphrodite's promiscuity with an instinctual ordering principle. While Aphrodite holds fast to the fertility of the swamp stage (using Bachofen's category), which is also represented by Eros in the form of a dragon, a phallic serpent-monster, Psyche possesses within her an unconscious principle which enables her to select, sift, correlate, and evaluate, and so find her way amid the confusion of the masculine. In opposition to the matriarchal position of Aphrodite, for whom the masculine is

anonymous... Psyche, even in her first labor, has reached the
stage of selectivity.[25]

This corresponds to Neumann's view that Psyche's story represents
a development toward consciousness well beyond the unconscious,
matriarchal state symbolized by Aphrodite as the Great Mother.

In the second task Psyche must gather wool from dangerous
sheep. Neumann sees the rams as the destructive power of the masculine, "the negative masculine death principle as experienced by the
matriarchate"[26] and the reed which aids Psyche as the feminine vegetative wisdom of growth. For Neumann, the feminine wisdom is to
wait, to avoid confronting the rams (the masculine) directly. Just as
with the first task, Neumann sees the fulfillment of this second task
as the product of a fruitful contact between masculine and feminine.
This interpretation is in accord with the Jungian theory that individuation depends on the integration of masculine and feminine in the
human psyche.

Neumann sees Psyche's third task as a quest for the water of life.
Psyche has to catch some of this water which defies containment.
Neumann understands this task as a summary of Psyche's overall
work: she is the vessel of individuation which is to give specific form
to the eternally moving energy of life, to encompass this overwhelming power without being shattered by it. Neumann interprets the
eagle who comes to Psyche's aid as a symbol of the masculine spirit
which moves Psyche even further toward the masculine-feminine
integration characterizing individuation: "The eagle holding the vessel profoundly symbolizes the already male-female spirituality of
Psyche, who in one act 'receives' like a woman, that is, gathers like a
vessel and conceives, but at the same time apprehends and knows
like a man."[27] Neumann maintains that each of the first three tasks
contributes to Psyche's growth in consciousness by incorporating
aspects of the "masculine."

Neumann reminds us that in myths and fairy tales there are
usually three tasks, but in this case there is also a fourth. The number
four is frequently a symbol of wholeness, and Neumann sees this as
the meaning of the last task, where Psyche must journey to the
underworld, a journey which represents a direct struggle with the
feminine principle embodied in the deadly alliance of Aphrodite-
Persephone. Neumann understands the tower which counsels Psyche on how to carry out this perilous journey as both feminine (as a
fortress) and masculine (as a phallic symbol). The tower, a structure
erected by human beings, represents the collective human culture,
which furnishes wisdom and instruction as a means to survive the
underworld journey.

Neumann also believes that the strength Psyche has accumulated by carrying out the first three tasks enables her to face this most difficult task of all—a direct battle with death or the underworld. Neumann's view is that the first three tasks represent a confrontation with the negative masculine principle manifested as "masculine promiscuity" (seeds), "the deadly masculine" (rams), and the "uncontainable masculine" (stream of life). In each case Psyche must overcome the negative "masculine" potential. According to Neumann this is a dramatic way of expressing the dangers encountered as the female attempts to incorporate masculine dimensions of the psyche.

Neumann interprets the beauty ointment which Psyche must fetch from the underworld as the eternal youth of death, the "barren frigid beauty of mere maidenhood, without love for a man, as exacted by the matriarchate."[28] He sees in this deathlike sleep the pull of narcissism which would regress Psyche from the woman who loved Eros back to the maiden lost in narcissistic love of herself.[29] According to Neumann, the only saving grace in Psyche's act is the intention to make herself pleasing to Eros. The key here is that Psyche places her desire for beauty in the service of devotion to her beloved and for no one else. This intent rescues Psyche's preoccupation with beauty from the anonymous realm of Aphrodite's fertility and narcissism and connects her to her own feminine centre. Neumann, like Jung, sees the essence of the feminine in personal relatedness, so for him, Psyche's spiritual development is only fulfilled in her individual love encounter with Eros, not in the successful completion of tasks, which would seem to be the prerogative of a male hero. Thus, paradoxically, it is through her failure to complete her task that she finds success in that she demonstrates her willingness to sacrifice even her life for her beloved.

At this point Neumann's psychological interpretation takes an unusual turn. Not only does Psyche save herself through love but she also redeems Eros by making him human. Neumann's interpretation appears to derive from his understanding of integrating transpersonal contents of the unconscious, where integration means humanizing such transpersonal contents as Eros and Aphrodite by bringing them into conscious relationship to the ego. This process alters the unconscious itself: "The tale of Psyche ends with the deification of the human Psyche. Correspondingly, *the divine Aphrodite becomes human, and so likewise Eros*, who through suffering prepares the way for union with the human Psyche" [emphasis added].[30] In terms of Neumann's schema, this means that the realm of the feminine has been transformed. The female psyche is no longer dominated by an impersonal fertility principle, symbolized by the old Aphrodite-Eros combination, and is now able to direct itself to individual love as personal encounter. From this perspective, Eros (as erotic love) must be saved from the transpersonal sphere of the Great Mother and ushered into the sphere of human love.

Considering that Neumann's work is a study of female development, his use of the terms masculine and feminine is very problematic. Some of the difficulty is due to his stereotypical use of gender terms. For example he speaks of the "masculine attribute" of "a stout heart and prudence beyond the prudence of woman"[31] and the "masculine world of consciousness."[32] He attributes Psyche's failure to carry out her task in the underworld to being a female: "Psyche fails, she must fail, because she is a feminine psyche."[33] And Neumann's inquiry into the reason for her failure is presented in equally sexist terms: "It is only an irresistible, deplorable feminine curiosity mingled with vanity that prevents her from fulfilling her mission as messenger in the service of the goddess's cosmetic needs, that impels her to open the box on which her whole fate depends."[34] The very context of Apuleius' novel, which many commentators feel centres around Lucius' curiosity (i.e., a man's curiosity), should have given Neumann pause before choosing the words "deplorable feminine curiosity." Even the tendency to despair becomes "feminine" in Neumann's view:

> Her naivete, as well as the type of scene to which she subjects Eros, her passionate murmurs, as well as her propensity for despair, are thoroughly feminine. Still more so is the quality of her love and will, which, though not unswerving as in men, are for all their suppleness amazingly tenacious and firm.[35]

And reason appears to be a masculine preserve in the following description of Psyche: "She professes her love and holds fast to her individual encounter with Eros, but at the same time, in opposition to all—masculine—reason, she discloses her primordial femininity."[36] Neumann even characterizes ego stability as a masculine virtue when he tries to explain why Psyche must show pity on her journey to the underworld:

> As the tower teaches Psyche, "pity is not lawful." If as we shall proceed to show, all Psyche's acts present a rite of initiation, this prohibition implies the insistence on "ego stability" characteristic of every initiation. Among men this stability is manifested as endurance of pain, hunger, thirst, and so forth; but in the feminine sphere it characteristically takes the form of resistance to pity. This firmness of the strong-willed ego, concentrated on its goal, is expressed in countless other myths and fairy tales, with their injunctions not to turn around, not to answer, and the like. While

ego stability is a very masculine virtue, it is more; for it is the presupposition of consciousness and of all conscious activity [italics
added].[37]

Neumann is right about the importance of ego stability in human
development and in initiation rites in particular, but he gives no reason why he refers to this as a "very masculine virtue." He presents
no argument or evidence to show that men are necessarily more sta-
ble in ego consciousness than women. It would be difficult to prove
such a generalization.

I call attention to some of these highly questionable assumptions
about the nature of feminine and masculine because they bear
directly on Neumann's interpretation of the Eros and Psyche tale.
When it is evident from the passages just considered that his understanding of masculine and feminine are so heavily laden with stereotypes, we should approach the gender-related aspects of his theory
with great caution.

Neumann makes a minor attempt to relate his interpretation of the
Eros and Psyche myth to its literary context when he connects it to
Lucius' initiation in the last book of Apuleius' novel. There he identi-
fies Lucius with Eros:

> In Eros as in Lucius, the development at every state starts not
> from the activity of the masculine ego, but from the initiative of
> the feminine. In both cases the process—for good and evil—is car-
> ried out by this feminine principle, in opposition to a resisting and
> passive masculine ego.[38]

As Eros is the son of the goddess Aphrodite, so Lucius becomes the
son of the goddess Isis through initiation, and this may partly
explain why Neumann supposes that Lucius' initiation is prefigured
by Eros' development in the course of the Eros and Psyche tale. Yet
in Neumann's unorthodox interpretation of Eros as the god who
becomes human in the tale, this is exactly the opposite of Apuleius'
story, where Lucius becomes identified with a god in the course of
initiation. In Eros' case, a god becomes human while in Lucius' case
a human becomes like a god. The more obvious parallel which commentators have pointed out is that Psyche is deified and, to some
extent, so is Lucius. But this parallel would not follow Neumann's
assumption that the Psyche tale illustrates female development. At
most, he is willing to admit that Lucius' initiation is complementary
to Psyche's transformation:

> While in the tale of Psyche the myth of feminine individuation
> leads to the supreme union of the feminine with the divine lover,
> Apuleius' novel, as though to complement this feminine initiation

with a masculine one, ends with the introduction of Lucius into the mystery of Isis, where the Great Mother manifests herself as Sophie and the Eternal Feminine.[39]

Neumann focusses on the immediate context of the Psyche tale to support his interpretation of it as a feminine initiation: an old woman tells the story to a young woman who is abducted on her wedding day by robbers seeking a ransom from her parents. Neumann emphasizes the fittingness of this tale as a consolation to the poor young woman. Just as Psyche is finally reunited with her beloved Eros after misfortune and suffering, so the woman can hope for such a positive outcome in her own case.

Neumann sees Lucius' initiation into the feminine mysteries of Isis as his identification with the son who is born from the Mother Goddess. Lucius is transformed into the son of Isis, Horus-Osiris, the Sun-Light-God.[40] For Neumann this transformation is linked to Lucius' original metamorphosis into an ass. A female is behind both transformations. The evil goddess of fate was behind the first change, while the good goddess Isis is responsible for his salvation. Beyond noting a parallel between the Eros and Psyche tale and Lucius' initiation Neumann does not go into detail about the psychological meaning of Lucius' initiation and transformation into the Sun god.

For Neumann the birth of Psyche's daughter at the end of the story has great significance. The daughter, named Voluptas (meaning Pleasure or Joy), represents the "birth of the divine child," which in Jungian terms is the Self, the "divine" fruit of the individuation process. The myth itself is not explicit as to whether the child of Psyche and Eros is divine, since its divinity was dependent upon the condition that Psyche keep the secret of Eros' identity and in the tale itself it is doubtful whether Psyche does keep the secret. Nevertheless, Neumann interprets her as the divine joy of mystical union and, together with the Eros-Psyche archetype, a perfect expression of the result of individuation:

> The archetype of Psyche united with Eros, taken together with the child Joy, strikes us as one of the highest forms that the symbol of the coniunctio has taken in the West. It is a youthful form of Shiva united with his Shakti. The hermaphrodite of alchemy is a later but lesser form of this image, because, as Jung has pointed out, it represents a monstrosity, contrasting sharply with the divine pair, Eros and Psyche.[41]

The hermaphrodite of alchemy is Hermes, who symbolizes the synthesis of opposites, at once both male and female, young and old. In this regard Neumann places his interpretation of the tale in the context of Jung's own search for symbol systems which represent historical antecedents to analytical psychology.

Neumann's interpretation can be seen as a creative commentary on a myth which evokes the main outlines of the individuation process described by Jung and, as such, continues to be valued by many depth psychologists. But we have also noted certain difficulties with Neumann's interpretation, especially regarding his assumptions about consciousness being masculine and the unconscious being feminine and, in particular, his view that the Psyche tale is the "central document of feminine psychology."[42] A major problem with Neumann's interpretation lies in the extent to which he removes the tale from the overall context of Apuleius' novel, but this is a tendency among all of the psychological interpreters of the Psyche tale we have seen thus far.

Marie Louise von Franz

After Neumann, Marie Louise von Franz has presented the most thorough psychological treatment of the Psyche tale in *A Psychological Interpretation of the Golden Ass of Apuleius* (1970). She differs from most of the other psychological commentators in that she insists on keeping the literary context of this story in the foreground: "For what I know about this type of literature allows me to think that it is neither legitimate nor even possible to interpret in isolation these passages at their deepest level of meaning because the novel is a whole."[43] The immediate context of the Psyche tale is that robbers have taken the bride, Charite, from her mother, and a drunken old woman who lives with the robbers tells the story to Charite in order to comfort her. Von Franz interprets Charite herself as representing Lucius' real feelings which have been tied up with the mother to this point in the story, and the robbers are masculine elements which work to free Lucius' from his mother complex.

The Psyche story itself, von Franz maintains, is an archetypal dream. She disagrees with Neumann's view of the tale as a literary insertion which doesn't belong in the context of Apuleius' novel. Von Franz believes that Apuleius chose to insert the fairy tale because it illuminates the masculine psychology of Lucius and even of Apuleius himself; in particular it expresses Apuleius' "initiation problem."[44] By this she means that the Eros and Psyche tale is an archetypal story about the coming together of the divine and the human—the essence of religious initiation. Yet von Franz does not consider the Psyche tale as a portrayal of successful divine-human union even though it ends with Psyche's deification on Mt. Olympus. According to von Franz, retiring to Mt. Olympus is equivalent to receding into the collective unconscious, and that is the opposite of bringing the divine-human encounter to reality. But as Lucius' archetypal dream, this story has had an effect on him. Von Franz suggests that for the first time Lucius' inner totality, or Self, emerged from the unconscious, touched his consciousness slightly, and then sank again into the unconscious.[45]

To support this view she notes that at the point in Apuleius' novel where the Psyche story appears, Lucius is only a passive onlooker in donkey form. As a donkey, he is not yet in a position to integrate the full human potential represented in the Eros and Psyche tale. It is only later when Lucius is again in human form that he is able to actualize the spiritual union of Eros and Psyche, to rescue this potential from the collective unconscious in his own initiation into the Isis mysteries.

Von Franz considers Aphrodite to be the combined archetype of the mother-anima. She joins these two archetypes because the anima derives from and is influenced by the mother archetype, and in their undeveloped state, the figures of the mother archetype and the anima are virtually the same.[46] To help clarify the close relationship between the two archetypes represented by Aphrodite, von Franz says that Aphrodite symbolizes the anima when it is connected with the mother while Psyche symbolizes the anima as it is gradually distinguished from the maternal image.[47] These archetypes do not connect with people's actual lives until they are activated by a human drama such as experiences with one's mother or with a lover. Von Franz says this whole process can be characterized as a descent of the god figure into the human realm, a kind of incarnation, and many neuroses are due to the ego's holding back this development.[48] From this viewpoint, healing coincides with a widening of consciousness to discover and incorporate the emotions and meaning these divine figures bring with them. In its most positive form this expansion of consciousness can be an ascent into religious experience, which is a central aspect of Apuleius' novel. Diagram 12 illustrates the psychological dynamics von Franz describes.

Because von Franz sees Psyche as the anima which seeks to become differentiated from the mother archetype, she considers Psyche to be, in a sense, a variant of Koré, the daughter of the Great Mother goddess. Von Franz points out that the daughter goddess is closer to the human than the Mother goddess, just as Christ is closer to the human than God the Father.[49] Thus von Franz speaks of Psyche as a *daimon*, a figure who is not strictly divine but mediates between the divine and the human. Von Franz also picks up on Merkelbach's view that Psyche is Isis and Aphrodite is also Isis, thus equating Psyche and Aphrodite. Von Franz presents this compli-

Diagram 12

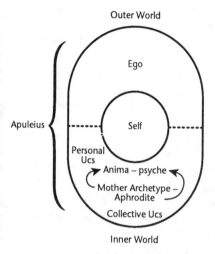

This diagram shows the personality of Apuleius. Psyche symbolizes Apuleius' anima differentiating itself from the Mother archetype (Aphrodite). This allows Apuleius to become more aware of his emotional life and his unconscious.

cated set of relationships to show that the Eros and Psyche tale is a variant of the *hieros gamos*, the heavenly marriage of royal brother and sister which also symbolizes the end result of the individuation process:

> One could therefore say that something from the collective unconscious voices the wish that a union between Eros and Psyche, the human incarnation of Venus, should take place. It is a sacred marriage because Venus is the mother of Eros, and if Psyche is Venus, it is the famous mythological *hieros gamos*, the sacred marriage between mother-daughter-sister and her own son, but this time in a partly incarnate form, so it is not only that the archetype of Venus tends towards approaching the human realm, but also that the archetype of the divine marriage should come down onto earth.[50]

Thus for von Franz, the Eros and Psyche tale shows a movement within the collective unconscious itself toward realizing (incarnating) the highest potential of individuation. She sees individuation, the process of developing psychological wholeness, at the heart of Lucius' religious initiation. Seen spiritually, Psyche, as the incarnation of the Great Mother goddess, represents Isis, who comes to save Lucius at the end of the novel. Seen psychologically, Psyche, as the anima, represents those feminine elements which Lucius must integrate in order to achieve psychological wholeness.

Von Franz understands both Psyche and Eros as *daimones*, who are minor gods, intermediaries between the human and the divine. She refers to Apuleius' paper on the *daimon* of Socrates in which he presents the theory about the *daimones*: they are capable of every kind of emotion, unlike the gods, and they can be influenced by human beings.

Eros is a multi-faceted figure for von Franz. In the first place she sees him as the god of love who moves the soul toward individuation.[51] Von Franz also briefly considers the possibility that Eros could represent the animus.[52] Since she has a traditional understanding of the animus as being the personification of a woman's unconscious psyche, it is difficult to see what psychological role Eros as animus would play in Lucius' development. Could Eros represent Psyche's animus, assuming for a moment that Psyche is a woman rather than Lucius' anima? Unfortunately, this question remains unanswered because von Franz does not develop the psychological implications of Eros as an animus figure.

Von Franz also deals with Eros' specific role in relation to Lucius' psychological struggle in the *Metamorphoses*. In this regard, Eros represents the *puer aeternus* archetype in Lucius. The *puer* has characteristics of a mother's boy who does not wish to grow up but prefers to stay with the eternal mother. According to von Franz, the *puer aeternus* is often found in a person with a strong mother complex such as Apuleius and the hero of his novel, Lucius.[53] Someone with a positive mother complex frequently has megalomaniacal fantasies to compensate for an inability to deal with real life and real women. The *puer* often leads a provisional life, always expecting one day in the future to do great things.[54] This aspect of Eros is brought out in his reaction to being burned by Psyche when he flies back to his mother and remains there while Psyche struggles to regain his love. However, von Franz also recognizes a potentially valuable role of the *puer* element in the personality, for it can bring a quality of youth, creativity and fresh insight to a person's life, if it is consciously integrated.

A person with a negative mother complex has too little of this *puer* element and so he tends to be cynical and not able to trust his feelings.[55] She considers Apuleius to be struggling with a negative mother complex, so his goal would be to find the *puer* element lacking in his personality. She sees this represented in the Psyche tale where Eros appears as the "remote bridegroom of the anima,"[56] the missing *puer* element for which Apuleius is searching. According to von Franz, in the Psyche tale, Eros himself has a "positive mother" complex in that he is dependent on his mother and has difficulty marrying because of her.

While Lucius does not consciously identify with the *puer aeternus*, it is at work in his unconscious. In this sense the Eros and Psyche tale is a portrait of what is emerging from within Lucius:

> Lucius has a negative mother complex. . . . He is not a *puer aeternus* in that sense, but, one step removed, he has the same thing in the unconscious. Very often if a man has a negative mother complex predominating in his visible attitude, he is cynical or negative about women, realistic in an even cold intellectual way. But if, in working on the problem, one tries to bring up his feeling if it has not been destroyed by the negative mother, then you see his real feelings are just the other way around, like the positive *puer aeternus*.[57]

When von Franz characterizes Eros in this way she focusses on a much less positive dimension of the tale than the *hieros gamos* meaning previously considered. But then von Franz does not see this tale as having a successful outcome, even though she recognizes its valuable psychological potential.

Von Franz sees the jealous sisters as the negative aspect of the anima. They represent negative elements in the mother complex which contaminate the anima, symbolized by Psyche.[58] Overall, these negative attitudes tend to counterbalance the positive, somewhat naive feelings represented by Psyche herself. Von Franz links the sisters with cynicism and the power drive, but she also recognizes that they have a positive role associated with self-preservation and realism.[59] The sisters' cynicism focusses on the unreality of Psyche's paradise and the likelihood that her lover is a dragon or snake. Von Franz says that even when the sisters slander Eros, calling him a monster, they correctly call attention to the fact that Eros' unreal paradise is too far away from reality and is, in some sense, inhuman and cold.[60]

So the sisters serve as a kind of self-preservative instinct to move Psyche out of this situation:

> Mythologically, there is no such thing as an unconscious paradise, and here there are the sisters who represent the impulse for self-preservation, and also a certain amount of realism. Self-preservation is an instinct we need, and if it is too much excluded it will break in and poison.[61]

For von Franz the skeptical attitude represented by the sisters contains the essence of Apuleius' entire novel.[62] The knife Psyche prepares to use against Eros is the rational devaluation which undercuts strong feelings of attachment. Von Franz sees this skeptical attitude as Apuleius' defence against his own sensitivity which only occa-

sionally surfaces when he is gripped by strong feeling, such as at the
end of the novel. Von Franz interprets the lamp, like the knife, as a
rational depreciation that undervalues the divine in the unconscious:

> The light of Psyche's lamp represents a conscious point of view
> that is like seeing Eros as no more than an animal (that is, "noth-
> ing but" sexuality: it is this that drives away the God). Moreover,
> the burning oil of the lamp deeply wounds him. In every under-
> valued interpretation, the psychic personifications and events of
> this sort dissimulate a secret emotional motive: the desire to
> escape from the "divine" aspect in all of the archetypal manifesta-
> tions of the deepest layers of the collective unconscious.[63]

It is clear that light often represents a conscious viewpoint, but the
light in the story shows Eros to be a god, and not the monster the sisters warned Psyche about. Thus, while von Franz is correct about a
certain conscious viewpoint undermining the divine dimension in
human experience, her interpretation of the lamp does not seem to fit
this particular context in the Psyche story. Here the lamp appears to
be a light of consciousness that is able to see through the sisters' lies
and show Eros' divinity.

Like Neumann, von Franz provides a detailed commentary on
Psyche's tasks. She interprets the pile of seeds which Psyche must
sort as the multiplicity of images and potential forms of the collective
unconscious.[64] So long as the archetypal contents remain unrealized
or unintegrated they continue to be chaotic potentialities which do
not benefit the individual person. According to von Franz, the feeling function must be developed to order and select the archetypal
images so that the meaningful and valuable material can be distinguished from the nonsense and destructive elements which
co-exist in the unconscious. Yet the feeling function, even when
developed, is not enough in this work. The ants which help Psyche
in her seemingly hopeless task symbolize an ordering principle
within the collective unconscious itself. Based on her clinical experience with integrating unconscious contents, von Franz maintains
that the feeling function somehow calls forth this secret order in the
collective unconscious.

In Psyche's second task, the reed which tells her the secret of col-
lecting wool from the dangerous sheep represents the hint of truth
coming from the collective unconscious. Von Franz agrees with
Merkelbach that the reed is connected with the Egyptian motif of
Horus, the rising sun, the king at the moment of renewing his king-
ship when he is reborn in his son. Since the reed represents Horus in
the hieroglyphs, she sees it as an expression of the solar principle of
becoming and therefore an anticipation of the truth of future life.

Von Franz sees this truth as part of the collective unconscious.[65] She interprets the ram as aggressive and unreflective impulsiveness which is often a quality of the anima. Just as Psyche discovers how to gather the wool indirectly, so the anima must be able to sort through emotions rather than simply acting them out, which would be the reaction of the ram. Von Franz interprets this task as a way of developing the ability to discover the significance behind a strong emotion, thus relating to and learning from the anima rather than being ruled by its emotions.

In the third task Psyche must fill a crystal vessel with the water of the Styx. For von Franz this water represents the psychic energy of the collective unconscious which cannot be held or manipulated by an individual's will. When Psyche despairs of accomplishing this task, the eagle of Zeus comes to her rescue. Von Franz interprets this eagle as the flight of spiritual intuition which often emerges from the depths of the unconscious just when the conscious mind appears to be incapable of acting by itself.[66] According to von Franz, Psyche's holding the water of the Styx signifies that when the anima keeps a person in touch with the depths of the unconscious, great creativity is possible.

In Psyche's final task, her journey to the underworld to obtain the beauty ointment, von Franz views the instructions about not taking pity on the figures who cry for help as a refusal of the anima to be caught up in sentimental feelings toward that which is already dying. She applies this symbol to the analyst as well as the analysand in the process of integrating unconscious contents. Retrospective sentimentality about past experience can interfere with the business of getting on with one's life and attending to the immediate needs of the present and goals for the future. For von Franz, Psyche's task represents the analytical journey into the unconscious as a search for those symbols which lead from an outgrown attitude into a new perspective on life.

Von Franz believes the beauty ointment itself is connected with the religious dimension of Apuleius' story. She refers to the sacramental function of creamy ointments in Egypt which were used to anoint the statues of the gods as a sign of devotion. So she sees the ointment as a symbol of the psyche's ultimate spiritual devotion which belongs only to the gods. When Psyche takes some of the ointment for herself, this is appropriating for the human being what belongs only to the gods. Von Franz has in mind here the situation where people try to exploit their dreams or the unconscious for their own purposes without giving respect and reverence to the religious mystery within their own souls. Psyche falls into a dangerous sleep when she tries to manipulate this sacred life substance for her own use.[67]

When Eros rescues Psyche from this deathlike sleep von Franz sees Eros as a symbol of the self archetype which is often activated during situations of extreme danger. Von Franz agrees with Merkelbach that here Eros prefigures Osiris, who appears in Lucius' final initiation at the end of the book. Even when von Franz interprets Eros as a symbol of the divine psychic centre of the soul, she is not optimistic about the meaning of Eros' triumph. Because von Franz equates Olympus with the unconscious, she concludes that when Eros takes Psyche to Olympus any gains Psyche has made are lost in the unconscious: "It seems that Lucius has not yet suffered enough for his Self to have achieved its full energy, and that he was not in any way ready for a deep religious experience."[68] This is a rather pessimistic conclusion from her study of the Psyche tale as the story of Apuleius' or Lucius' anima development. She sees in the Eros and Psyche tale a solution to Apuleius' or Lucius' problem which she has characterized as his negative mother complex, but in her opinion this solution is not realized in the human realm. It remains a kind of archetypal thought experiment which doesn't find fulfillment in reality.

Von Franz also interprets the birth of Voluptas more negatively than does Neumann. Where he sees the child as the fruit of mystical union, she says it represents lust.[69] Von Franz adds an unusual twist to this aspect of the story. She says that the child would have been a boy, not a girl, if Psyche had kept the secret of Eros' identity.[70] In this event, the boy would have been a symbol of the self archetype in relation to Lucius. Even if this birth of the self would have taken place in Olympus, which for von Franz is equated with the unconscious, it would still be more positive than the birth of a girl who represents the rebirth of an anima aspect, namely sensuous love.

So, as the Eros and Psyche story ends, von Franz concludes that the time is not yet ripe for the self archetype to emerge into consciousness, where it could have an effect on Lucius' life. Von Franz appears to be unduly pessimistic when she interprets Eros primarily as an expression of the *puer aeternus* archetype and when she considers union with Eros to be potentially pathological, but the great value of her interpretation is that she constantly refers the Eros and Psyche story back to its context in the *Metamorphoses* and to Lucius' own struggles and development.

Ann Ulanov

Ann Ulanov, another Jungian analyst, treats the Eros and Psyche story in *The Feminine in Jungian Psychology and Christian Theology* (1971). Her approach modifies Neumann's interpretation in that she sees this tale as a description, not of a woman's development, but of anima development in man:

> The story of Eros, or Amor, and Psyche is interpreted by Erich Neumann as a description of feminine development within a woman. With appropriate modifications of interpretation, I think the story is more accurately read as the development of a man's anima. As with any myth, there are many levels of understanding. My own interpretation is based on the fact that this story is one episode in a larger narrative of a man's psychological transformation; the all-embracing context is masculine.[71]

This statement shows Ulanov's concern with the relation of the Eros and Psyche tale to the story of Lucius' transformation in the *Metamorphoses*. While Neumann does briefly relate this tale to Lucius' initiation, the overall context of Apuleius' novel does not influence his fundamental line of interpretation. On this point Ulanov is more like von Franz, who recognizes that the psychological interpretation of a story should bear in mind its literary context.

Ulanov believes Psyche represents the anima, but it is not clear whether Psyche symbolizes *Lucius'* anima and is therefore the personification of his unconscious. If Psyche did represent Lucius' anima, this could shed light on the psychological dynamics of his transformation in the Isis mysteries, but Ulanov does not apply her psychological insights in any detail to Lucius' transformation. She holds that, secondarily, Psyche may refer to women as well as a man's anima.[72]

For Ulanov, the beginning of the Psyche tale describes the emergence of the anima out of the matriarchal collective unconscious represented by Aphrodite (Diagram 13, A). A man's initial independence from the maternal unconscious comes from his anima, as an intermediate feminine symbol. Psyche as an anima figure represents this more human form of the man's unconscious, which allows him to relate to the unconscious rather than be dominated or overwhelmed by it. Aphrodite's rage symbolizes the reaction of the conservative side of the unconscious, which works against differentiation or development.[73] According to Ulanov, the way Aphrodite holds onto her son with long and fervent kisses illustrates the regressive aspect of the unconscious, "the strong incestuous flavor of mother love in its regressive phase, and, intrapsychically, the lure of unconsciousness."[74] But what does her son, Eros, symbolize in his close tie to Aphrodite? On the one hand, this relationship could represent the proximity of human love to the unconscious, and especially the Mother archetype; on the other hand, it could represent the problem of the young male trying to differentiate himself from his mother. Ulanov recognizes the ambiguity of the Eros figure in this tale:

> The problem of interpreting the symbolism of Eros psychologi-
> cally is a complicated one, because Eros is himself confused in the
> story. He is not sure whether he is love incarnate, and thus a deity,
> merely a human son at the beck and call of his mother, or prima-
> rily a male who falls in love with a human female and thus must
> fall into space-time relationships. These confusions are acted out
> in the story. Eros runs errands for his mother and retreats to his
> mother; he defies his mother by taking Psyche for himself, but he
> also hides her from his mother. He excites Psyche into achieving
> her adult womanhood and yet is himself humanly dependent on
> her in order to achieve his own autonomy.[75]

This accurately summarizes the multiple roles of Eros in the tale and highlights the complexity of any psychological interpretation of the Eros figure.

This ambiguity leads Ulanov to interpret Eros primarily as an ado-lescent male who "alternately thinks he is all these things: a mama's boy, love incarnate, *the* male, a god, an ordinary man."[76] Here she sees Eros as the young man, in love for the first time, whose relation-ship to the feminine changes from revolving around a greater parent (mother) figure to a more autonomous and individual relationship. This shift also causes an inward change in the way he relates to his own anima, the feminine within. Ulanov considers this inner change crucial because it frees the male ego from identification with the unconscious and allows for an individual relationship to the uncon-scious through the anima. Such an interpretation would seem to shed light on Lucius' transformation and initiation in the *Metamor-phoses*, but I have already pointed out that Ulanov does not highlight this. Psyche symbolizes the emergence of the "transformative anima" which leads to a man's spiritual development by initiating and mediating a relationship to his unconscious.

For Ulanov, the jealous sisters represent neglected feminine ele-ments in a woman or in the anima (Diagram 13, C). When they press Psyche to look at Eros in the light, they represent a move to deepen consciousness and Eros-in-the-dark symbolizes the non-related qual-ity of man's erotic passion. Ulanov considers this scene pivotal, since it precipitates differentiation. The difficulty with this interpretation is that Psyche as the anima differentiates herself from the male ego and Eros (as erotic love) so that they may be integrated in conscious rela-tionship. But the psychological centre of integration is the ego, not the anima, and so the psychological dynamics are hard to picture in relation to the Psyche tale.

Diagram 13

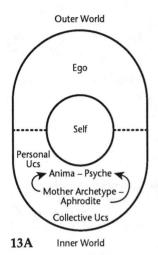

13A   Inner World

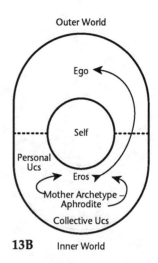

13B   Inner World

13C   Inner World

This diagram shows a man's anima development: (A) indicates the separation of the anima (Psyche) from the Mother archetype (Aphrodite); (B) shows that Eros (as the drive to involvement) also becomes differentiated from the Mother archetype so as to be at the disposal of the ego; (C) shows the sisters as neglected elements in the unconscious which help to separate the anima and the drive to involvement from the Mother archetype.

According to Ulanov, Psyche's development represents the anima becoming an independent centre of experience and intentions, which permits an individual relationship between consciousness and the anima (Psyche) and eventually leads to the emergence of the self archetype (Diagram 14). The anima must be strong enough to mediate the collective unconscious to the ego without itself being swamped by the unconscious contents. Ulanov believes that Psyche's despair and suicidal thoughts at each stage of fulfilling her tasks represent the danger of regressing into unconsciousness.

Diagram 14

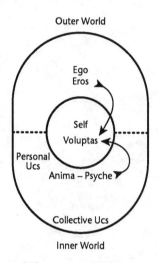

This diagram shows that Eros (as the drive to involvement and the ego's relationship to the anima) joins with Psyche (anima) to produce Voluptas (a symbol of the realized self archetype).

Like most of the Jungian interpreters, Ulanov devotes considerable attention to the psychological meaning of Psyche's tasks. She interprets the seeds Psyche sorts in the first task as the male's promiscuous tendencies, and the ants who help sort them represent the anima's instinctive ability to order the countless potentialities of the psyche. Psyche's second task, gathering wool from the sheep, represents the anima's ability to blunt the male's aggressive tendency in order to direct this power to relationships. For Ulanov, this symbolizes the developed anima's wisdom in avoiding the stalemate of intrapsychic polarization by instructing the male's ego on procedures of correct timing and learning how to let things pass in order to gather only their essence.[77]

In the first task the anima develops the capacity to tame the male's sexual instinct and in the second it learns to channel the male's power instinct. Psyche's third task, filling the crystal vessel with waters from the dangerous spring, represents the anima's ability to give form to the boundless vital energy, and especially the spiritual elements, of the collective unconscious. In this way, Psyche as anima becomes the vessel of individuation for the male. For Ulanov, Zeus' eagle who aids Psyche is a symbol of male friendship which can help a young man in his struggle for independence from the mother.

Ulanov interprets Psyche's fourth task, entering the underworld, as a symbol of the anima's role in mediating the reality of death which the ego must accept. When Psyche is instructed to resist the dead man seeking help on the underworld journey, this stands for the anima's need to respond to an actual and immediate love rather than to remain attached to ancestral spirits or the spirit of the mother. According to Ulanov, Psyche must resist the weaving women just as the anima must serve reality and not get lost in the world of fantasy, wishing and dreaming. When Psyche disobediently opens the beauty ointment, her positive intention saves her: she seeks not simply to become beautiful, but to be beautiful for Eros. For Ulanov this represents the anima serving masculine eros, the drive for involvement, rather than the anima becoming lost in narcissistic self-idolization.

Psyche's bold act evokes courage and determination in Eros, who rescues Psyche from the sleep which overcomes her. For Ulanov this shows the reciprocity between anima and ego: the masculine ego saves the anima from immersion in the unconscious, just as in the first three tasks the anima protects the ego by mediating the power of the unconscious that threatens to overwhelm it.

Ulanov speaks of the deification of both Psyche and Eros at the end of the tale, but this seems confusing because Eros is divine from the beginning of the story. Here Ulanov again calls attention to the ambiguity of the Eros figure by speaking of his deification. Eros represents not only an archetype of the divine but also the human ego: "Eros symbolizes both the transpersonal archetype of relatedness to a deity, that is, a nonhuman principle, and also the human masculine ego that depends on the anima to free its eros drive from the maternal unconscious."[78] For Ulanov, the marriage of Psyche and Eros represents the union of the anima and the now-differentiated ego, which is so central to the individuation process described by Jung, and she quotes Neumann on the relationship of the Psyche tale to the mystical union described in the world's religions: "her final abandonment and the god who approaches as a savior at this very moment correspond exactly to the highest phase of mystical ecstasy, in which the soul commends itself to the godhead."[79] The general thrust of Ulanov's interpretation is that Eros primarily represents an aspect of the masculine ego, namely the drive for involvement with others and the world, but some of her comments about the role of the divine in human transformation leave the door open for an interpretation of Eros as a god, or at least a symbol of the relationship to God. She speaks of the marriage of Eros and Psyche as a "kind of paradigm of the union of the soul and God."[80]

The fruit of the union of Eros and Psyche is the daughter called Voluptas (Joy or Pleasure) who is, according to Ulanov, both human and divine. As I noted in my discussion of Neumann, Apuleius' story itself is not clear on the divine or human status of the child Voluptas. Ulanov follows Neumann by interpreting the child as at least partly divine, and she agrees with him that Voluptas represents the joy that is experienced in mystical union. The divine character of the child born to Psyche seems to correspond well with Jung's view that the self archetype is not empirically distinguishable from the god-image. In Jungian thought, the relationship between the conscious mind and the unconscious (personified by the anima) results in the establishment of the transcendent function and the emergence of symbols of the self archetype. The child Voluptas would symbolize not only the joy of mystical union, but also the transcendent function itself (Diagram 14). If the self archetype is indistinguishable from God and is, in some sense, the result of union of the ego and the anima, this could explain why Neumann and Ulanov assume that Psyche's child is divine.

James Hillman

In *The Myth of Analysis* (1972) James Hillman treats the Eros and Psyche story as a metaphor for what takes place between people and within the person in psychological creativity, whether that be in analysis or in life outside the analytical setting. He does not see it primarily as a metaphor of feminine psychology in women, as Neumann does, nor as a story about anima development in men, as Ulanov and von Franz do. The Eros and Psyche story is equally valid for both men and women wherever "soul making" occurs.

To understand Hillman's perspective on Eros and Psyche it is necessary to consider how he modifies certain aspects of traditional Jungian thought. Hillman disagrees with Jung's idea that the anima exists only in men as the personification of their unconscious:

> Although Jung has given us this concept of the anima, he has limited it by definition to the psychology of men. Empirically, the anima shows first where a man's consciousness is weak and vulnerable, reflecting his interior contrasexuality as a feminine inferiority—he whines and bitches. However the archetype of the anima cannot be limited to the special psychology of men, since the archetypes transcend both men and women and their biological differences and social roles.[81]

Hillman notes that Jung considered the anima to be an "empirical concept whose sole purpose is to give a name to a group of related or analogous psychic phenomena" and in Hillman's analytical experience this group of psychic phenomena are not confined to men.[82] Hillman points out that part of the difficulty with distinctions between the psychological terms used by Jung is that "soul," "psyche," "anima" and "animus" all mean "the soul" and thus could be confused with the religious idea of the soul in Christianity. Hillman reminds us that although Jung wished to give conceptual clarity to the words "psyche" (as the totality of all psychic processes), "anima" (as signifying the personification of a man's unconscious) and "animus" (as signifying the personification of a woman's unconscious), these words are symbols which evoke meanings apart from any technical definitions assigned to them.

Hillman's own view is that the anima is related to psyche as potential to actual. Through dialogue and intercourse with the feminine aspects represented by the anima, psyche develops. "Therefore, latent within all the anima confusions is the psyche, straining to awaken; and this psyche, as the old tale tells us, was a beautiful, moody, suicidal, rather inexperienced girl, in naive relation with her sisters and the goddesses."[83] So anima is in the process of becoming psyche. In Hillman's interpretation of the Eros and Psyche tale, using the same Jungian diagram, Psyche would represent both the anima (Diagram 15, A) and the total psyche of any human being (Diagram

Diagram 15

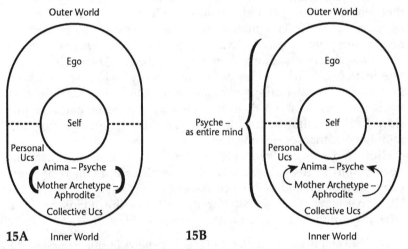

15A Inner World   15B   Inner World

This diagram shows: (A) that early Psyche (as anima) is still undifferentiated from Aphrodite (Mother archetype) and (B) Psyche develops both as the differentiated anima and the entire mind (conscious and unconscious).

15, B), especially someone involved in psychological creativity. Hillman is not concerned with how this interpretation might depart from the tale as it appears in Apuleius' narrative, since he does not present the same kind of detailed and systematic treatment of the tale we find in the works of Neumann or von Franz. He deals more with how the Eros and Psyche myth illuminates the process of psychological creativity than with how psychology illuminates the myth as it is found in Apuleius' *Metamorphoses*. Consequently he draws from sources other than Apuleius to broaden his description of the way Eros and Psyche relate to each other.

Hillman builds on Merkelbach's research, which emphasizes the initiatory aspect of the Eros and Psyche tale. Merkelbach considers the Psyche tale to be a mystery text which refers to initiation into the mysteries of Isis. Hillman sees Psyche's experiences as describing the initiatory path of psychological creativity. Both forms of initiation, that of the mystery religions and that of psychological creativity, involve the transformation of consciousness, or what Hillman calls "soul making."

Hillman interprets Eros as a broad realm of psychic reality, extending from the spiritual to the physical. Eros represents a divine function which operates between the gods and which allows the gods to enter into participation with humans; he brings the transpersonal realm to the individual. In this sense he is like Hermes, a psychopomp, the principle of intercourse between the divine and the human.[84] According to Hillman, Eros himself is part of a world neither wholly archetypal and divine nor wholly personal and physically human.[85] He is a masculine creative principle necessary for heightened psychological activity and is not to be confused with the feminine relatedness Jungians often speak about: "The phallic aspect of eros points to its male essence. This quality has sometimes been forgotten by analytical psychology, especially when eros is contrasted with logos and is then associated with the lunar and feminine side."[86] Here Hillman avoids some of the "Jungian" ambiguity found in Neumann's treatment of Eros.

Hillman draws on Plato's view of Eros as a *daimon*, the inner cautionary spirit. Eros as *daimon* is "the inexplicable moment of intervening inhibition and prescience that engenders psychic reality."[87] In Hillman's view, Eros is both the driving and the inhibiting force often present in creativity and other aspects of life:

> The compulsion-inhibition ambivalence shows in ritual, in play, and in mating, eating and fighting patterns, where for each step forward under the urge of compulsion there is lateral elaboration of dance, of play, of ornamentation—a "breather," which delays, heightens tension, and expands imaginative possibility and aesthetic form.[88]

So Eros represents a force which broadens the psyche by contradictory movements of drawing her forward and holding her back, eventually moving her toward awareness of her archetypal background. Hillman sees Eros not only as the contrasting forces which expand psyche by introducing her to the archetypal world, but also as the force that generates the symbols which surmount the opposites con-

Diagram 16

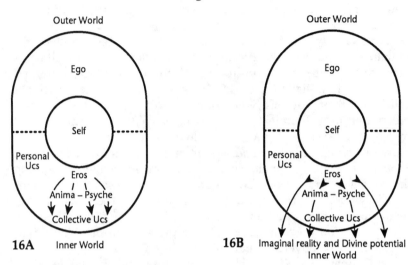

16A   Inner World   16B   Imaginal reality and Divine potential
                                          Inner World

This diagram shows that: (A) Eros (as a driving and inhibiting force) broadens Psyche (anima) by expanding her into the deep unconscious and (B) Eros also relates her to potentially divine levels of imaginal reality.

stituting the archetypal realm. In this regard Hillman considers Eros to be the transcendent function, that product of the individuation process which mediates between the conscious and unconscious. Although Hillman does not hold the "monotheistic role"[89] of the self archetype in the same high esteem as Jung does, nevertheless he values Eros' role as a synthesizer of opposites. Hillman himself prefers a polycentric psychology which recognizes that it is "the gods who clothe themselves in our complexes and speak through them."[90] Hillman is very much at home with language that personifies psychological contents as the activity of the gods and at times it seems as though he recognizes the possibility that the gods may have a transcendent reality independent of the human psyche (Diagram 16, B).

Hillman's thought is particularly important for the psychology of religion on this point. He sees Eros as the link to the transpersonal realm of the gods and as the key to participation in the imaginal world through which people experience the gods. He also says "what transpires in our psyche is not of our psyche."[91] In this regard, Eros coming in the night is a way of affirming the reality of contact with the divine which may occur in dreams, even though Hillman considers this reality of divine contact as something experienced through the imagination.[92] Hillman's affirmation of this possible divine contact through Eros *could* highlight the relationship of the Eros and Psyche tale to Lucius' story, since Lucius encounters the

divine in Isis. Yet Hillman is not concerned with possible implications of his interpretation for the story of Lucius in the *Metamor-*
phoses.

I have already noted Hillman's agreement with Merkelbach on the
initiatory meaning of the Psyche tale in Apuleius' novel. Hillman's
interpretation of the role of Eros as link to the gods brings to mind
Lucius' call to initiation in the last book of the novel. There Lucius is
called in dreams by Isis, who comes in the night and shows him
mercy and love. From a Christian perspective, this redemptive call
by Isis might seem like grace, but Hillman states that "grace depends
more on *caritas* and *agape* and less upon eros."[93] In Hillman's view,
Eros would not be the ideal god to characterize the descending
movement of grace from God because Eros represents an upward
spiral, symbolizing the urge of the individuation process as a movement starting from the human and reaching to the divine.[94] So this
places limits on how far Hillman's interpretation of Eros could illuminate Lucius' conversion and initiation.

For Hillman, the relationship between Eros and Psyche describes
an initiation which changes the structure of consciousness. While
Hillman grants that in Apuleius' novel the Psyche tale relates to
Lucius' initiation into the Isis mysteries, he interprets the fundamental meaning of this tale primarily as a symbolic portrayal of the
psychological and erotic ordeals experienced in neurosis: "Neurosis
becomes initiation, analysis the ritual, and our developmental process in psyche and eros, leading to their union, becomes the mystery."[95] Initiation in our day is more likely to occur in neurotic suffering and its treatment in analysis than in the setting of institutional
religion. For Hillman, neurosis involves the withdrawal of eros from
the psyche, leaving a person without hope or energy, loveless and
with a sense of guilt and separateness.[96] Psyche's tasks represent the
soul-work which prepares for reunion with Eros. Although he does
not discuss the meaning of each of Psyche's tasks, Hillman does say
that her tasks better facilitate an enduring connection of Eros to culture and history. By this he means that the psyche filters Eros' creative thrust in a way that gives lasting form to what would otherwise be a momentary impulse.[97] Thus, Psyche's tasks develop her to
the point where she can be an effective container for the inspiration
of the gods.

Hillman interprets Aphrodite as the great goddess who represents
a different kind of love from that of Eros. She is more serving and
accepting, and less differentiated than Eros. She symbolizes, on the
positive side, endless fecundity, while on the negative side, demand-
ing emotionality and notorious promiscuity.[98] For Hillman, Aphrodite represents an antipsychic component in love, as seen in her con-

stant opposition to Psyche. This is close to Neumann's view that Aphrodite represents love as the fertility principle as opposed to love as personal encounter.

Hillman interprets the birth of Psyche's child, Voluptas, as the pleasure deriving from psychological creativity, whether this be in the experience of saints, mystics, poets or ordinary people. According to Hillman, this emphasizes that creativity may be closely related to pleasure. This underscores Hillman's psychological theory that soul making through Eros (giving life to the imaginal) is more important than "making" consciousness and strengthening the ego by withdrawing projections from the imaginal realm.[99]

For Hillman, the deification of Psyche at the end of the tale underscores the primacy of the archetypal powers who rule Eros and psyche; it does not symbolize the immortality of those who accomplish the process of individuation, but rather affirms that soul making is related to the divine and that psychological creativity is a goal in itself. In arguing his case, Hillman presents a very creative interpretation of the Eros and Psyche story, while straying far from the details of Apuleius' version. Yet Hillman captures the initiatory significance of the myth in a way that remains true to the spirit of Apuleius' tale as an archetypal recapitulation of Lucius' initiation into the mysteries of Isis. So even where Hillman does not provide nearly the detailed analysis of the Eros and Psyche story as do Neumann, von Franz or Ulanov, his interpretation contributes to a greater appreciation of the myth's relation to creativity and the realm of the gods.

Robert Johnson

Robert Johnson's *She* (1976) is a popular discussion of the Psyche tale. He follows Neumann's lead very closely, but attempts to modify Neumann's use of the term feminine. He calls the Psyche tale ". . . one of the best elucidations available of the psychology of the feminine personality"[100] but then goes on to say that he is speaking of femininity in men as well as in women. Thus he appears to include in his term "feminine personality" those psychological characteristics in a man which Jung has termed "anima." These two cases would appear as in diagrams 17 and 18.

Johnson interprets Psyche's marriage of death as a reflection of a woman's attitude toward marriage in that the maiden in her must die. He generalizes the meaning of this symbol as the end of a woman's naivete at different times in her life, not just when she marries. Like Neumann, he sees Eros' insistence on remaining unknown in the darkness as a desire to avoid conscious relationship, and the

Diagram 17

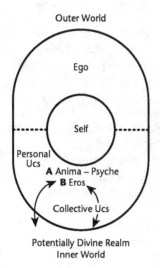

This diagram shows a man's personality where: (A) Psyche represents the anima (as the personification of a man's unconscious), and (B) Eros (as the experience of love) is the intermediary between humans and the divine.

Diagram 18

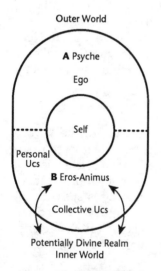

This diagram shows a woman's personality where (A) Psyche represents a woman's conscious mind and (B) Eros is the animus (as personification of a woman's unconscious) which mediates the divine realm.

sisters who push Psyche out of this dark paradise as ambiguous figures who may be positive shadow elements.

Johnson interprets the light and the knife Psyche uses to unmask her mysterious lover as masculine symbols. He notes two opposite meanings of the knife: 1) It may represent discrimination and clarity for cutting through fogbanks in a personal relationship, thus improving it, or 2) It may represent sarcastic and cutting remarks which tend to destroy a relationship.[101] Oddly enough Johnson attributes the negative pole of this masculine knife symbol, the sarcastic, to women or the anima in men,[102] as if to suggest that sarcasm is more predominant in women or a feminine characteristic in men. It is not clear why he says this. It could be because Psyche's sisters represent female elements in her who motivate her use of the knife. Since Johnson sees the knife as a masculine symbol, he might just as easily have attributed cutting remarks to men or the animus of women.[103] Though not always so obvious as with Neumann, we also encounter in Johnson the problem of gender stereotyping psychological characteristics.

Johnson's observations about the light symbol are poetic and creative, though beyond the context of the Psyche myth. He sees the light as a woman's presence, which bestows meaning and value on the events of the man's day,[104] the light that sees the god in a man.[105] Johnson adds that a man who is in good relationship with his own femininity, his anima, doesn't rely so heavily on the outer woman for this sense of worth. What Johnson refers to here as femininity seems to be simply the human. A woman is to bestow meaning on the events of the man's day. He does not suggest who is to bestow such meaning on the events of the woman's day, i.e., the man's "femininity" should bestow value on the woman's activities.

These ideas reflect a particular cultural and economic pattern of society: The man is to go out into the ruthless world, while the woman maintains a humane refuge at home with the children. This attitude reflects Jung's own bias regarding the Logos arena for men and the Eros arena for women.[106] In regard to the woman's light showing the god in a man, it seems that Johnson is speaking of the basic need for the presence of another person to recognize and bring out the divine potential in the human being. To characterize this fundamentally human activity as "feminine" does not help to clarify the psychological dynamics of spiritual development.

Johnson, like the other analysts, sees Eros as a multi-faceted symbol. He interprets Eros as 1) the experience of love, 2) a woman's animus and 3) an archetypal god. He notes that in our secular society people have increasing difficulty experiencing God in religion, but they often encounter the power of God in love. According to Johnson, Eros, as the experience of love, is the principle intermediary between humans and God.[107] Being in love opens a person to the superpersonal world of the archetypes or the divine and is often experienced as an intrusion that upsets the person's familiar world. A person can be possessed by Eros as an archetypal deity just as by any of the other archetypes of the collective unconscious (Diagram 19). For Johnson, the particular significance of the Psyche tale is that it represents the first time that a mortal experiences an archetype directly and lives. The tasks of Psyche show how she is transformed by this experience of Eros.

Diagram 19

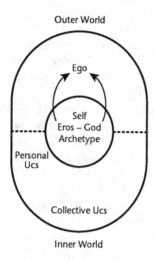

This diagram shows a person possessed by Eros as the god archetype. In such a case the ego is taken over by the deep unconscious.

Yet another meaning of Eros, according to Johnson, is that he represents a woman's animus (See diagram 18, B). In this case Psyche is held in a state of animus-possession until she lights the lamp of consciousness. Whether Eros is interpreted as an archetype of the divine or as the archetype of the animus would make little difference in terms of Jungian strategy for dealing with the psychological situation portrayed. In both cases, conscious relation to, rather than possession by, or obsession with, the archetype would be the goal. Psyche's lamp symbolizes this conscious, critical, relation to Eros as the archetype of the divine or as animus. Assuming Eros is the animus, he personifies and mediates the unconscious and as such he might be the one responsible for sending Psyche help at critical times while she performs her tasks.[108] While this explanation of Psyche's helpers fits the Jungian hypothesis of Eros as animus, it is hard to find evidence in Apuleius' text that Eros is responsible for sending help to Psyche.[109]

Johnson sees Psyche's first task, sorting the mixed seeds, as a symbol of dealing with the unconscious. The ants, being primitive, earthy symbols, represent the feminine instinct for handling the influx of material from the unconscious and relating it properly to consciousness. This leads Johnson to theorize again about the role of masculine and feminine: "The masculine component in personality, in man and woman, deals primarily with the outer world, while the feminine component deals primarily with the inner world."[110] Since he offers no evidence for such speculation, we can only imagine its source. Sociologically, the traditional role of men working "out" in the world and women "in" the home might be one source. Here Johnson's ideas reflect a traditional cultural dualism, which he does not support with either argument or evidence. Equally puzzling is his statement: "Sorting out the influx of emotions, moods and archetypes for the family is a beautiful feminine act."[111] This equation of feeling and emotion with the "feminine" is as dubious as the former linking of feminine and the inner world. What is particularly problematic about such statements by depth psychologists is that they are presented as truisms or folk-wisdom with little, if any, critical reflection on the culturally conditioned character of these ideas and almost no attempt to demonstrate their basis in fact.

In Psyche's second task Johnson sees the ram as an ambiguous power, capable of saving a person from a difficult parental situation on the one hand, but on the other hand, capable of sweeping aside a frail ego and destroying it. According to Johnson, modern humanity has identified with the ram in its assumption of power over nature[112] and Psyche's art of getting only the left-over fleece from the boughs is a symbol of achieving just the right amount of power without losing perspective of deeper values. Unfortunately, Johnson deflects this important insight by going on to discuss the difference between masculine, focussed, consciousness and feminine, diffused, awareness.

Johnson considers Psyche's third task, filling a crystal goblet with water, a model of the way a woman should deal with life's endless possibilities: "I think that this task is telling us how the feminine must relate to the vastness of life. She may take only one goblet of water. The feminine way is to do one thing and to do it well."[113] Johnson reminds us how much the fragile and precious crystal is like the human ego. If the goblet represents the ego, Psyche's act symbolizes the care necessary to prevent the ego from harm in its encounter with life and the unconscious. This interpretation would seem appropriate if Johnson did not link it with his view that this method of psychological limitation is somehow "feminine."

In the fourth task, Johnson sees Psyche's journey to the underworld as a symbol of psychological death, which is involved in the transition from one level of development to another. For Johnson, the tower which instructs Psyche about her journey represents the conventions and traditions of a culture; the beauty ointment she seeks may be a woman's preoccupation with beauty or attractiveness. Psyche's attempt to keep some of the beauty ointment for herself is a temporary regression to the old feminine consciousness. Although this failure brings on a deadly sleep, it is not a permanent condition and, according to Johnson, this serves to remind us that failure is a necessary part of growth.

The strength of Johnson's *She* lies in his art of telling this age-old tale in a lively and simple manner to a wide audience. A major weakness of this work lies in its unreflective support of the gender stereotypes which shore up sexual-social inequality. In this regard Johnson merely reflects certain cultural and economic patterns and thus does not get at a deeper psychological meaning of the story. It is difficult to see what he gains by gender-labelling such characteristics as sarcasm and curiosity. Even when a characteristic such as sarcasm is symbolized in a dream as a certain man or woman, it is dangerous to generalize such a personal or cultural representation as a comment about what is the psychological nature of masculine or feminine, and even more problematic to attribute such characteristics to male and female. Finally, Johnson, like most of the psychological commentators, does not relate his interpretation to the literary context of the story as it appears in Apuleius' *Metamorphoses*.

Jean Houston

Although not a Jungian analyst, Jean Houston considers the Eros and Psyche tale from a Jungian perspective in *The Search for the Beloved* (1987). For her, this story tells about a major development in the history of human consciousness, the awakening of the soul to its divine potential. Houston is not concerned at all about the literary context of the Psyche tale in Apuleius' novel as she seeks out the current implications of this myth for our own growth. Like Ulanov and Johnson, she interprets the myth as a story about the development of the feminine principle in both men and women.[114] Like Hillman, she views Psyche's situation as a myth of psychological creativity, offering clues to our own growth.

In Houston's interpretation, Aphrodite represents the old order, the "tyranny of all old dependencies and unreflected archetypes"[115] (see diagram 20, A). She also represents the great divide between the divine and the human, yet ironically at the same time she prepares for bridging that gap. For Houston, Psyche symbolizes consciousness, and especially a feminine element in consciousness. Aphrodite is Psyche's initiator, preparing her for the *hieros gamos*, the sacred marriage, wherein the human psyche will realize its godlike possibilities.

Houston sees Eros as a force within the soul which longs for development and a connection to something beyond the personal self. Eros leads the soul to the gods and brings the gods, as patterns of creativity and possibility, into the soul (Diagram 20, B).[116] In this sense Eros, the intermediary between the human and divine, "must create the world-in-between, providing sacred time and space to do the work of love and transformation."[117]

Diagram 20

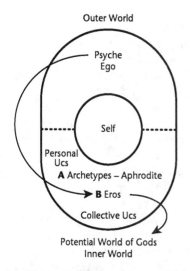

Outer World

Psyche
Ego

Self

Personal
Ucs

A Archetypes – Aphrodite

B Eros

Collective Ucs

Potential World of Gods
Inner World

This diagram shows: (A) Aphrodite as undifferentiated archetypes in the collective unconscious and (B) Eros as a psychopomp leading the conscious mind (Psyche) to contact with the gods.

Houston likens this world-in-between to a chrysalis from which a butterfly emerges. She interprets the magical castle where Psyche is transported as just such a place of gestation. Houston does not offer textual evidence when she connects Psyche's timeless period with Eros in the dark of night and Psyche's ability to accomplish her seemingly impossible tasks. Here Houston adds to the psychological interpretation of the marriage-of-darkness by seeing it not simply as an unconscious attachment and a function of the fertility principle or as a symbol of the ravishment of a virgin, but also as the creative ground out of which great achievements are born. She notes that the secret of this creative darkness lies in spending just the right amount of time there: staying there too long can mean decay or even madness; too little time there can result in lack of creative inspiration.

The sisters who ultimately push Psyche out of her unconscious paradise represent a positive force, according to Houston. They symbolize the doubts that arise when a situation is too one-sided and unconscious.[118] For Houston, the fact that Psyche sought out the sisters supports the view that they represent a realization in Psyche herself that her exclusive life of rapture in the darkness is missing something important. They represent Psyche's own awareness that she has spent long enough in that place of gestation. Diagram 20 illustrates Houston's interpretation. Houston considers the lamp and

knife to indicate that Psyche must use both the feminine and masculine parts of herself. The oil of the lamp symbolizes the feminine
essence of the plant world. This produces the light that illuminates
transpersonal dimensions of other persons and allows their innate
beauty to appear. This interpretation is similar to Johnson's, but
Houston adds that both "men and women can hold for each other
the lamp of mutual light and mutual remembrance."[119] In this way
she avoids the gender stereotyping of the lamp symbol which is part
of Johnson's interpretation. Houston agrees with other Jungian commentators that the knife represents a symbol of either discrimination
or destruction, depending on the user's intentions.

When Houston comments on Psyche's tasks she is especially concerned to bring out their enduring relevance for psychological and
spiritual growth today. Reflecting on these tasks, which most of the
Freudian interpreters pass over in silence, is the central part of Houston's work. She has devised psychological exercises associated with
each task to allow us to gain insight into their meaning. The tasks
which Aphrodite sets symbolize the "psychological and erotic
ordeals through which all of us are put in our search for union and
completion";[120] they are a series of initiations designed to deepen
consciousness. Psychologically, Houston sees Psyche's tasks as
engaging the animus. Although she does not discuss this aspect of
Jungian theory, she appears to agree with Hillman that both animus
and anima are in the unconscious of each person. Houston says that
the lesson women should learn from Psyche's labours is to develop a
true relationship with the masculine principle (animus) in themselves; men should learn "to engage the anima with sufficient animus so that the anima is luminous and not effete and the psyche is
deepened, not weakened."[121]

Houston interprets the ants who help Psyche sort the mixed seeds
in Psyche's first task as an instinctive ordering principle which operates beyond known resources to select, evaluate and order life. To
gain an experiential sense of this ordering principle she suggests that
we sit with a pile of mixed seeds and take an hour or so to sort them.
By observing what happens in this process, how the instinctual self
takes over, what emerges in fantasy, and what the various seeds
come to symbolize, we can get a direct feeling of how this instinctive
organizing principle works in our own lives.

In Psyche's second task, Houston sees the rams and their fleece as
powerful and dangerous masculine energies which have to be
redeemed in order to be integrated. The reed which instructs Psyche
on the secret of gathering the remaining fleece clinging to the bushes
represents the deep wisdom of the psyche regarding growth and

appropriate timing. Houston also offers a very interesting interpreta-tion of the time of day when Psyche is to accomplish her task. To acquire the fleece, Psyche is to wait until evening when the rams are asleep. According to Houston, the evening corresponds to twilight states of consciousness which give access to the wisdom of the deep unconscious. These alternate states of consciousness are in direct contrast to the ordinary state of "suntime (daylight) consciousness" which corresponds to the time of day when Psyche would be unable to gain what she needs. To illustrate the meaning and relevance of this task, Houston suggest a lengthy guided fantasy to give first-hand experience of the wisdom available through altered states of consciousness.

Psyche's third task is to fill a crystal vessel with the water of life. Houston speculates that the dangerous dragons who guard the spring may be a "mythic representation of our own ancient reptilian brain with its insistence on repetition and ritual."[122] The eagle who comes to Psyche's rescue represents a far-sighted perspective which is able to select just the right place to dip into the water of life. Hous-ton accepts Robert Johnson's view of the goblet as a symbol of the fragile ego and she also agrees with him that the wisdom of this task is to take the water of life one goblet at a time. To provide insight into the meaning of this task Houston recommends a guided fantasy in which we imagine ourselves as an eagle flying over the river of our lives to gain perspective on various life incidents.

Houston views the instructions given to Psyche for her fourth task, the journey to the underworld, as a guide to initiation. Like other Jungian commentators, she interprets the tower which provides these instructions as a symbol of a culture's wisdom, including its various rules and disciplines.[123] Houston understands the tower's warning to resist the many figures requesting help along the way as the need to curb availability and focus energy for critical tasks in psychological development. When Psyche opens the jar of beauty ointment on her return trip, she falls back into the sleep of old con-sciousness and returns to old habits.[124] But this is typical of develop-ment and not necessarily pathological, according to Houston, who sees this deep sleep as a period of gestation preparing for a new full-ness of life. Here Houston departs far from the text in offering her optimistic interpretation of Psyche's deadly sleep after opening the beauty box.

To experience the power of Psyche's adventure in the underworld, Houston has designed an initiation rite which attempts to re-enact Psyche's journey. Houston has adapted each of the tower's warnings to the demands of modern life which impede psychological growth and she suggests a combination of fantasy and ritual which aims at re-enacting the sacred marriage. Houston understands by this marriage of Eros and Psyche an historical event in consciousness where the gods come closer to humanity and human beings are transformed by their relationship to the divine. In contrast to von Franz's rather pessimistic conclusions about the meaning of the Psyche tale, Houston seems remarkably sanguine. Her statement, "If this myth teaches us nothing else, it shows that help is always present,"[125] captures her positive view of the meaning of this myth.

Despite the fact that Houston seems almost totally unconcerned about the literary context of this tale in Apuleius' *Metamorphoses*, she has arrived at an understanding which fits very well with the role of this myth in prefiguring Lucius' initiation into the mysteries of Isis. Houston's interpretation of the Eros and Psyche tale is designed to put people directly in touch with the timeless wisdom of this story. She seeks to participate to some extent in this mythical drama by contacting that deep level where this myth continues to live and influence people. The problem with such an interpretation is that there is no guarantee her experiments will lead to similar "immediate experiences" of the Eros and Psyche myth for more than a handful of people. From a therapeutic point of view, such an attempt to discover the enduring influence of this myth might be intriguing, yet Houston's strong focus on immediate experience has distanced her considerably from the original literary context of the tale. While some of her imaginative exercises may have value and therapeutic justification, they generally have little to do with the structure of the myth as it is presented by Apuleius. In this regard Houston appears to use the Eros and Psyche myth primarily as a springboard for her own developmental agenda.

To summarize this chapter, the Jungian interpretations emphasize the way the Eros and Psyche myth symbolizes certain aspects of psychological and spiritual development. Generally they focus on feminine development, whether that be understood as the development of 1) a woman, 2) the feminine aspects of a man's personality, or 3) the phylogenesis of feminine consciousness. This development is variously characterized as a movement toward love as personal encounter beyond the fertility principle (Neumann), Apuleius' (or Lucius') attempt to free himself from his mother complex (von Franz), the growth of a man's "transformative anima" which can relate him to the divine (Ulanov), soul making and increasing psychological creativity (Hillman), nourishing and strengthening a woman's ego and cultivating a man's spiritual life (Johnson), and transforming human consciousness by relating it to the divine (Houston). These interpretations follow, in one way or another, Jung's theory of the archetypes as a collective heritage which influences the individual's psychological and spiritual life. Jungians stress those elements of the myth which highlight the role of the archetypes in psychological development, namely Psyche's tasks, her deification and the birth of Voluptas. Like the Freudians, all of the Jungians except von Franz virtually ignore the literary context of the myth.

Notes

1 See the discussion re the parallels between Psyche and Lucius in the first chapter.

2 *Amor and Psyche—The Psychic Development of the Feminine* (New York, 1956), p. 146.

3 Ibid., p. 86.

4 Ibid., p. 78.

5 Jung defines the shadow as "the negative side of the personality, the sum of all those unpleasant qualities we like to hide together with the insufficiently developed functions and the contents of the personal unconscious" (CW 7, p. 66).

6 *Amor and Psyche*, p. 73.

7 Ibid., p. 75.

8 Ibid., p. 73.

9 "The Myth of Psyche," *Arethusa* 9 (1976): 111.

10 *Amor and Psyche*, p. 92.

11 Again, on p. 107, although he also refers to Psyche's unconscious forces, he speaks of Psyche as the ego: "Yet with her the unconscious forces play a more conspicuous part than in the development of masculine consciousness; the independent activity of Psyche as an ego is less powerful than in the corresponding careers of masculine heroes, as for example those of Heracles or Perseus."

12 Ibid., p. 141.

13 *The Origins*, p. 42. James Hillman has also commented on this peculiarity of Neumann's theory: "An Apollonic definition of consciousness occasions an unconscious that is Nietzschean or, to say the least, a province of the Great Mother. The identification of consciousness with the heroic-Apollonic mode forces one into the absurdities of Neumann" (*The Myth of Analysis* [Evanston, IL., 1972], p. 289).

14 This diagram is adapted from Jacobi's *The Psychology of C.G. Jung* (London, 1943), p. 122.

15 *Amor and Psyche*, p. 108.

16 The "paternal *uroboros*" refers to the "procreative thrust whereby the initially undifferentiated unconscious begins to differentiate itself with the beginning of evolution in time" (*The Origins and History of Consciousness* [New York, 1954], pp. 18-20).

17 *Amor and Psyche*, pp. 108-109. This section may be somewhat confusing to the reader due to Neumann's ambiguous use of the term "Eros." Neumann himself does not seem to be troubled by this ambiguity.

18 Jung defines the contamination of unconscious contents in this way: "The displacement and overlapping of images are as great in alchemy as in mythology and folklore. As these archetypal images are produced directly by the unconscious, it is not surprising that they exhibit its contamination of content to a very high degree. The best instances of this interconnection of everything with everything else can be found in dreams, which are very much nearer to the unconscious even than myths" (CW 14, p. 293).

19 *Amor and Psyche*, p. 90.

20 Ibid., p. 91.

21 *The Origins*, pp. xxiii-xxiv.

22 There is some question here as to whether Neumann's understanding of the divine order and its relationship to the collective unconscious is similar to Jung's view. This question is made even more complex when we realize that there is considerable debate about Jung's own position on this matter. See the summary of this debate in my *Dreams in the Psychology of Religion* (Lewiston, NY, 1987), pp. 110-14.

23 *The Origins*, p. 190.

24 Ibid., p. 338.

25 *Amor and Psyche*, pp. 95-96.

26 Ibid., p. 99.

27 Ibid., p. 105.

28 Ibid., p. 118.

29 Bettelheim also calls attention to the narcissistic state symbolized by Psyche alone in Eros' magical palace (*The Uses of Enchantment*, p. 293).

30 *Amor and Psyche*, p. 92.

31 Ibid., p. 110.

32 Ibid., p. 130.

33 Ibid., p. 121.

34 Ibid., pp. 120-21.

35 Ibid., p. 97.

36 Ibid., pp. 123-24.

37 Ibid., pp. 112-13.

38 Ibid., p. 151.

39 Ibid., p. 151.

40 Ibid., p. 150.

41 Ibid., pp. 144-45.

42 Ibid., p. 160.

43 *A Psychological Interpretation of the Golden Ass of Apuleius* (Zurich, 1970), p. 2.

44 Ibid., pp. 61-62.

45 Ibid., p. 64.

46 Ibid., p. 70.

47 Ibid., p. 81. Von Franz recognizes the interconnectedness of all the archetypes, not just the anima and mother archetypes: "I represented the archetypes as contents, or nuclei, in the unconscious. But they are more likely in a kind of soup in which everything is contaminated with everything else. Thus an archetype which is in the unconscious is identical with the whole unconscious. It is its own contrast; it is everything, masculine and feminine, dark

and light, and its own opposite. Everything overlaps; only when an archetype approaches the threshold of consciousness does it become more distinct" (Ibid., pp. 81-82). This description highlights the complexity and ambiguity of a Jungian interpretation of Apuleius' novel and the Eros and Psyche story in particular.

48 Ibid., p. 71.
49 Ibid., p. 75.
50 Ibid., p. 73.
51 Ibid., p. 66.
52 Ibid., p. 108.
53 Ibid., p. 19.
54 Ibid., p. 78.
55 Ibid., p. 78.
56 Ibid., p. 78.
57 Ibid., pp. 86-87.
58 Ibid., p. 79.
59 As with Neumann, there is no reflection on the sisters as sexual anxiety or sibling rivalry which is so important to the Freudian interpretations.
60 Ibid., p. 84.
61 Ibid., p. 90.
62 Ibid., p. 90.
63 Ibid., p. 85.
64 Ibid., p. 91.
65 Ibid., pp. 84-85.
66 Ibid., p. 99.
67 Ibid., p. 104.
68 Ibid., p. 109.
69 Ibid., p. 87.
70 Ibid., p. 86.
71 *The Feminine in Jungian Psychology and Christian Theology* (Evanston, IL, 1971), p. 215.
72 We shall see that Robert Johnson adopts this same position regarding the symbolic meaning of Psyche: she represents both the anima and woman.
73 Ibid., p. 219.
74 Ibid., p. 219.
75 Ibid., p. 218.
76 Ibid., p. 218.
77 Ibid., p. 234.
78 Ibid., p. 238.
79 Ibid., p. 239.
80 Ibid., p. 239.
81 *Myth of Analysis*, p. 50.
82 Hillman is not the only Jungian who holds that anima/animus exist in both men and women. See Edward Whitmont's "Reassessing Femininity and Masculinity: A Critique of Some Traditional Assumptions," *Quadrant* 13, 2 (1980): 119-21.
83 *Myth of Analysis*, p. 52.

84 Ibid., p. 70.

85 Ibid., p. 70.

86 Ibid., p. 65.

87 Ibid., pp 72-73.

88 Ibid., p. 75.

89 Hillman criticizes Jung's emphasis on the self archetype and its equation with monotheism as a narrowing of psychology. For Hillman, excessive focus on the self archetype relegates everything else, including the rich variety of images and gods in the psyche, to second place; all of the talk in analytical psychology about unity, growth, development, individuation, integration, centring, and the self does not do justice to the multiplicity and complexity of the psyche. See A. Samuels' discussion of Hillman in *Jung and the Post-Jungians* (London, 1985), pp. 106-10.

90 *The Dream and the Underworld* (New York, 1979), p. 129.

91 *Myth of Analysis*, p. 104.

92 For the psychology of religion the question remains as to the ontological status of the gods experienced in the imaginal realm. Is the reality of the gods limited to the imaginal realm or is this realm the psychological locus for humans' experience of, and union with, God or the gods?

93 Ibid., p. 83.

94 Jung himself reflected on how the individuation process might be seen in terms of the traditional language used in the debate over salvation through grace or through good works. Jung's answer to this apparent dilemma was that the conscious mind does the work of attending to and integrating material from the unconscious, but the whole process itself depends on the grace (co-operation) of the unconscious in presenting the conscious mind with images and stories which are the stuff of transformation, the material to be integrated. In other words, individuation (psychological "salvation") requires both grace and works. See "The Difference Between Eastern and Western Thinking," CW 11, p. 488.

95 *Myth of Analysis*, p. 95.

96 Ibid., p. 94.

97 Ibid., pp. 111-12.

98 Ibid., p. 67.

99 Ibid., p. 87.

100 *She: Understanding Feminine Psychology* (New York, 1976), p. 1.

101 Ibid., p. 27.

102 Ibid., p. 27.

103 The animus is the personification of the woman's unconscious as male figures.

104 *She*, pp. 28-30.

105 Here there is no trace of the lamp as a symbol of sexual curiosity which is prominent in the Freudian interpretations.

106 June Singer, another Jungian analyst, is very aware of Jung's gender stereotypes and criticizes him on this point in *Androgyny* (New York, 1976), p. 35.

107 *She*, p. 37.

108 Ibid., p. 41.

109 Only the eagle who assists Psyche in filling the crystal goblet owes Eros a debt and can therefore be considered as "sent by Eros."

110 *She*, p. 51.

111 Ibid., p. 52.

112 Ibid., p. 56.

113 Ibid., p. 61.

114 *The Search for the Beloved* (Los Angeles, 1987), p. 154.

115 Ibid., p. 155.

116 Ibid., p. 157.

117 Ibid., p. 158.

118 Ibid., p. 159. Unlike the Freudians, Houston does not speak of sibling rivalry or sexual anxiety in regard to the symbolism of Psyche's sisters.

119 Ibid., p. 160.

120 Ibid., p. 161.

121 Ibid., p. 165.

122 Ibid., p. 164.

123 Ibid., p. 166.

124 Ibid., p. 167.

125 Ibid., p. 164.

4 The Eros and Psyche Myth and the Psychology of Transformation

Primary Psychological Insights of Earlier Approaches

In the face of the diverse psychological interpretations of the last two chapters I would now like to propose a chart summarizing the main points of the Eros and Psyche myth. This will provide an overview of the various psychological readings of the story and also some perspective on how they relate to each other.

There are particular features of these interpretations which stand out as we compare them. The first striking feature is that most of them assume the story tells us something about the "feminine," whether about women or the feminine aspects of men. In the range of psychological interpretations, Psyche may be a woman, an adolescent girl, women in general, consciousness, a psychotic's mind, the anima (or personification of a man's unconscious), a dream or fantasy ego or the highest psychic qualities of the human mind.

With the Freudian interpretations the story is viewed from the perspective of Psyche's fantasy or dream. Psyche is presented as the main figure with whom the reader identifies. Barchilon interprets Psyche as an adolescent girl, and most other Freudian interpreters consider the story to be the fantasy of a young woman. Riklin is the only one among the Freudians not to insist that the point of view of the myth is primarily that of a female. For Riklin, the character of the story as psychotic wishfulfillment overrides any particular sex or gender considerations in the story.

The Jungians tend to view the Eros and Psyche story as a symbolic portrait of feminine development from an in-depth perspective. Neumann sees Psyche as representing both the development of any particular woman and the phylogenetic development of female consciousness in general. Both developments reflect the shift from love as part of an impersonal fertility principle to love as an expression of personal encounter. In Neumann's view, the Psyche tale portrays this significant change in the history of human consciousness as an evolution of the matriarchate and, because the myth is still active in the collective unconscious, it helps individual women to achieve the

113

Chart 1

Psychological Interpretations of the
Eros and Psyche Myth

Author	Story symbolizes	Psyche	Eros	Aphrodite	Sisters	Voluptas	Tasks
Freudian Interpretations							
Riklin 1908	a psychotic's wishfulfillment	psychotic's mind	a hallucinating wishfulfillment	persecutor	figures in contrast to hero	—	life difficulties; escape hallucination
Schroeder 1917	a girl's erotic dream	a girl	man; penis; monster	—	—	—	—
Barchilon 1959	an adolescent girl's anxieties	an adolescent girl	man; father; sex as beastly	—	sexual anxieties	—	—
Bettelheim 1976	a woman's reaching for consciousness	a woman; rational soul	sexuality	regressive form of sexuality	sexual anxiety	—	process of overcoming sexual anxiety
Hoevels 1979	a woman's Oedipal fantasy	a woman	man; penis; father-substitute; serpent	rival mother; object of Psyche's death wish	sibling rivals; objects of Psyche's death wishes	—	working out the guilt due to death wishes

Jungian Interpretations

Neumann 1956	female development	woman (ego, total psyche, an archetype)	eros within the psyche; paternal uroboros; man	unconscious; bad mother archetype	matriarchal stratum in the psyche; Psyche's shadow	mystical joy	aspects (stages) of female's development
von Franz 1970	anima development	Apuleius' (and Lucius') anima	animus; *puer aeternus* aspect of self archetype	unconscious; mother archetype	self-preservative instinct	sensual lust	aspects of anima's development
Ulanov 1971	anima development	anima	drive to involvement; archetype of deity	unconscious; mother archetype	neglected, undifferentiated feminine elements	symbol of self archetype	stages of anima's development
Hillman 1972	soul-making; psychological creativity	anima (becoming psyche)	masculine creative principle; daimon linking gods to humans	fecundity; promiscuity; emotionality	—	pleasure of creativity	aspects of soul-making
Johnson 1976	female and anima development	woman and man's anima	man; woman's animus; *puer aeternus*; God-archetype	unconscious; mother archetype or complex	Psyche's shadow	joy or ecstasy	aspects of inner development
Houston 1987	female and anima development	woman and man's anima	drive toward development and expression; psychopomp linking personal self to beyond	unconscious; unreflected archetypes	doubts arising from a one-sided situation	source of instinct, wisdom and culture	psychological ordeals in search of completion

goal of love as personal relationship in the particular circumstances of their lives. Houston also emphasizes the phylogenetic significance of this story, although she depicts this development, not as a change in the character of female love, but as a stage in history where human consciousness is transformed by its relationship to the divine (symbolized by Psyche's union with the god Eros). Hillman, Johnson and Houston all agree that the story pertains to the feminine aspects of men as well as to women.

Only von Franz and Ulanov keep the overall context of the *Metamorphoses* in mind and see Psyche as a representation of a man's psyche or soul. Ulanov speaks of Psyche as the "transformative anima" because when she finally breaks free from the domination of Aphrodite, she is able to marry Eros and experience spiritual transformation. The "transformative anima" differentiates itself from the rest of the unconscious (symbolized by Aphrodite) and then mediates for the man a relationship to the divine (symbolized by Eros). Ulanov and von Franz both recognize what the recent non-psychological studies of the *Metamorphoses* have shown, namely, that the Eros and Psyche myth is intimately related to the story line of the frame narrative in which it is set. As we saw in Chapter 1, critics have characterized this relationship variously as summary, recapitulation or anticipation of the story of Lucius' wanderings and religious initiation in the *Metamorphoses*. The Jungian view that a man's unconscious is usually personified by female figures fits well into this line of interpretation, since Psyche's story then can be viewed as symbolizing the development of Lucius' soul.

While Ulanov recognizes the literary context of the tale, she applies this realization only as a starting point, to the extent of seeing the Eros and Psyche myth as a portrait of male development, not to shed light on the story of Lucius in the *Metamorphoses*. Von Franz, on the other hand, provides a thorough and systematic treatment, not only of the Eros and Psyche myth, but also of the entire *Metamorphoses*. She considers the Eros and Psyche myth as an archetypal dream which sheds light on the psychological state of both the author, Apuleius, and his thinly veiled autobiographical character, Lucius.[1] In her view, the Eros and Psyche myth represents only one of a number of stories inserted into the frame narrative, and she interprets all of these stories as dreams which illuminate Apuleius' psychological condition.

After Psyche, the other controlling figure in the story is Eros. The diversity of opinion on what he represents is as great as with Psyche. He may be sexuality, a beastly aspect of sex, a projection of sexual anxiety or of repressed sexual curiosity, a father-image or father-substitute, the hallucinatory wishfulfillment of a psychotic, the son of a goddess, the male ego, a *daimon* which unites humans and the gods, the creative principle in the mind, the animus (or personification of a woman's unconscious), the *puer aeternus* archetype or an aspect of the self archetype. Hillman's statement that Eros is not clearly defined seems to be quite an understatement in light of this diversity of psychological interpretation. The range of meanings here is mind-boggling and demonstrates the incredible malleability and multi-faceted nature of this symbol.

The Freudian interpretations of the Eros figure are no doubt influenced by Freud's use of the term "Eros" to represent the "love instinct" as well as (later) the "life instincts" (which include the preservation of the self and the species as well as ego and object love).[2] Freud's impact can be seen in Bettelheim's study, where Eros represents sexuality in its broadest sense. In this case, the goal of psychological development is symbolized by the marriage of Psyche and Eros, which represents the union of the most highly developed aspects of the psyche with the sexual dimensions of the person.

Schroeder and Barchilon, who interpret the Eros and Psyche myth as a picture of a girl's sexual anxieties, also appear to be influenced by Freud's view of Eros, though they are more concrete than Bettelheim in their understanding of Eros. For them, Eros symbolizes the physical and potentially dangerous aspects of sex. They focus on Eros as he is presented in the marriage-of-death sequence and as represented by Psyche's jealous sisters. Here Eros symbolizes the penis and the girl's fear that sex is beastly.

Hoevels has developed the sexual perspective on Eros in the greatest depth. For Hoevels, Eros epitomizes the Oedipal fantasy, which includes the girl's wonder at and fear of her father and the mystery of sex symbolized by his body. Repressed infantile sexual curiosity which the girl cannot admit even to herself lends power to this fantasy. Hoevels focusses on the snake as a symbol of Psyche's Oedipal projection of the danger of the father's penis from the vantage point of a child's fear and curiosity. Even Riklin, who does not interpret the story primarily as a woman's fantasy or development, considers Eros in sexual terms as a psychotic's erotic tactile hallucination.

These interpretations show how Freud's general psychological theory has helped to shape the Freudian understanding of the Eros figure along sexual lines. Much as in the interpretation of a dream, the Freudian associations to the Eros symbol give context and specific content to the meaning of this figure, and consequently, to the psychological meaning of the entire story. These associations seem to have more influence on the Freudian interpreters of the Eros and Psyche myth than the classical understanding of Eros or Cupid as a mischievous and spoiled child, which seems to be part of Apuleius' own characterization of Eros. In contrast to Freud, Jung emphasized the connective aspect of Eros, as he frequently referred to Eros as the "capacity to relate."[3] Jung criticized Freud for "the imprudence of trying to lay hold of unconfinable Eros with the crude terminology of sex."[4] He thought that Freud was partly correct, but one-sided:

> Eros is a questionable fellow and will always remain so.... He belongs on one side to man's primordial animal nature which will endure as long as man has an animal body. On the other side he is related to the highest forms of the spirit. But he thrives only when spirit and instinct are in right harmony.[5]

Jung attempted to do justice to both sides of Eros by focussing on his relational aspect, but he seems to have given more weight to the spiritual than to the sexual side of Eros.

There is great diversity in the way the Jungian interpreters follow Jung's lead in comprehending the Eros figure. Neumann sees Eros as the tendency to relatedness in a woman's psyche and Ulanov considers one aspect of Eros to be the male's drive to involvement in the world. But Ulanov and most of the other Jungians stress the spiritual side of Eros in his role as a *daimon*, a link between the human and the divine. Ulanov considers Eros in his most spiritual sense to symbolize the God archetype, and Johnson speaks of Eros as the experience of human love which provides many people today with their only contact with the divine. Johnson, like Ulanov, associates Eros with the God archetype (or self archetype, as it is usually called in Jung's psychological system) and Houston also sees Eros as a symbol of the force in the soul which connects a person to the divine.

For Jung, images of the self or God archetype in the psyche are theoretically, but not practically, distinguishable from God as symbolized in the world's religions. In one of the most intriguing passages from Jung's writings, he wrestles with the question of how to understand the relationship of the God archetype to a traditional view of the transcendent God in Christianity and other theistic religions:

> It is only through the psyche that we can establish that God acts upon us, but we are unable to distinguish whether these actions emanate from God or from the unconscious. We cannot tell whether God and the unconscious are two different entities. Both are border-line concepts for transcendental contents.... The (self) archetype produces a symbolism which has always characterized and expressed the Deity.... Strictly speaking, the God image does not coincide with the unconscious as such, but with a special con-

tent of it, namely the archetype of the self. It is this archetype from which we can no longer distinguish the God-image empirically.[6]

This means that in Jung's view of psychological experience, the various images of God may be symbols of real divine presence. Therefore, when Ulanov, Johnson and Houston connect Eros to the self or God archetype, they see him as one of these symbols which may render God present.

Hillman understands Eros as a *daimon* joining humans to the gods (as a region of the imagination), but it is not clear how he conceives the relation of this imaginal realm to God as the transcendent reality described in many of the world's religions. It seems as though Hillman considers the archetypes primarily as personifications of forces acting in the psyche and the world. Although he speaks about the gods, and, Eros as a god, he relates Eros to the highest human spiritual and creative experiences with no connection to a traditional notion of a transcendent God.

Von Franz believes that Eros represents an aspect of the self archetype (God archetype) as well as of the *puer aeternus* archetype. While both of these archetypes may be sources of creativity, von Franz does not see Psyche's encounter with Eros as symbolizing a positive religious experience. When we remember that von Franz sees the Eros and Psyche story in the context of the *Metamorphoses* and as an archetypal dream revealing the psychological condition of Apuleius, her interpretation of Eros as an expression of the *puer aeternus* archetype shows that she considers Eros and union with him as problematic, if not pathological. According to von Franz, Eros as a symbol of the *puer aeternus* archetype represents Apuleius' mother-bound condition and his psychologically underdeveloped state. As a figure symbolizing the self archetype, Eros potentially represents Apuleius' (and Lucius') quest for union with God. But since Eros takes Psyche off to Olympus, which von Franz construes as the realm of the unconscious, she interprets their marriage in Olympus as an indication that Apuleius' spiritual quest remains in the collective unconscious and never reaches the level of conscious realization in his life.

All of the interpreters include some account of both Psyche and Eros. However, this is not the case with the other figures and events of the tale. Not only are some elements of the tale given little attention, but others are ignored altogether. The most conspicuous example of this is the almost complete absence of commentary among the Freudian interpreters on Voluptas, the child born to Psyche. A glance at the chart shows how this figure is brushed aside. Another example is the way Hillman passes over the sisters in his treatment of the tale so that he does not deal with the sibling rivalry and sexual anxiety which are so central to Hoevels' interpretation.

The role of Aphrodite, too, seems to be overlooked in the interpretations of Schroeder and Barchilon. We can also see that Psyche's tasks, which play such a large part in the Jungian interpretations, are not dealt with at any length in the Freudian approaches. For the Freudians, the tasks are, at most, considered as working out guilt arising from death wishes or as overcoming sexual anxieties. Barchilon does not mention Psyche's tasks at all and Riklin dismisses them as life's difficulties; in none of the Freudian commentaries is there any kind of detailed analysis of the symbols involved in Psyche's tasks.

Now let us consider for a moment the role of some of these secondary elements in the different interpretations and why they vary so greatly. Once the interpretations of the characters Psyche and Eros are established, the other elements of the myth seem to fall into place almost automatically. After Psyche and Eros, the most important figure in the myth appears to be Aphrodite. The Freudians vary considerably in their estimate of the importance and role of Aphrodite in the myth. Riklin interprets her as a symbol of a psychotic's paranoia. She represents the witch or step-mother figure who is so often the persecutor in fairy tales. For Schroeder and Barchilon, who construe the myth as a portrait of a girl's anxiety, Aphrodite is given no place whatever. They both understand the girl's anxiety in relation to fears about the beastly and potentially dangerous aspects of sex. Their view of the dynamics of sexual anxiety concentrates on the girl's fantasy of the male as monster, not on fear of an older woman as a threatening mother or mother-in-law figure. Consequently they see no function for Aphrodite in this mythical expression of female sexual anxiety.

Bettelheim recognizes the aspect of sexual anxiety symbolized in this myth but he interprets the myth primarily in terms of the psyche's growth in consciousness. In this framework, Aphrodite is associated with a kind of incestuous love which is opposed to the development of consciousness. While Bettelheim does not devote much attention to the role of Aphrodite, he clearly understands her as a rival who symbolizes a regressive form of sexuality. Her primitive sexuality stands in sharp contrast to the mature sexuality which is integrated into a fully developed personality. According to Bettelheim, integrated sexuality is symbolized by Eros' marriage to Psyche.

Hoevels sees Aphrodite as the rival mother in the context of a feminine Oedipus complex. When the Eros and Psyche myth portrays Aphrodite as setting impossible and deadly tasks for Psyche, Hoevels interprets this as a woman's fantasy in which she projects her own death wishes onto her rival. For Hoevels, this myth shows the degree to which these Oedipal fantasies and projections appear beyond any shadow of a doubt to be absolutely real, and so the blame is effectively shifted to the other person. Thus Aphrodite, portrayed as cruel and heartless in the Eros and Psyche myth, is in Hoevels' view actually innocent and merely the victim of a young woman's Oedipus complex and the web of fantasies surrounding that complex.

For the Jungian interpreters, Aphrodite is not understood in relation to the Oedipus complex but rather as a symbol of the older and more regressive aspects of the unconscious. Neumann identifies her with the maternal source of life and the fertility principle. In this regard she represents the Great Mother archetype, which can provide comfort and security, but also resists the growth of consciousness. According to Neumann, in the history of the human race this archetype played a crucial role in insuring human survival, but now it may retard individual women from realizing their own conscious potential. Since Neumann interprets the Eros and Psyche myth as a portrait of female development, he sees Aphrodite as the original state of the female psyche before individual consciousness and the capacity for interpersonal love began to emerge.

The other Jungians understand Aphrodite along these same general lines, with some modifications. Von Franz sees Aphrodite as the Great Mother archetype, which is mixed with all the various contents of the unconscious before any kind of differentiation occurs. In this light she speaks of Aphrodite as depicting both the Mother archetype and the anima before the anima begins to separate itself from the Mother archetype in the male's psychological development. When von Franz interprets the Eros and Psyche myth as a reflection of Apuleius' psychological situation, she believes Aphrodite's domination of Psyche indicates that Apuleius is under the control of the Mother archetype and that his individual personality cannot find its unique and independent expression as a result of this. It is only when the anima begins to distinguish itself from the Mother archetype (as symbolized by Psyche completing Aphrodite's tasks and marrying Eros), that von Franz finds some hope for Apuleius' psychological predicament.

Ulanov, like von Franz, supposes that Aphrodite symbolizes the undifferentiated collective unconscious. The uncomplimentary portrait of her as raging and incestuous in the Eros and Psyche tale emphasizes the regressive character of this undeveloped psychological state. Johnson does not deal much with the Aphrodite symbol but he, too, considers her to represent the unconscious, and especially the Mother archetype. Hillman also emphasizes the relatively primitive and undifferentiated character of Aphrodite. He believes that she primarily symbolizes those psychic forces which work against expansion and creativity. Houston agrees with these other Jungian interpreters that Aphrodite stands for undifferentiated and unintegrated archetypal material. She adds that Aphrodite represents dependencies and the old order, both of which tend to hold the psyche back from development. In this regard Aphrodite expresses an early state of development where there is a great divide between the human and the divine. Nevertheless, Houston believes that Aphrodite plays a positive role by forcing on Psyche tasks which eventually strengthen her and thus prepare her for union with the divine as symbolized by marriage to the god Eros.

Psyche's sisters play a large role early in the Eros and Psyche myth, and all but two commentators (Schroeder and Hillman) include some account of their psychological significance. Among the Freudians, the sisters express either sexual anxieties or sibling rivalry. For Bettelheim they merely give voice to a woman's concern about the place of sexuality in her life and how it relates to her cherished values. They symbolize a potential for conflict within the female psyche. Barchilon goes further and considers the sisters as irrational fears in a woman's psyche which confuse her, upset her psychic equilibrium and may even lead her to unreasonable actions. Schroeder sees no place for the sisters in his understanding of the story as an erotic dream and Riklin considers them only in so far as they offer a dramatic contrast to a psychotic's wishfulfillment. For Riklin, the way the sisters are destroyed in the myth symbolizes the possible threat to the psychotic of not having wishes realized. From this vantage point it makes sense that the sisters may represent underlying anxieties which menace the psychotic.

The most unusual interpretation of Psyche's sisters is found in Hoevels' reading of the tale. He sees them as objects of sibling rivalry in that Psyche has arranged in her fantasy to make them appear evil, guilty and deserving of their terrible fate. The key point for Hoevels is that the myth embodies Psyche's death wishes against her rivals. Hoevels is the only interpreter to view the sisters as referring to people in the external world rather than as subjective elements within the psyche. For him, the story illustrates how a woman manages to create an incredible fantasy to get rid of her rivals and blame them for what she has done to them.

Among the Jungian commentators only Hillman finds no place in his interpretation for Psyche's sisters. Neumann considers them from both a phylogenetic and an ontogenetic perspective. In the former case, they are symbols of patriarchal slavery and represent an antagonistic early stage in the development of consciousness where feminine aspects of the psyche are not yet integrated and are dominated by "male" values. For Neumann this is symbolized by both sisters being unhappily married to men whom they do not love and who demand much from them. In the life of any particular woman, the sisters represent a matriarchal stratum of the psyche which does not trust men. Neumann also speaks of them as Psyche's shadow, which means that in the story they would represent aspects of Psyche's own unconscious and projected negative attitude towards men (and towards Eros).

Johnson follows this view of the sisters as Psyche's shadow. Ulanov, who understands the myth as a portrait of anima development in men, does not speak of the sisters as Psyche's shadow (since the shadow is usually thought of as the ego's shadow, and not the anima's shadow), but merely as neglected and undifferentiated feminine elements in a man's psyche. In this regard her understanding of the sisters does correspond to the general definition of a person's shadow. Ulanov sees a positive aspect to the sisters in that they inadvertently spur Psyche on to see Eros in the light which symbolizes greater conscious development in a man's psyche.

Von Franz also recognizes the positive role of the sisters when she interprets them as a self-preservative instinct. By this she means that the sisters alert Psyche to the one-sidedness of her relationship to Eros. They shake Psyche out of her complacency and warn her that enjoyment of the dark paradise with her lover is too compartmentalized and isolated from the rest of her world and reality. In regard to the dynamics of Apuleius' psyche the sisters represent doubts which call into question his identification with or preoccupation with the *puer aeternus* archetype.

Insofar as von Franz interprets Eros as an aspect of the self archetype, the sisters and their negativity signify that Apuleius' spirituality is still too deeply locked in the unconscious, presumably because of his mother-bound condition, which von Franz repeatedly emphasizes. In this case the sisters represent an urge within Apuleius which might stimulate him to adopt a more conscious and critical relationship to his mother complex as well as to the divine. In the *Metamorphoses*, Lucius appears to have undergone exactly such a development in his adventures and finally in his conversion experience as he outgrew his immersion in magic and opted for the disciplined path of the goddess Isis. But von Franz does not credit Lucius any more than Apuleius with a genuine spiritual transformation, so even though the sisters play a partially positive role and represent a critical force spurring on Apuleius (and Lucius), this is not enough to rectify their underdeveloped psychological condition.

Houston understands the role of the sisters in much the same way as does von Franz. She, too, stresses their positive value in pushing

Psyche out of her unconscious paradise with Eros and into a conscious relationship with him. Houston believes that the sisters symbolize Psyche's doubts about remaining in the dark (i.e., in an unconscious state), no matter how pleasurable it may seem at times. For Houston, then, the sisters are like Aphrodite in that they force Psyche to grow even though on the surface of the narrative they are depicted as plotting against her.

One of the most puzzling figures in the Eros and Psyche myth is Voluptas, the daughter born to Psyche at the very end of the story. While she has no active part in the myth itself, some commentators find her to be a crucial symbol of the outcome of the story. As the daughter of Psyche and Eros she is the fruit of their union and symbolizes the quality or significance of their relationship. The Latin word "voluptas" means pleasure, delight or enjoyment and this shapes the psychological interpretations of her place in the myth.

Hillman understands Voluptas to symbolize the pleasure which ensues when the creative principle contributes to "soul making" (the process of relating the psyche to its archetypal depths). Neumann interprets her as a symbol of the mystical joy which results from the process of psychological development. As woman's capacity for love progresses from the fertility principle to personal encounter, her ability to experience joy grows. By referring to the mystical character of this pleasure, Neumann emphasizes that the psychological process of development and integration actually corresponds to the spiritual path which religious mystics have described. Johnson makes this point even more emphatically when he speaks of Voluptas as the ecstasy of Psyche discovering her divinity.

Houston relates Voluptas to an ancient meaning of the word, namely, "plunging into life," which she understands to be the result of Psyche's search for and union with Eros. This child, according to Houston, symbolizes how the soul discovers its source of instinct and wisdom as it plunges into life, without knowing in advance where this quest will lead. For Ulanov, Voluptas represents the self archetype which produces its characteristic images more and more clearly in the course of individuation. From this vantage point, there is something of a parallel between the Psyche myth and Jung's view of psychological transformation: Just as Psyche and Eros join to produce Voluptas, so the analysand encounters the anima (Psyche as the personification of a man's unconscious) and thereby "produces" the transcendent function. The full realization of the self archetype develops from this process.

Jung has argued that alchemical symbolism actually describes this process of psychological transformation as the marriage of Sol (the sun as representing consciousness) and Luna (the moon as representing the unconscious) which produces Mercury as the result of this union. Mercury (or Hermes) symbolizes the synthesis of psychological opposites such as good and evil, young and old, feminine and masculine, conscious and unconscious, etc. Thus the Eros and Psyche myth, like alchemy, can symbolically represent the overall process of psychological transformation. Ulanov calls attention to this by interpreting Voluptas as a symbol of the self archetype.

Von Franz is the only Jungian who interprets Voluptas negatively. She understands Voluptas, not as a joyous symbol of realized psychological or spiritual transformation, but rather as an aspect of the anima. Because von Franz considers the Eros and Psyche myth as symptomatic of Apuleius' (and Lucius') underdeveloped psychological state, she sees Voluptas as a symbol of sensual lust. Here von Franz construes the daughter symbol to represent a "derivative aspect" and she focusses on the sensual dimension of the word "voluptas." In this light, Voluptas symbolizes Apuleius' lasciviousness, which he expresses through Lucius' sexual curiosity in the early part of the *Metamorphoses*, as well as the many bawdy stories contained in that work.

As I have already mentioned, the Freudians virtually overlook the role of Voluptas in the Eros and Psyche myth. This may be a bit surprising, since Voluptas as delight or pleasure might seem to fit in with a generally sexual interpretation of the story as a woman's fantasies, dreams or anxieties. Yet sexual fulfillment is not the primary object of these fantasies, since the Freudians, for the most part, read this myth as an expression of repressed sexual impulses, projections and reaction formations. This is particularly evident in the views of Schroeder and Barchilon, where Eros symbolizes monstrous sexual fantasies, or in Hoevels' interpretation of Eros as a projection of repressed infantile curiosity. With such an understanding of Eros, it is no wonder that Psyche's relationship to Eros would hardly be symbolized by joy or delight. Bettelheim combines both the anxiety-producing character of sexuality as well as its highest potential in his interpretation of Eros; nevertheless, he still does not find a place for the symbolism of Voluptas as the result of Psyche's union with Eros. Riklin's notion that the myth represents a psychotic's hallucinatory wishfulfillment does not extend to seeing Voluptas as the possible pleasure or joy in such an hallucination. So it would appear that Voluptas is ignored in these psychological commentaries primarily because, as a symbol, she does not fit in with their general line of interpretation.

The final major category appearing in the chart is Psyche's tasks. Here, as with the Voluptas symbol, we find a very different emphasis between the Freudian and Jungian commentators. In most of the Jungian interpretations a great deal of space and attention is devoted to the symbolism and meaning involved in each of Psyche's tasks. By contrast, two of the Freudians (Schroeder and Barchilon) say nothing at all about the tasks and their meaning, while the others merely characterize the tasks in vague terms, without going into a detailed analysis of the symbolic elements of the tasks.

All but one of the commentators who deal with Psyche's tasks see them as a process of development. The particular meaning of this development ranges all the way from overcoming sexual anxieties and guilt due to death wishes (among the Freudians) to the broadening of consciousness and the unfolding of the unconscious (among the Jungians). Specifically, Bettelheim sees Psyche's tasks as a woman's struggle to reach for greater consciousness without cutting herself off from deep sexual needs. The incredibly difficult nature of Psyche's tasks illustrates how much effort is required to overcome sexual anxieties and recognize the key role which integrated sexuality plays in achieving true wisdom.

Hoevels, on the other hand, sees Psyche's tasks as the inevitable price a woman must pay for lack of psychological insight into her Oedipal fantasies. From Hoevels' perspective, Psyche is responsible for generating the entire story though, of course, she is not aware of this. Psyche is the one who has unconsciously arranged to steal Eros from his mother/wife and who has projected her own death wishes onto her sisters and Aphrodite. According to Hoevels' application of Freudian theory, Psyche must find a way to deal with the enormous underlying guilt resulting from such Oedipal fantasies of ridding the world of all rivals. Psyche manages to have her Oedipal fantasy and deal with her guilt at the same time by incorporating into the fantasy the almost overwhelming struggles which allow her to work out her guilt as a kind of punishment. The only other Freudian who deals with Psyche's tasks to some degree is Riklin, who views them as difficulties which the psychotic encounters in life. In Riklin's view, the dramatic and magical way in which Psyche is rescued in each of the tasks betrays their character as "escape hallucinations" in which the psychotic's power of wishing allows life's difficulties to be solved magically in an hallucinatory fashion. This avoids having to deal with such problems in reality.

Most of the Jungians have gone into great detail regarding the symbolic meaning of Psyche's tasks. I shall not go into all of these symbols here, as I have already described some of their interpretations of various elements such as the seeds, the ants, the wool, the water of the Styx, the eagle, the beauty ointment and the journey to Persephone's home in the underworld. Among the Jungians, the main differences in interpreting these tasks have to do with whether they see Psyche as symbolic of the conscious or the unconscious mind.

Neumann insists most strongly of all that the Psyche myth represents a female's development of her conscious mind, and so he views Psyche's tasks as the great struggle involved in a woman differentiating her conscious mind from the seemingly overwhelming unconscious from which it emerges. For Neumann, woman's struggle to individuate seems even more difficult than it is for a man because woman is more closely associated with nature, fertility and the unconscious. Psyche's tasks are determined by Aphrodite precisely because she represents the Great Mother archetype or woman as immersed in nature and fertility.

Johnson and Houston see the Psyche myth as a development of the feminine in both women and men. From their Jungian perspective this means that the Eros and Psyche myth represents for women the development of their animus (as the personification of their unconscious). For Johnson and Houston, the meaning of Psyche's tasks applies equally to the growth of woman's conscious mind and man's unconscious mind, so they do not constantly spell out how the meaning of particular tasks would be different for women or men. Because Johnson seems to have no difficulty characterizing certain psychological qualities as masculine and feminine, he generally views Psyche's tasks as symbolically expressing the development of "feminine traits," whether they be closer to consciousness in a woman or more deeply buried in the unconscious of men.

For Houston, Psyche's tasks represent the ordeals we encounter as we search for psychological completion and union with the divine. In the exercises which she includes in her work, Houston shows how the tasks are actually initiations to deeper levels of consciousness. Hillman believes Psyche's tasks represent the difficulties involved in the process of soul making. Where Houston sees the tasks in terms of deepening consciousness, Hillman underscores the importance of not trying to rescue the dreams and reveries of the unconscious in order to accomplish the work of broadening consciousness. He treats the tasks as the great problems involved in immersing oneself in the world of unconscious images and stories. Often this process leads to what Hillman refers to elsewhere as "pathologizing," by which he means identifying with a particular archetype and experiencing in the imaginal realm the full force of the archetype. This process eventually leads the soul into the depths of the underworld just as Psyche's task of fetching the beauty ointment led her to Persephone's door in the land of the dead.

Ulanov and von Franz see the tasks as stages of anima development. Ulanov describes how the anima mediates a man's unconscious to his conscious mind and how, in order to do this adequately, the anima must acquire certain psychological characteristics in the process of development. Psyche's tasks represent this growth: sorting seeds (channeling the male's sexual instinct), gathering wool (blunting the male's aggressive tendencies), filling the vessel with water from the river of death (referring to the anima as the vessel of individuation in her capacity to give form to the boundless elements in the unconscious, which is often called the "land of the dead"), and journeying to the underworld (referring to the anima's role in mediating the reality of death to the male ego). For a man's complete psychological and spiritual development to take place, his anima must have acquired all of the strengths symbolized by those tasks.

Von Franz is more specific than Ulanov in her interpretation of Psyche's tasks as symbolizing the development of the anima. For von Franz the tasks refer, not only to men in general, but especially to Apuleius' psychological state and his anima in particular. According to von Franz, Psyche's first task symbolizes the need for Apuleius to develop his feeling function, which largely governs the ability to order and select just the right archetypal materials for his growth. Von Franz believes Psyche's other tasks call attention to Apuleius' need to come to terms with his strong emotions and his deep unconscious. Although she interprets Eros' rescue of Psyche in the final task as an intervention of the self archetype, nevertheless she concludes that the gains which Apuleius and Lucius made in the course of undergoing these developmental "tasks" are eventually lost in the unconscious, and so Apuleius and Lucius do not accomplish the potential for personal self-realization in the Eros and Psyche myth.

From this overview we can see that the interpretive framework determines which aspects of the story have relevance, that is, which symbols express some of the dynamics described in a particular psychological theory. This is seen particularly in the way Jungians emphasize Psyche's tasks to strengthen their case for the myth symbolizing feminine development. With the Freudians, the emphasis on the anxiety which is involved in the marriage-of-death scene supports their focus on the Oedipal elements in the myth as a woman's fantasy. The significant point here is not simply that the analysts call particular attention to different elements of the myth, but that they give these elements a central function in their psychological explanations. Each of these interpretations seizes on one or another aspect of the story which supports a particular view of Psyche and Eros, and the interpretations appear to be as much determined by Freudian and Jungian psychological theory as by the drama described in the myth itself.

The Literary and Religious Context of the Metamorphoses

In the first chapter we have already seen many references to the literary context of the Eros and Psyche myth. There we considered how the recent literature has emphasized links between the Eros and Psyche myth and the story of Lucius as set out in Apuleius' *Metamorphoses*. We saw the variety of ways authors have discussed these parallels between Psyche and Lucius, and that, in general, they concluded the Eros and Psyche myth symbolically recapitulates, summarizes or reflects Lucius life and character, at least to some extent. Since the literary setting appears to be so closely related to the Eros and Psyche myth, and because this study has argued that literary context may be a significant way to control or limit the tendency to project psychological theory onto the myth, we shall consider the main outlines of Lucius' story in the *Metamorphoses* here.

Apuleius' *Metamorphoses* is a remarkable tale of how a young man, Lucius, with a great curiosity about witchcraft, undergoes many adventures (including being transformed into a donkey) which eventually lead to religious conversion and initiation into the cult of Isis. Even from the broadest outline of the story, it is evident that the literary context is religious in character. The *Metamorphoses* is ultimately the story of a profound religious experience. In fact this book still provides scholars of history and religion with the fullest account from antiquity of the initiation ceremonies and mysteries connected with the cult of the Egyptian goddess Isis.

The narrative is told by Lucius in the first person and begins with Lucius travelling to Thessaly on business. Thessaly is of particular interest to Lucius because it is thought to be the birthplace of magic and witchcraft. Lucius' curiosity is particularly aroused when he learns that his host's wife, Pamphile, is a witch, and he seduces the serving woman, Fotis, in order to learn more about Pamphile and discover the secrets of magic.

One night he watches the witch strip her clothes, apply a magic salve, and transform herself into an owl. Later, Lucius attempts a similar feat with the help of Fotis, but she inadvertently gives him the wrong jar of ointment, and Lucius turns into a donkey instead of a bird. Fotis tells Lucius not to panic, because she knows the antidote which will return him to human form: he must eat roses. Fotis intends to bring him some roses at dawn, but before she has a chance to do so, Lucius is taken away by thieves who break into the compound. This misfortune means that Lucius is unable to get the antidote of roses and this is the beginning of his many trials while locked in the body of an ass.

The immediate context of the Eros and Psyche myth occurs early in Lucius' story. While he is in the form of a donkey in the robbers' cave he hears the myth told by an old lady who works for the bandits. She tells the story in order to comfort a young woman whom the robbers have taken prisoner. This unhappy woman, Charite, the only daughter of wealthy parents, was about to be married when the robbers seized her for ransom. Later Charite and Lucius are rescued, but that is not the end of their trials.

As a donkey Lucius passes from owner to owner. Generally his life is miserable, as he is beaten and overworked by many of the people who keep him. Among his various owners are herdsmen, a band of homosexual priests of Cybele, a miller, a soldier, a gardener and cooks. Towards the end of these adventures Lucius is taken to the gladiatorial games at Corinth, where he is supposed to copulate with a condemned woman and then be attacked by wild beasts. Lucius is horrified at this prospect and plans an escape. Because he is so tame nobody keeps an eye on him, and so he manages to edge towards the gate and suddenly gallop off at full speed when the opportunity presents itself. He does not stop until he is miles away on a secluded beach at Cenchreae. There he stretches out his exhausted body in the sand and sleeps.

He awakens with a sudden start to see a magnificent full moon over the sea. Lucius believes this overwhelming sight of the moon to be a visible image of the goddess, and he implores her help to release him from his miserable existence as a donkey. After he prays earnestly either to be returned to his human form or to be allowed to die, he falls asleep again. A dream soon emerges in which the goddess Isis appears as a beautiful woman. She comforts Lucius and promises to deliver him from his donkey form. Isis instructs him to join in a procession in her honour (celebrating the reopening of the navigation season) which is to take place the next day, and there he is to pluck the roses from the hand of the High Priest leading the procession.

Isis assures Lucius not to worry about how this will all occur because at the same time that she is in his dream vision she is simultaneously instructing the sleeping High Priest on his role in Lucius' transformation. Isis also demands that Lucius dedicate the rest of his life to her in return for her help in changing him back into human form. All goes exactly as the goddess said it would, and Lucius' bestial form fades miraculously away. He immediately becomes a loyal devotee of the goddess and is guided by her in dreams and visions. After an appropriate period of contemplation and preparation, Lucius is called by the goddess to be initiated into her cult. Later, in

Rome, Lucius receives a dream vision calling him to be initiated into the cult of Osiris, and Osiris assures him in another dream that he will become a famous lawyer. The *Metamorphoses* ends on this positive note.

This brief summary cannot do justice to the richness and variety of the *Metamorphoses*, since it is only intended to establish the general framework within which the Eros and Psyche myth is set. I have purposely not gone into the many stories which are told in the course of Lucius' adventures because this would lead us too far astray from the Eros and Psyche myth itself. It is necessary only to mention here that the astounding array of stories in the *Metamorphoses* has led some literary commentators to conclude that the book really has no serious or religious intention but is merely designed to entertain readers. Such a view, however, seems extreme and treats too lightly the overall framework of the novel, especially the last part, which deals at length with Lucius' conversion.

Now, in relation to the overall narrative, M. L. von Franz has suggested that the Eros and Psyche myth is best understood as an archetypal dream reflecting Lucius' and Apuleius' psychological situation.[7] We have already examined von Franz's interpretation and found it to be the most firmly grounded in the *Metamorphoses*. Although in Chapter 3 we saw that her interpretation relies on certain assumptions which seem contrary to the actual story, her initial perspective on the Eros and Psyche myth as an archetypal dream appears to be the most promising way to take the literary and religious context of the *Metamorphoses* into account when interpreting the myth. Such a viewpoint would also be consistent with both Freudian and Jungian approaches to the basic similarities between myth and dream interpretation discussed at the beginning of Chapter 2.

The Eros and Psyche Myth as Lucius' Dream

In the context of the *Metamorphoses*, the psychological implications of the Eros and Psyche myth as a dream would refer primarily to the experience of Lucius and, in particular, his religious conversion and initiation into the cult of Isis. The intention of this section is not to give a complete interpretation of the Eros and Psyche story as a dream, but primarily to show the general direction of where such an interpretation might lead in attempting to preserve 1) important insights of earlier psychological commentators and 2) the literary context of the myth.[8]

An important aspect of interpreting dreams is to consider the overall structure of the dream plot in order to determine how it might resemble the dreamer's life. In this case we would reflect upon the relationship of the Eros and Psyche story to Lucius' life. The structure of the Eros and Psyche story might be summarized in this way:

> Psyche's situation: beautiful but unhappy
> Aphrodite's jealousy and action against Psyche
> Crisis: marriage of death
> Turn-about: Eros' castle and love
> Sisters' jealousy and action against Psyche
> Crisis: lamp scene where Eros departs
> Psyche's wandering and tasks—despair, help
> Crisis: beauty box and Psyche's death sleep
> Turn-about: Eros rescues Psyche
> Psyche marries Eros, is deified and Voluptas born

Here we see cycles of difficulty, crisis and turn-about which propel Psyche's development toward divinization. In a dream interpretation we would ask: how does this pattern relate to Lucius' life? In his experience there are also such cycles of difficulty, crisis and turn-about.

For example, this cycle seems to be epitomized in Lucius' experience of the Festival of Laughter early in the *Metamorphoses*. There he is on his way home after a pleasant evening of eating and drinking when the wind blows out the light his slave is carrying. When Lucius reaches the home where he is staying, he sees what appears to be three men trying to break into the house, so he draws his sword and thrusts it at them until they fall at his feet. Then he staggers to his room and falls asleep immediately. Upon waking the next morning he remembers the fight and panics, imagining how he will be tried and condemned to death. People knocking at his gate interrupt this revery and they take him along a winding path in front of thousands of laughing people.

Lucius feels like a sacrificial victim as he is taken to the theatre to stand trial and there attempts to defend himself by making up a story about how three men attacked him and threatened to kill those in the house. He begs for mercy, but the court demands vengeance and prepares to torture Lucius to get the names of any accomplices. Lucius loses all hope when he is ordered to uncover the corpses lying in the court-room theatre, but at the moment he pulls back the shroud, everything changes:

> Good gods! O what a sight was there! What an incredible joy! What an abrupt reversal of my fortunes! I, who had already felt myself enrolled on Proserpine's ledgers, one of Death's chattels—I, stupefied at the seesawing of fate, gaped, unable to explain, or even to express intelligibly, the unexpected spectacle (Bk. III, 9).[9]

Lucius can hardly believe his eyes as he discovers that the three corpses are really only inflated wine skins and the entire incident and trial are a hoax.

This adventure early in the story reflects Lucius' experience of fortune's fickleness, as he is suddenly thrust into a crisis situation which is dramatically resolved. This pattern resembles Psyche's marriage of death or even her tasks, where she is rescued just as she despairs and appears to be lost. Fortune plays this apparently cruel practical joke on Lucius, just as Aphrodite arranges Psyche's ordeals. But the Festival of Laughter is really only a harmless foreshadowing of the absurd play of fate which brings Lucius to the major disaster of his life when he is inadvertently turned into an ass through a grave error in the use of magic.

We may consider the overall structure of the Eros and Psyche story, when treated as an archetypal dream, to be a symbolic representation of what is currently happening to Lucius at the point in the narrative where the tale is inserted and we might expect that the dream, in general, casts light on Lucius' entire life. As dreams reflect both current and long-term issues in the dreamer's life, the Eros and Psyche story as a dream would reflect not only Lucius' recent disaster of being transformed into an ass, but also the long-range consequences of that event. This long-term view of a person's life is often presented as myth.

Carl Jung believed that an individual is deeply influenced and motivated by a central myth or myths which emerge in dreams.[10] Just as Jung asked of his own experience at its deepest level, "What is the myth that is living itself out through me?" so we might ask, which myth is living itself out through Lucius' experience? If the answer to this question is the myth of Eros and Psyche, then it serves not only to symbolize his "sacrilegious curiosity" and suffering, but also to offer a glimmer of hope, because the *entire* myth, not just the negative aspects symbolized by Psyche's marriage of death or Eros leaving Psyche, would have an impact on him. From the point of view of a personal myth patterning Lucius' life, the most striking feature of the Eros and Psyche myth is that despite human failings and seemingly endless struggles, there is finally salvation.

A primary concern in examining the overall structure of a dream is the resolution of the plot. With the Eros and Psyche story the resolution lies in the divine initiative towards the end of the tale. Just when all hope seems lost and it appears that Psyche is left for dead, Eros comes to rescue her:

> And there she (Psyche) lay without the slightest stir, a corpse asleep.
>
> But Eros' wound had now healed into a scar; and he himself could not bear his long separation from Psyche. So he slipped out through the high window of his chamber, where he was enclosed. His wings strengthened by their rest, bore him even swiftlier than before, as he hastened to find his Psyche. Delicately purging her of the Sleep, which he put back in its original lair, the box, he roused Psyche with a charming prick of his Arrow (VI, 21).[11]

This sequence seems to anticipate that moment in Lucius' own life when he is at his wits end and the goddess Isis saves him from despair and death.

Beyond examining the dramatic structure of the dream, an analyst would attempt to discover the dreamer's associations to each of the major symbols in the dream. While we do not have Lucius present to provide us with his personal associations to the Eros and Psyche story, we may draw from the *Metamorphoses* itself to determine possible associations and dimensions of reference for each major symbol.

Psyche

Considering that the Greek word "psyche" refers to the soul, Psyche herself most likely represents Lucius' soul or mind, either his entire soul or the anima (the personification of his unconscious psyche), especially as it is becoming increasingly more conscious. In classical Jungian theory, a man's unconscious is personified by a feminine figure, called the anima, the Latin word for soul. For Jung, the anima was a bridge to the unconscious, or a personified guide who leads a person to a deeper encounter with the unconscious. In dreams the anima figure frequently appears as a woman who helps the dreamer or leads him in the transformation process.

So Psyche, as a symbolic figure in Lucius' dream, could be thought to represent the vicissitudes of his life. Lucius is like Psyche in that he is ripe with potential, but isolated. The following description of Psyche might well characterize Lucius' life before his conversion experience:

> Meanwhile Psyche, for all her manifest beauty, reaped no benefit from her pre-eminence. She was gazed at by all, praised and mazed; but no man, king or prince or even commoner, raised any pretensions to her hand in marriage. They admired her as a sample of divinity, but only as men admire an exquisitely finished statue.... Psyche, lonely lass, sat sad at home, mourning her forlorn fate, weak in body and sick at heart; and she hated the beauty that gave pleasure to all the world save herself (IV, 32).[12]

When Lucius is attached to magic, he is unable to commit himself deeply to another person or to the divine. At this point he, like Psyche, has no real relationship to the external world. For Psyche this stage of isolation continues with the marriage of death where she finds herself without normal human companionship in the magical castle with Eros. Here she has no developed conscious relationship to Eros, since she cannot even see him, and she waits in fear as he operates on his own without her active participation. This situation resembles Lucius' involvement with Fotis and magic, which is not consciously developed but ruled by lust and curiosity. The following passage shows how Lucius' experience of Fotis is characterized primarily by sexual desire:

> She (Fotis) leaped into bed, and saddling and bridling me she rode agilely into pleasure. In the process she showed herself to possess a spine of pliant lubricity, and she satiated me with the enjoyment of Aphrodite-on-a-swing, until stretched at the last gasp of ecstasy with languid bodies we fell twined in a warm and mortal embrace, pouring out our souls.
>
> In these and like entanglements, without a sigh of sleep, we came up to the confines of light, charming away moments of lassitude with the winecup, once more awakening desire and replenishing delight. And a good many more nights we spent in devices similarly pleasant (II, 17).[13]

It is also noteworthy that Apuleius uses the imagery of Aphrodite to describe Lucius' relationship to Fotis, since in the dream, at the subjective level of interpretation,[14] Aphrodite might be thought of as the force of lust which torments Lucius, which again links Lucius' Psyche-dream to his life.

Lucius' interest in magic is closely tied to his sensuous attachment to Fotis. He tries to gain her aid in acquiring some of the witch's magic ointment by insisting that this would demonstrate her love for him:

> I grasped the hand of Fotis, and laying it upon my eyes I said, "Please let me enjoy a great and singular proof of your affection towards me, while the chance beckons. Get me a little of that same ointment. Please, by these your nipples, my honey-darling, do this, and I shall stand at your side a winged Eros by my Aphrodite" (III, 22).[15]

Here we see mixed together the two appetitive drives of lust and curiosity, and Lucius identifies himself with the Eros who hovers around Aphrodite, which seems to reflect Eros as he is in the first part of the Eros and Psyche tale, where he is still very much under the domination of Aphrodite. This is the Eros who possesses Psyche in the dark early in the tale and forbids her to see him, that is, to know him consciously. The taboo against Psyche seeing Eros would be an effective way for a dream to express symbolically Lucius' manner of relating to others primarily out of lust and curiosity, that is, Eros in the dark.

When Psyche directs the light of the lamp on Eros, she sees the beauty of relationship for what it can be (symbolized by her enchantment with Eros), but when the oil from the lamp burns him and he sees that she has broken the taboo, he flies from her:

> The god, thus burnt, leaped out of bed; and spying the scattered evidences of Psyche's forfeited truth, he made to fly mutely out of the clasp of his unfortunate wife. But Psyche, as he rose into the air, caught hold of his right leg with both hands and clung there, a wailing drag upon his upward flight. Into the cloudy zones they soared, until her muscles gave way and she dropped to the earth (V, 23-24).[16]

As a dream segment this might well portray how Lucius' expectations are lifted off the ground in his relationship with Fotis and magic, only to fall back in complete despair, lacking not only false hopes inspired by lust and magic, but now even bereft of the normal capacity for human relationship. This is a symbolic way of portraying Lucius' transformation into an ass, whereby he entirely loses the ability to relate to the world in a human way. The sorrow and despair of Psyche without Eros is a dream-like reflection of Lucius wandering in the body of an ass at the hands of fate. In this situation Lucius is primarily a passive spectator in life as he observes what is happening around him.

Eros

Eros as the God of love is represented in the story as a winged infant who defies social customs:

> So anon she summoned her son, that winged lad, the naughty child who has been so spoilt that he despises all social restraint. Armed with flames and arrows he flits in the night from house to house. He severs the marriage-tie on all sides; and unchastised he perpetrates endless mischief; and he does everything save what he ought to do (IV, 30).[17]

Apuleius clearly recognizes the humour in this characterization of the Olympian god Eros as a bad boy, yet if we consider the divine dimension of Lucius' dream, these important elements of the divine stand out: The divine is closely related to love and is contacted in human love. We also see that there is an aspect of the divine which is at odds with social convention and cannot be understood according to the expectations of society. Some may also see humour in the mischievous side of the divine which refuses to be bound by human expectation.

Perhaps the most striking feature in this portrayal of the divine is that God loves the human psyche, although initially this is experienced as a love in the dark. What might be the significance of such a characterization of divine love? The first point evident in this portrayal is that humans are not in control of this encounter. Eros takes the initiative and determines the time and character of the meetings. The experience of the divine only in the darkness also indicates that this is not primarily a conscious relationship between the psyche and God.

The Freudian emphasis on the sexual bearing of the Eros symbol should also be taken into account in attempting to determine its relationship to Lucius' life and his religious experience. It plays either a direct role in Lucius' motivation early in the *Metamorphoses*, where Lucius is driven by lust, or an indirect role in his strict chastity in the service of Isis at the end of the story. In the latter situation Freudians would probably speak of such rigid control, or denial, of sex as a form of sublimation. It is also possible that a Freudian perspective would emphasize the regressive function of this sublimation in a manner similar to the way Freud characterized mystical experience as a return to primary narcissism in *The Future of an Illusion*. In this view, Lucius' religious experience might be deemed both a kind of sublimation and, at the same time, a regression to a state of narcissism.

The Jungians generally focus on the relational elements of the Eros symbol, which emphasizes that the way Eros behaves with Psyche in the myth reflects Lucius' relationship to his world, in his pre-asinine adventures as well as in his painful experience in the body of an ass. For Jungians, individuation ultimately occurs through relationship with the various contents of the unconscious, such as the anima, the shadow, the persona and the self or God archetype.

Most of the Jungian interpreters (von Franz, Ulanov, Johnson and Houston) see the Eros symbol as a reflection of the psyche's potential transformation in the individuation process. Here they focus on the self-transcendent aspect of the psyche which brings the human being in relationship to the divine. This transformative, self-transcendent experience is beautifully symbolized in the image of winged Eros which brings together all of the elements symbolized by Eros, namely, the sexual, the relational and the self-transcendent. When this insight is applied to the way the Eros and Psyche myth reflects

Lucius' story, it seems entirely probable that the myth provides another level of representing Lucius' experience of the divine.

Psyche's Tasks

The tasks of Psyche might well represent the way Lucius recovers his involvement in the world but now, as conscious relationship, no longer ruled by lust and sacrilegious curiosity. This aspect of the Eros and Psyche dream characterizes both Lucius' current situation at the time he experiences the tale as well as his future developments. Here it is possible to apply aspects of Neumann's interpretation of Psyche's tasks to Lucius' development. Psyche's first task of sorting seeds can be seen as a symbolic reference to Lucius' need to channel his promiscuity. Jack Lindsay also hints at this association when he freely translates part of Venus' instructions as "separate this *promiscuous* mass of seeds"[18] (emphasis added). While it is clear that in Lucius' world his promiscuous behaviour is not considered sinful in a Christian sense, it is incompatible with his future life as a priest of Isis.

The ants who come to Psyche's rescue may represent the unconscious forces which are realigning themselves to prepare Lucius for his future relationship with Isis. The ants are described in the *Metamorphoses* as "nimble daughters of the all-producing earth,"[19] thus connecting them with the generosity of the earth. Ants are traditionally known for a kind of wisdom and orderliness which is tied to the instincts.[20] Such associations support the idea that this task refers to a reorganization of Lucius' instinctual life. Von Franz's notion that sorting seeds refers to sorting the mixed elements in the collective unconscious may apply to Lucius' need to reorganize his instinctual life or to distinguish between the powers of magic and the power of Isis.

Psyche's second task of gathering the fleece from the dangerous rams could shed light on Lucius' situation if we understand the fleece not simply as impulsive power, but as the power of transcendence which is not to be found directly in the form of magical power, but indirectly in service to Isis.[21] The golden fleece is also linked to the elusive hidden treasure, which may be understood as wisdom or strength of spirit.[22] In this sense, Psyche's task symbolizes qualities which Lucius is to acquire in the course of his journey to Isis.

In the Eros and Psyche story the power associated with the fleece is deadly only if it is sought in the wrong way.

> While burning in the rays of the sun, they borrow his heat; they range in formidable frenzy; and with buttings of their sharpened horns and rocklike heads, or (as oft happens) with their poisonous

bites, they worry men to death. Then wait till the sun of noon has slackened the reins of his heat—till the spirit of the river breathes out a lulling influence, and beasts sleep. Lie hidden meanwhile under the shade of that lofty plane-tree which drinks from the same breast of waters as myself (VI, 12).[23]

This closely resembles Lucius' development, where he is meant to experience the transcendent power of Isis, but only at her bidding. The wisdom Lucius is to achieve lies in the appropriate attitude and timing. The reed which offers Psyche this wise counsel is characterized in the story as the "nurse of sweet music" (*musicae suavis nutricula*), so that the harmonious flow of music symbolizes the proper attitude and timing Lucius must learn in the development of his spiritual life. Isis' approach through dreams and visions establishes the proper timing for Lucius' encounter with the divine. Psyche's third task, filling the crystal vessel with deadly black water from the Styx, the river of the infernal regions, might well be understood as a dream portrayal of Lucius' future spiritual death in preparation for rebirth and character transformation. At the subjective level of interpretation the crystal vessel may symbolize the fragile nature of the psyche, which is threatened in the process of this transformation. The transparency of crystal as "matter that can be seen through" may also refer to the union of opposites which is involved in dying spiritually to gain new life.

The extraordinary help Psyche receives in accomplishing this task is linked to divine providence and to the eagle who brought the beautiful prince Ganymede to Zeus:

> But the agony of the innocent soul is apparent to the mastering eyes of Providence. For the royal bird of high Jove (swooping eagle) suddenly appeared, coming with wide-spread wings, mindful of his ancient obligations to Cupid—by whose agency he had rapt-up the Phyrgian lad to be Jove's cupbearer (VI, 15).[24]

Ganymede, like Psyche, was a human who was taken to heaven and joined to the divine. This allusion links the divinization of a human to the task of fetching water from the river of the dead, that is, undergoing spiritual death. The eagle also represents the watchful eye of Providence, which guides the human soul through this dangerous process. As a segment of Lucius' dream this might symbolically express the divine light of Isis, which brings Lucius through his spiritual death to new life in the goddess.

The eagle who comes to Psyche's aid emphasizes the mortal danger involved in gaining even a drop of this deadly water:

Ah, simple one, unlearned in the world's ways, how can you hope ever to dip a finger or snatch one drop of this holy and no-less murdering stream? Have you never heard that these Stygian waters are dreaded by all the gods, including Jove himself; and that as you mortals swear by the Power of the Gods, so the gods swear by the Majesty of Styx? (VI, 15)[25]

If this task represents channeling the stream of vital psychic energy, as Neumann believes, it shows that Lucius must learn the secret of giving expression to this moving force without being destroyed by its overwhelming power.[26] The difference between Lucius tapping this power through dabbling in magic may be contrasted with being open to such power through the disciplined service of Isis.

Both Psyche and Lucius are brought to the brink of despair and suicide in the course of their struggles. As Psyche contemplates the seeming impossibility of her final task, she climbs a high tower from which to jump and end her misery. The tower, characterized as "far-seeing" or "being able to exercise foresight" (turris illa prospicua), comes to Psyche's rescue by giving her detailed instructions on how to survive the journey to the underworld. As a dream symbol the tower stands in contrast to the elements of nature which previously helped Psyche, namely the ants, the reed and the eagle. The tower represents a work of human culture which is able to give perspective to the soul's immersion in the underworld experience preceding spiritual rebirth.

From its long-range view, the tower tells Psyche to look beyond the immediate impulses of pity (nec tu tamen illicita afflectare pietate) and desire for comfort and luxury. The tower warns Psyche: "She (Proserpina) will bid you seat yourself on cushions and eat a luxurious meal. But you must sit on the ground and ask for a scrap of brown bread" (VI, 19).[27] In short, this journey requires constant vigilance if the spiritual seeker is not to be swept away by the forces of the underworld. As a dream reflecting Lucius' life, this sequence shows him that he has to learn to control his impulses of lust and greed in his spiritual search. In fact, his awareness of the required abstinence for an encounter with transcendence causes him to hesitate before being initiated.

Psyche's descent into the underworld in order to get the box of beauty ointment from Persephone is undoubtedly also connected to the death-resurrection theme in the process of transformation. The ointment may be related to the religious dimension of transformation, which as von Franz pointed out, refers to the way the Egyptians gave life to statues of their gods by anointing them with a cream-like substance.[28] Since this ointment comes from the underworld, Neumann believes that it may promise something like the eternal youth of death.[29] This may again link Psyche's fate to Gannymede, who was a human who remained eternally young when transported to the world of the gods. But in Psyche's case the ointment clearly represents an aspect of the underworld which is not appropriate for her, even though it may be greatly prized by the goddess Aphrodite.

The deadly sleep which overcomes Psyche as she takes for herself some of this ointment again highlights the danger involved in Lucius' spiritual journey and the respect necessary for dealing with aspects of the unconscious. This ointment belongs to the underworld and the gods and can be deadly to mortals. Psyche's taking the ointment for herself may characterize Lucius' early curiosity where he wishes to acquire for himself the power of magic. As a dream segment, this task could be warning Lucius not to be presumptuous in seeking the power of the otherworld, but to wait for appropriate power under the direction of Isis. Also, if Jung is correct about the psychological significance of the number four, then the fact that there are four tasks might also underscore the idea that they are designed to lead Lucius to psychological wholeness.

Aphrodite

At the subjective level, Aphrodite appears to represent the Mother archetype and the inertia of the unconscious. In Lucius' situation Aphrodite symbolizes the antagonism between his conscious development and his desire to remain in the unconscious embrace of the mother. It is this dynamic at the subjective level which prompts von Franz to emphasize Lucius' mother complex and to attribute his lack of personality development to this complex. For von Franz, Aphrodite represents the anima as still connected with the mother, in other words, the unconscious in a yet undifferentiated state. On the one hand, Aphrodite does have the mythological association with fecundity and promiscuity and there is a part of Lucius which strongly resists any efforts to develop his capacity for relationships beyond this mode. This might be thought of as the negative aspect of the Great Mother which Neumann stresses when he identifies Aphrodite with the Bad Mother.

But on the other hand, in the Eros and Psyche dream, Aphrodite also forces Psyche to develop herself through the tasks she sets for her. The motivation of jealousy which is so much a part of Aphrodite's behaviour in this story means that Psyche possesses something valuable which Aphrodite does not have. In relation to Lucius' psyche this probably refers to his capacity for consciousness, at the core of which is his rational will. The power to discriminate in sorting seeds and in learning the timing crucial to acquiring the rams' fleece points to the powers of consciousness. The Eros and Psyche dream shows that Lucius must use these powers to regulate his relationship to sex and transcendence so that he is no longer simply under the domination of lust and greed for magical power.

So the positive aspect of Aphrodite, even though she appears to be primarily negative in the dream, is that she, like blind Fortune tormenting Lucius, pushes the psyche toward development. This is very much the view of the priest of Isis in Book 11, who addresses these words to Lucius:

> At last, Lucius, after the long days of disaster and the heavy storms of fortune you have reached the haven of peace and the altar of mercy. Neither your high lineage, nor your pride of place, nor your learning, profited you one jot. You gave yourself to the slavery of pleasure in the lewdness of hot-blooded youth; and you have reaped the reward of your unprospering curiosity. Nevertheless, blind Fortune, persecuting you with horrors and snares, has led you in her shortsighted malice to this beatitude of release. Let her go now and rage as madly as she will; but let her seek another object for her hate. For terror and calamity have no power over him whose life the majesty of our Goddess has claimed for her service (XI, 15). [30]

Here the priest brings together these contradictory aspects of Lucius' experience. It is blind Fortune who has tormented Lucius just as Aphrodite harassed Psyche, and it is precisely when Lucius was under the sway of Aphrodite's power, or the mother complex, that he was led by lust and greed for power into his horrible fate of being imprisoned in the body of an ass. But just as Aphrodite's interference ultimately led to Psyche's experience of Eros, the tasks and ultimately her victorious union with the divine, so Fortune has led Lucius through his suffering to the experience of Isis.

The Sisters

Psyche's sisters might be thought of as those characteristics which led Lucius to his divided state, symbolized by a human mind in the body of an ass. At the subjective level of interpretation they would primarily represent the lust and restless curiosity which push him to experiment with magic. [31] The sisters play a role similar to that of Aphrodite. They, too, are closely tied to jealousy, and for much the same reason—that as shadowy, undeveloped aspects of Lucius' psyche they are not able to exercise the conscious will which is part of Psyche's destiny. In other words, they have no connection to Eros as conscious relationship.

As shadow elements, the sisters can at best express a kind of pseudo-will which is like the autonomous character of unconscious complexes. As sisters of Psyche they are related to her nature as a centre of will and action, but they never experience Psyche's unique tie to Eros as the subject of conscious relationships. Ironically, it is at their bidding that Psyche is forced to assume a different relationship to Eros, but then this is not unlike the unconscious factors in the form of ants, the reed and the eagle, which operate behind the scenes to allow Psyche to complete her tasks of development.

The sisters, like Aphrodite, may show symbolically how psychological (character) transformation is effected by realignments in the unconscious which prepare the way for changes in consciousness and behaviour. As unintegrated aspects of Lucius' psyche, such as his curiosity and lust, the sisters seem to be negative, yet indirectly push him towards Isis through horrifying experiences with magic. In this way they make things so bad for Lucius that he comes to the point of despair and finally calls upon the queen of heaven for help.

Voluptas and Deification

The child, Voluptas, appears as the fruit of the union of Psyche and Eros. At the subjective level this seems to characterize the joy which Lucius experiences as he ends his condition of inner division, symbolized by a human mind in the body of an ass, and is again able to relate to others. Specifically, Apuleius uses the term "voluptas" to characterize the pleasure Lucius finds in contemplating the goddess Isis: "Having tarried there for a few days longer, I enjoyed the ineffable pleasure (inexplicabili voluptate) of the image of the goddess, to whom I was now pledged by a favour that could not be repaid" (XI, 24).[32] This context supports the interpretation of Voluptas as a symbol of the joy in Lucius' mystical experience. William James emphasizes that ineffability is one of the four fundamental characteristics of mystical experience and it is precisely in relation to Lucius' pleasure that this term occurs.

Psyche's deification at the end of the story is closely related to her marriage to the god Eros and the birth of their daughter, Voluptas, especially where some Jungians associate Voluptas with the self archetype. Here Jung's notion of the emergence of the self archetype in the course of psychological development and character transformation seems applicable.

Jung does not make any judgment about the ontological status of the self archetype since he considers this to be the province of philosophers and theologians, not psychologists. But he does maintain that various symbols of the self archetype which appear in dreams are, in practice, indistinguishable from the God-image:

We cannot tell whether God and the unconscious are two different entities. Both are border-line concepts for transcendental contents. But empirically it can be established, with a sufficient degree
of probability, that there is in the unconscious an archetype of
wholeness which manifests itself spontaneously in dreams, etc.
Consequently, it does not seem improbable that the archetype of
wholeness occupies as such a central position which approximates
it to the God-image. The similarity is further borne out by the
peculiar fact that the archetype produces a symbolism which has
always characterized and expressed the Deity. These facts make
possible a certain qualification of our above thesis concerning the
indistinguishableness of God and the unconscious.[33]

So Psyche's deification might well be a symbolic expression of the
potentially divine aspect of the psyche which Jung calls the self
archetype.

Even if the self archetype is not considered to be divine, it generates the symbols of the highest level of psychological transformation.
So, from this perspective, if the Eros and Psyche story is Lucius'
dream, it seems to portray dramatically the realization of Lucius'
highest potential. In this regard the dream appears to forecast in a
very general way what may be seen as the development of Lucius'
psyche.

But we might also recognize a more specific precognitive aspect of
the Eros and Psyche myth as it relates to Lucius' experience.
Apuleius was well aware of the importance of precognitive dreams
in the ancient world, and he arranges for them to play a significant
role in Lucius' dream life. The distinction between predictive and
non-predictive dreams is perhaps the oldest form of dream classifica-
tion, and C.A. Behr holds that the ancient concern with predictive
dreams is one of the main differences between ancient and modern
dream interpretation.[34] While modern dream analysis has focussed
almost exclusively on the psychological meaning of dreams, this
does not mean that the paranormal dimensions of dreams have been
completely overlooked even in this century.[35] In the Eros and Psyche
dream the precognitive level of interpretation seems to be particularly apparent in regard to the course of Lucius' trials as they finally
issue in his conversion and initiation. Psyche's deification could
symbolically indicate Lucius' future transformation. As Lucius
encounters the goddess Isis he develops a transforming relationship
which leads him to the initiation in which *he* is symbolically deified.
Lucius' symbolic "deification" (spiritual transformation) is highlighted in the imagery of his initiation, where he becomes identified
with Isis' son, Horus, the sun god. In regard to this crucial aspect of

Lucius' experience, the Eros and Psyche dream would be considered a symbolic or allegorical type of precognitive dream as opposed to the type which shows or tells the foreknown event exactly as it happens.[36] In the symbolic type of precognition there is much room for interpreting how the dream foresees a future event, and the multi-leveled character of symbols is evident in the attempt to determine the subjective or objective reference of particular symbols within the dream.

Those authors who have suggested that the origin of the Eros and Psyche story is possibly to be found in the nightmare may have hit upon a truth regarding an aspect of the divine-human encounter in the Isis religion, namely, that one of the fundamental modes of experiencing the divine is at night in the dream. From the perspective of the conscious psyche, a dream is for the most part an arena of experience, outside of conscious control. Not only must the dreamer await the time of the dream experience but also only a limited dream ego is available for the encounter. While it is true that in dreams magical transformations can occur and that the dream ego is capable of remarkable feats, such as going through walls or flying, it is also true that the person often does not have full or even partial use of ego functions, such as logical thinking, volition or action. It is possible that the characterization of Psyche's encounter with the divine Eros in the dark might well imply all of these limitations or restrictions on Lucius' experience of the goddess Isis.

Conclusion

As we look back at the various psychological interpretations of the Eros and Psyche myth considered in this study, one of the most prominent characteristics noted has been selective perception based on Freudian and Jungian theoretical perspectives. Thus, in Freudian theory, where sexuality, sibling rivalry and the power of wishes predominate, the analysts concentrate on Eros (as sexuality), the sisters (as rivals and anxieties) and Psyche (as the initiator of fantasy, wishes and dreams). Among Jungians, who emphasize the bridging role of the anima and the wise spiritual guidance of the unconscious, we find commentators focussing on Psyche's tasks and deification, Eros (as a link to the divine) and Voluptas (as the joy emerging from inner development).

All of the psychological commentators have discovered some truths about the nature and dynamics of the human mind hidden in the Eros and Psyche myth. The great variety of interpretations illustrates both the multi-leveled character of the symbols themselves as well as the degree to which analysts project their own theories and preoccupations onto the story. This is very similar to the way dream interpretation involves the analyst to such a degree that the analyst must constantly guard against reading too much of himself or herself into the meaning of the dream. At the beginning of Chapter 2, we considered this tendency, along with other similarities between interpreting myths and dreams.

There is no sure way to avoid completely this "creative contact" between the analyst and the symbolic material to be interpreted, particularly when both dreams and myths invite the analyst to encounter profound aspects of his or her own inner life. A careful dream analyst always checks with the dreamer, the context of the analysis and other of the person's dreams to determine whether a particular interpretation is on the mark. The "verification process" is somewhat different in myth interpretation because we can only indirectly check an interpretation with the creator of a myth in the sense of locating the historical and cultural context in which the myth and its symbols arose.

A number of the psychological commentators on the Eros and Psyche myth attempted to recover this context in the course of their investigations, and I have tried to point out how this helps to ground their interpretations. With the Eros and Psyche myth, further interpretive context is provided by Apuleius' *Metamorphoses*, yet only von Franz continually refers her interpretation back to that primary context. Hers seems to be the most sound approach to controlling the interpreter's projections, although there can never be an absolute guarantee against reading oneself into an interpretation of this kind of symbolic material. In fact, some scholars believe that an objective interpretation of such material is impossible.

Now, as we seek to consolidate the insights of past psychological interpreters with reference to literary context, we see two general lines of contribution. On the one hand, the Freudians from the beginning have been aware of the relationship of this myth to the development and management of the sexual instinct, while the Jungians have emphasized how this myth illustrates the transforming role of the archetypes.

We have seen that among the Freudians the range of specific interpretations is great, but the unifying thread is the sexual interpretation which revolves around the symbol of Eros as sexuality in its vast range of meanings, and the entire story as reflecting the vicissitudes of the sexual instinct in the development of the human being. Although most of the Freudian interpreters have applied the dynamics of the myth to a woman's development, Riklin seems to recognize a wider application of the myth to both women and men.

Bettelheim, Schroeder, Barchilon and Hoevels have provided some support for the view that the Eros and Psyche myth sheds light on the psychology of an adolescent girl's anxieties about sex. Hoevels' argument is particularly convincing in regard to the dynamics of a female's Oedipal fantasy. But it seems that this specific perspective has little relation to the literary context of the myth in the *Metamorphoses*.

The Freudian emphasis on the sexual character of the Eros symbol may help to focus on the prominent but elusive role of the sexual element in Lucius' transformations. In reading the *Metamorphoses* there can be little doubt that the sexual instinct and religious (sacrilegious) curiosity are the primary psychological determinants of Lucius' behaviour. Lust draws Lucius to sexual adventure and curiosity involves him, more deeply than he ever anticipated, in the magical world of witchcraft and religion.

The relationship of these two motivational elements in Lucius would not be entirely clear from the Freudian perspectives we have examined in Chapter 2, primarily because these commentators showed little, if any, interest in applying their insights to Lucius' life in the *Metamorphoses*. But the implications of the fundamental Freudian perspectives would lead to an interpretation of Lucius' religious experience in terms of the development of his sexual instinct, and this instinct would be related to his curiosity about magic and witchcraft.

Early on in the story Lucius is ruled by the sex instinct and a curiosity about the dark area of the unknown symbolized by witchcraft. In Freudian terms Lucius' ego appears to be dominated by id impulses in the early stages of the *Metamorphoses*. From a Freudian perspective, one could argue that both of these areas (sex and magic) are id-based. Lucius being changed into a donkey could be seen as a powerful symbol of his id (animal instincts) controlling his personality.

But Lucius' psychological dynamics appear to change greatly as a result of his dream encounter with the goddess Isis. Since dreams are so closely related to the id and the pleasure principle in Freudian thought, it might not be too much of an overstatement to say that Lucius is transformed by virtue of the id—by what he meets there and its effect on him. From a Freudian point of view Lucius' behaviour after transformation shows a management of his sexual instinct which was apparently not available before his conversion. His religious life entailing celibacy or sexual abstinence might be considered as a particular form of sublimation of the sexual instinct. Freud himself, of course, would not be inclined to value very much the particular form that this id energy assumed, since for him religion was so closely related to psychological regression and pathology. The magical power of Lucius' dreamworld and its intrusion into his waking life would probably convince Freudians that Lucius was still not a psychologically healthy person. This is very much the way the Freudian Riklin interprets the Eros and Psyche myth.

That sex is so closely related to religion in Lucius' story might suggest to a Freudian that this is but one more instance where sex is seen to be a primary factor in human psychology. That sexuality as represented by Eros might include the highest human qualities (as in Bettelheim's Freudian interpretation) also broadens the potential application of sexual symbolism to Lucius' story. At the far end of these "highest human qualities" one could conceivably find religious experience, but that would depend very much on a person's worldview. In the worldview expressed in the *Metamorphoses*, the divine is involved in the symbols of Eros and Aphrodite as gods in Greek mythology and Isis and Osiris as gods in Egyptian religion. Even a Freudian perspective applied to the Eros and Psyche myth in relation to Lucius' experience might take seriously Lucius' claim to religious conversion and the mythical expression of that experience as the deification of the psyche in relation to the god Eros.

Freudians might object to a description which appears to divinize the psyche or Eros, as in the case of the mythical story, but there is little doubt they would be inclined to refer such descriptions of Psyche and Eros to their insight about the centrality of the sexual instinct in human development. This insight might be seen as the most fruitful contribution that the Freudians have made in relation to the Eros and Psyche myth, and preserving this insight in relation to the *Metamorphoses* is bound to keep a psychological interpretation of religious transformation well grounded in the body, that is, giving the body its due in regard to religious experience.

The Jungian interpreters have generally focussed on the way the Eros and Psyche myth shows the impact of central archetypes on human development. Most of the Jungians have viewed Psyche as a symbol of the anima, and they see her role in the myth as a key to the way human beings come to full self-realization or individuation. Both Ulanov and von Franz have recognized that this main insight can shed light on the dynamics of Lucius' psychological experience. Some of the Jungians (Ulanov, Johnson and Houston) also emphasize the relationship of the Eros symbol to the self or God archetype, and this has particular application to the religious context of the *Metamorphoses*.

Eros as related to the God archetype can be understood as a part of a symbolic portrayal of Lucius' spiritual transformation. The facts 1) that Jung had a high regard for direct religious experience, and 2) that he attempted to account for such experience in psychological terms mean that, initially at least, it is not difficult to see how Jungian psychological dynamics can be applied to Lucius' experience. Four of the Jungian commentators (von Franz, Ulanov, Johnson and Houston) on the Eros and Psyche myth make explicit reference to the way this myth deals, in one way or another, with the coming together of the human and the divine. So even where these commentators themselves have not focussed on the relationship of the myth to Lucius' religious experience, it is only a short step to apply the dynamics of the human relationship with the divine symbolized in the Eros and Psyche myth to Lucius' religious conversion and initiation.

We have seen that the mythical level of description (as exemplified in the Eros and Psyche story) characterizes Lucius' psychological and spiritual transformation as his divinization or deification. It is interesting to note that certain humanists use precisely this kind of mythical speech, the language of deification, to describe the process and results of self-actualization or self-realization. For instance, when we examine the kind of language Abraham Maslow uses to speak about the transformation of the psyche, we see that he chooses words like "the great mystic experience," "the great illumination," living "in heaven," "being on easy terms with the eternal and the infinite," experiencing oneself as "a god, a perfection . . . sacred, divine."[37]

At the same time Maslow also emphasizes the "naturalness" of this self-transcendence. In fact Maslow's ability to combine the human with the divine, or to put it more precisely, to appreciate the simultaneity of human and divine aspects of reality in a single psychological state, seems to be part of what makes his writing so compelling. He uses language traditionally reserved for religion and the gods of mythology to characterize the farther reaches of human potential.

Maslow seems to be very much at home with the kind of mythical and religious language that Apuleius employed when he selected the Eros and Psyche myth to be the striking centrepiece of his tale about Lucius' psychological and religious transformation. The most "religious" meaning of the Eros symbol in the context of the *Metamorphoses* would seem to represent Lucius' conversion experience as a kind of divinization. Such an interpretation would see the divinization of the psyche by the god Eros as a fundamental expression of the dynamics of psychological transformation. As Houston and Ulanov have already pointed out convincingly, the Eros symbol functions in relation to the self archetype or the God archetype. In this light, the Eros symbol and its relation to the psyche express mythically what Jung has called the dynamics of individuation.

From this viewpoint Eros may symbolize the divine which draws human beings and finally leads to their divinization. Marriage with Eros is the symbol of union with the divine which portrays Lucius' union with Isis. In Apuleius' veiled description of Lucius' initiation, he describes how Lucius is transported to the gods of the underworld and the gods of the upperworld: "I approached the confines of death. I trod the threshold of Proserpine; and borne through the elements I returned. At midnight I saw the Sun shining in all his glory. I approached the gods below and the gods above, and I stood beside them, and I worshipped them" (XI, 24).[38] Jung emphasized that the human being is unable to say definitively whether or not such a dream image or religious experience comes from one's unconscious or from a transcendent realm which corresponds to what the world's religions have spoken of variously as God, the Great Spirit, the divine, the ultimate or the absolute. Jung seems to have been open to the possibility that a psychological symbol such as Eros could conceivably allow the divine to reveal itself. From this vantage point, the miracle wrought by Eros in deifying Psyche cannot be completely separated from the miracle worked by Isis in divinizing Lucius, as is so explicitly expressed in the scene of Lucius' initiation into the cult of Isis, where he is portrayed as the divine sun:[39]

> In my right hand I carried a torch with rearing flames and my head was garlanded gracefully by a crown of gleaming palms whose leaves stood out like rays. When I had thus been adorned like the sun and set up in the manner of a divine statue, suddenly the curtains were drawn and the people crowded to behold me (XI, 24).[40]

Here we can see how the context of the *Metamorphoses* invites us to consider carefully the religious implications of the Eros and Psyche myth.

In summary, this study has presented the case that the Eros and Psyche myth, when interpreted as Lucius' archetypal dream in the context of the *Metamorphoses*, has more focus than when viewed only as a universal story about "Everyperson." A more contextual reading does not deny the major insights of earlier psychological interpretations, but applies them to a specific case or event, namely, Lucius' conversion. Such a contextual focus seems to place the myth within a more limiting, but at the same time a more firmly grounded, interpretive framework.

In this literary and religious framework, the Eros and Psyche symbols, in all of their aspects, can be seen as a mythological description of Isis leading Lucius to divination through ritual initiation. Such an interpretation draws upon the main insights of both Freudian and

Jungian interpreters of the Eros and Psyche myth. Here we acknowledge that the Freudian interpretation, with its focus on Eros as sexuality, highlights the role of sex in Lucius' life, first enticing him into the realm of magic and then being sublimated in his chaste devotion to Isis. With the majority of Jungians the focus is on Eros as relationship. They see Eros' departing and returning as symbolic of Lucius' initial incapacity for deep personal relationship followed by his transforming relationship with, and commitment to, the goddess Isis.

These two lines of interpretation are not necessarily contradictory, but rather complimentary. They highlight two different aspects, the sexual and the interpersonal, of Lucius' transformation experience. The contextual interpretation advocated in this study recognizes both of these crucial elements in Lucius' conversion. This interpretation sees winged Eros as a symbol of transformation which portrays how Lucius' psyche, as it becomes related to the divine, transcends both animal and human potential.

In conclusion, this study has attempted to show that the most promising lines of interpreting the Eros and Psyche myth psychologically appear to follow the lead of those recent non-psychological studies which emphasize the relationship of the Eros and Psyche story to Apuleius' *Metamorphoses*. Future psychological studies will shed more light on the meaning of the Eros and Psyche myth to the degree that they also take into account Apuleius, his main character, Lucius, and the enduring story of spiritual transformation recorded in the *Metamorphoses*.

Notes

1 Scholars still debate the degree of identity between Apuleius and his chief character, Lucius, but R. Th. Van der Paardt speaks for the majority when he says: "Anyone who knows that the author of the novel is from Madauros, cannot but conclude that a confusion or blending of author and narrator has taken place" ("The Unmasked 'I': Apuleius' *Metamorphoses* XI, 27," *Mnemosyne* 34 [1981]: 97). The last book of the *Metamorphoses* which contains the classical account of religious experience and initiation into the cult of Isis is generally agreed upon as autobiographical.

2 S. Freud, "The Theory of the Instincts," in *An Outline of Psychoanalysis*, SE XIII, pp. 148-49.

3 *Mysterium Coniunctionis*, CW 14, p. 178.

4 *Two Essays on Analytical Psychology*, CW 7, p. 28.

5 Ibid., p. 28.

6 *Answer to Job*, CW 11, pp. 468-69.

7 Von Franz, *A Psychological Interpretation of the Golden Ass* (Zurich, 1970), p. 61. Von Franz sees the *Metamorphoses* as largely autobiographical, and thus she

does not distinguish sharply between the psychological situation of Lucius and that of his creator, Apuleius.

8 I shall provide a more complete interpretation of this myth as a dream in a future monograph on the religious dreamworld of the *Metamorphoses*.

9 "Di boni, quae facies rei! Quod monstrum! Quae fortunarum mearum repentina mutatio! Quamquam enim iam in peculio Proserpinae et Orci familia numeratus, subito in contrariam faciem obstupefactus haesi nec possum novae illius imaginis rationem idoneis verbis expedire" (III, 9). In this chapter the English translations of the Latin text of the *Metamorphoses* are taken from Jack Lindsay's *Apuleius: The Golden Ass* (Bloomington, 1960) unless otherwise noted. The only change I have made in these translations is to substitute the Greek names of the gods for the Roman names in order to be consistent with earlier references to Eros and Aphrodite.

10 "What we are to our inward vision, and what man appears to be *sub specie aeternitatis*, can only be expressed by way of myth. Myth is more individual and expresses life more precisely than does science. . . . I can only make direct statements, only 'tell stories.' Whether or not the stories are 'true' is not the problem. The only question is whether what I tell is my truth. . . . That is why I speak chiefly of inner experiences, amongst which I include my dreams and visions." (*Memories, Dreams, Reflections* [New York, 1973], pp. 3-4).

11 "et iacebat immobilis et nihil aliud quam dormiens cadaver. Sed Cupido iam cicatrice solida revalescens nec diutinam suae Psyches absentiam tolerans, per altissimam cubiculi, quo cohibebatur, elapsus fenestram, refectisque pinnis aliquanta quiete, longe velocius provolans Psychen accurrit suam, detersoque somno curiose et rursum in pristinam pyxidis sedem recondito, Psychen innoxio punctulo sagittae suae suscitat" (VI, 21).

12 "Interea Psyche cum sua sibi perspicua pulchritudine nullum decoris sui fructum percipit. Spectatur ab omnibus, laudatur ab omnibus, nec quisquam, non rex, non regius, nec de plebe saltem cupiens eius nuptiarum petitor accedit: mirantur quidem divinam speciem, sed ut simulacrum fabre politum mirantur omnes . . . sed Psyche virgo vidua domi residens deflet desertam suam solitudinem, aegra corporis, animi saucia, et quamvis gentibus totis complacitam odit in se suam formositatem" (IV, 32).

13 "inscenso grabatulo super me sessim residens ac crebra subsiliens, lubricisque gestibus mobilem spinam quatiens, pendulae Veneris fructu me satiavit, usque dum lassis animis et marcidis artubus defatigati simul ambo corruimus inter mutuos amplexus animas anhelantes. His et huiusmodi colluctationibus ad confinia lucis usque pervigiles egimus, poculis interdum lassitudinem refoventes et libidinem incitantes et voluptatem integrantes: ad cuius noctis exemplar similes astruximus alias plusculas" (II, 17).

14 At the subjective level of dream interpretation the characters of a dream are considered to be aspects of the dreamer's own personality, or in this case, aspects of Lucius' personality.

15 "arrepta manu Fotidis et admota meis luminibus, 'Patere, oro te,' inquam 'Dum dictat occasio, magno et singulari me affectionis tuae fructu perfrui et impertire nobis unctulum indidem, per istas tuas papillas, mea mellitula,

tuumque mancipium irremunerabili beneficio sic tibi perpetuo pignera, ac iam perfice ut meae Veneri Cupido pinnatus assistam tibi" (III, 22).

16 "Sic inustus exiluit deus visaque detectae fidei colluvie prorsus ex osculis et manibus infelicissimae coniugis tacitus avolavit: at Psyche statim resurgentis eius crure dextero manibus ambabus arrepto, sublimis evectionis appendix miseranda et per nubilas plagas penduli comitatus extrema consequia tandem fessa delabitur solo" (V, 23-24).

17 "Et vocat confestim puerum suum pinnatum illum et satis temerarium, qui malis suis moribus contempta disciplina publica, flammis et sagittis armatus per alienas domos nocte discurrens et omnium matrimonia corrumpens impune committit tanta flagitia, et nihil prorsus boni facit" (IV, 30).

18 "Discerne seminum istorum passivam congeriem . . ." (VI, 10).

19 "terrae omniparentis agiles alumnae" (VI, 10).

20 See Ad de Vries, *Dictionary of Symbols and Imagery* (Amsterdam, 1984), p. 16.

21 Neumann also connects the fleece to "destructive magic powers" but he emphasizes more the masculine and solar significance of the fleece. Because he believes that Psyche represents a female's development, he views this task as showing the importance of a woman incorporating masculine aspects of her psyche, not as a warning against the use of magic to gain access to the transcendent. *Amor and Psyche*, p. 98.

22 De Vries, *Symbol Dictionary*, p. 220.

23 "quoad de solis flagrantia mutuatae calorem truci rabie solent efferri cornuque acuto et fronte saxea et nonnunquam venenatis morsibus in exitium saevire mortalium. Sed dum meridies solis sedaverit vaporem et pecua spiritus fluvialis serenitate conquieverint, poteris sub illa procerissima platano, quae mecum simul unum fluentum bibit, latenter abscondere" (VI, 12).

24 "Nec Providentiae bonae graves oculos innocentis animae latuit aerumna: nam primi Iovis regalis ales illa repente propansis utrimque pinnis affuit rapax aquila, memorque veteris obsequii, quo ductu Cupidinis Iovi pocillatorem Phrygium sustulerat" (VI, 15).

25 "At tu simplex alioquin et expers rerum talium, speras te sanctissimi nec minus truculenti fontis vel unam stillam posse furari vel omnino contingere! Diis etiam ipsique Iovi formidabiles aquas istas Stygias vel fando comperisti, quodque vos deieratis per numina deorum, deos per Stygis maiestatem solere!" (VI, 15).

26 *Amor and Psyche*, p. 106.

27 "ut et molliter assidere et prandium opipare suadeat sumere. Sed tu et humi reside et panem sordidum petitum esto" (VI, 19).

28 *A Psychological Interpretation of the Golden Ass*, pp. 103-104.

29 *Amor and Psyche*, p. 118.

30 "Multis et variis exanclatis laboribus magnisque Fortunae tempestatibus et maximis actus procellis ad portum quietis et aram misericordiae tandem, Luci, venisti: nec tibi natales ac ne dignitas quidem, vel ipsa qua flores usquam doctrina profuit, sed lubrico virentis aetatulae ad serviles delapsus voluptates, curiositatis improsperae sinistrum praemium reportasti. Sed utcumque Fortunae caecitas, dum te pessimis periculis discruciat, ad religiosam istam beatitudinem improvida produxit malitia. Eat nunc et summo furore saeviat, et cru-

delitati suae materiem quaerat aliam: nam in eos quorum sibi vitas in servitium deae nostrae maiestas vindicavit, non habet locum casus infestus" (XI, 15).

31 At an objective level (external reference) they could refer to the witch, Pamphile, and Fotis in her unwitting role in his metamorphosis into an ass.

32 This English translation is from J. Griffiths' *The Isis Book. Metamorphoses 11* (Leiden, 1975), p. 101. "paucis dehinc ibidem commoratus diebus inexplicabili voluptate simulacri divini perfruebar, inremunerabili quippe beneficio pigneratus" (XI, 24).

33 *CW* 11, pp. 468-69.

34 C.A. Behr, *Aelius Aristides*, pp. 171-73

35 Those involved in both the therapeutic and the paranormal investigation of dreams have dealt with the telepathic and precognitive potential of dreams. For example, Emilio Servadio, former president of the Italian Psychoanalytic Society, states that there have been large numbers of well-substantiated paranormal dreams studied since the nineteenth century ("The Dynamics of So-called Paranormal Dreams," in *The Dream and Human Societies* [Berkeley, 1966], p. 110) and much case material on telepathic and precognitive dreams has been published by both the British and American Societies for Psychical Research. With reference to the precognitive dimension of the Eros and Psyche dream, it is interesting to note that modern ESP evaluators reject the more symbolic representations of dreams expressing paranormal foreknowledge. Also see M. Ullman, S. Krippner and A. Vaughan, *Dream Telepathy* (New York, 1973) and J. Eisenbud, *Paranormal Foreknowledge* (New York, 1982).

36 By the time of Apuleius' *Metamorphoses*, three categories of predictive dreams were differentiated: 1) the allegorically predictive dream which required an interpreter to decipher the symbols of the dream, 2) the straightforward predictive dream in which future events take place as they appeared in the dream, and 3) the dream oracle in which the divine appears and foretells some future event. C.A. Behr, *Aelius Aristides*, p. 173.

37 *The Farther Reaches of Human Nature* (New York, 1971), pp. 267-68.

38 "Accessi confinium mortis et calcato Proserpinae limine per omnia vectus elementa remeavi; nocte media vidi solem candido coruscantem lumine; deos inferos et deos superos accessi coram et adoravi de proxumo" (XI, 24).

39 Von Franz emphasizes the multi-form imagery of this initiation by connecting the sun god with Isis' divine son, Horus. She states that this sun symbolizes the spiritual goal of the goddess Isis. *A Psychological Interpretation of the Golden Ass*, p. 154.

40 Here the English text is taken from J. Griffiths' translation in *The Isis Book. Metamorphoses 11* (Leiden, 1975), p. 101: "at manu dextera gerebam flammis adultam facem, et caput decore corona cinxerat, palmae candidae foliis in modum radiorum prosistentibus: sic ad instar solis exornato me et in vicem simulacri constituto, repente velis reductis, in aspectum populus errabat" (XI, 24).

Selected Bibliography

Primary Sources

Editions and Translations

Adlington, Wm., trans. *The Golden Ass of Apuleius.* Introd. C. Whibley. London, 1893.

Beaujeu, J., trans. *Apulée. Opuscules Philosophiques et Fragments.* Paris, 1973.

Bétolaud, V., trans. *Les Métamorphoses ou l'âne d'or.* Paris, 1883.

Butler, H., trans. *The Metamorphoses or Golden Ass of Apuleius of Madaura.* 2 vols. Oxford, 1910.

Gaselee, S., ed. *Apuleius, the Golden Ass.* With an English translation by W. Adlington. London, 1915.

Graves, R., trans. *The Golden Ass.* Harmondsworth, Eng., 1986.

Griffiths, J., trans. *The Isis Book. Metamorphoses 11.* Leiden, 1975.

Grimal, P., trans. *Apulei Metamorphoses IV,28-VI,24: "Le Conte d'Amour et Psyché."* Paris, 1963.

Helm, R., ed. *Apuleii Opera Quae Supersunt.* Vol. 1. *Metamorphoseon* Libri XI. Leipzig, 1931.

Hildebrand, G.F., ed. *Apuleii Opera Omnia.* 2 vols. Leipzig, 1842.

Lindsay, J., trans. *Apuleius: The Golden Ass.* Bloomington, Indiana, 1962.

Médan, P., ed. *Apulée Métamorphoses.* Livre XI. Paris, 1925.

Robertson, D.S., ed. *Apulée. Les Métamorphoses.* 3 vols. Trans. P. Vallette. Paris, 1940-45.

Taylor, T., trans. *The Fable of Cupid and Psyche.* Los Angeles, 1977.

Vallette, P., ed. and trans. *Apulée. Apologie, Florides.* Paris, 1924.

Secondary Sources

Abraham, K. "Traum und Mythus. Eine Studie Zur Voelkerpsychologie." In *Psychoanalytische Studien,* pp. 261-323. Frankfurt am Main, 1971.

Abt, A. *Die Apologie des Apuleius von Madaura und die antike Zauberei.* Naumburg, 1907.

Alpers, K. "Innere Beziehungen und Kontraste als 'Hermeneutische Zeichen' in den Metamorphosen des Apuleius von Madaura." *WJA* 6 (1980): 197-207.

Anderson, G. *Studies in Lucian's Comic Fiction.* Leiden, 1976.

Anderson, W. "Zu Apuleius' Novelle vom Tode der Charite." *Philologus* 68 (1909): 537-49.

Angus, S. *The Mystery Religions*. New York, 1975.

——. *The Mystery Religions and Christianity*. London, 1925.

Bachofen, J. *Myth, Religion and Mother Right*. New York, 1967.

Baltrusaitis, J. *La Quête d'Isis*. Paris, 1967.

Barchilon, J. "Beauty and the Beast: From Myth to Fairy Tale." *Psychoanalysis and the Psychoanalytic Review* 46, 4 (1959): 19-29.

Beaujeu, J. "Sérieux et frivolité au 11e siècle de notre ère: Apulée." *BAGB* (1975): 83-97.

Becher I. "Der Isiskult in Rom—ein Kult der Halbwelt." *ZAS* 96 (1970): 81-90.

Behr, C. *Aelius Aristides: The Complete Works*. Vol. 1. Leiden, 1986.

——. *Aelius Aristides and the Sacred Tales*.Amsterdam, 1968.

Bergman, J. *Ich Bin Isis*. Uppsala, 1968.

——. *Isis-Seele und Osiris-Ei*. Uppsala, 1970.

——. "Zum 'Mythus von der Nation' in den sog. hellenistischen Mysterienreligionen." *Temenos* 8 (1972): 7-28.

Bernhard, M. *Der Stil des Apuleius von Madaura*. Amsterdam, 1965.

Berreth, J. *Studien zum Isisbuch in Apuleius' Metamorphosen*. Ph.D. Diss. Tuebingen, 1931.

Bettelheim, B. *The Uses of Enchantment: The Meaning and Importance of Fairy Tales*. New York, 1977.

Bidney, D. "Myth, Symbolism, and Truth." In *Myth: A Symposium*, edited by T. Sebeok, pp. 3-24. Bloomington, IN, 1955.

Bieler, L. "Psyches dritte und vierte Arbeit bei Apuleius." *AP*, pp. 334-69.

Binder, G., and R. Merkelbach, eds. *Amor und Psyche*. Darmstadt, 1968.

Birley, A. "Apuleius: Roman Provincial Life." *History Today* 18 (1968): 629-36.

Bjorck, G. "Onar idein: De la perception de la rêve chez les anciens." *Eranos* 44 (1946): 306-14.

Bleeker, C. "Isis as Saviour Goddess." In *The Saviour God*, edited by S. Brandon, pp. 1-16. Manchester, 1963.

Bluemner, H. "Das Maerchen von Amor und Psyche in der deutschen Dichtkunst." *Neue Jahrbuecher fuer das klassische Altertum* 11 (1903): 648-73.

——. "Textkritisches zu Apuleius Metamorphosen." *Philologus* 55 (1896): 341-52.

——. "Zu Apuleius Metamorphosen." *Hermes* 29 (1894): 294-312.

Boehme, J. "Hundt, Der Traumglaube bei Homer." *Gnomon* 11 (1935): 466-73.

Bohm, R. "The Isis Episode in Apuleius." *Classical Journal* 68 (1972-73): 228-31.

Brzenk, E. "Apuleius, Pater and the Bildungsroman." *AA*, pp. 231-37.

Brotherton, B. "The Introduction of Characters By Name in the Metamorphoses of Apuleius." *Classical Philology* 29 (1934): 36-52.

Brown, N. "Psychoanalysis and the Classics." *Classical Journal* 52 (1957): 241-45.

Brown, R. "The Tales in the 'Metamorphoses' of Apuleius—A Study in Religious Consciousness." Ph.D. Diss. Florida, 1977.

Buechsenschuetz, B. *Traum und Traumdeutung im Alterthume.* Wiesbaden, 1967.

Buerger, K. "Zu Apuleius." *Hermes* 23 (1888): 489-98.

Burkert, W. *Ancient Mystery Cults.* Cambridge, Mass., 1987.

Bursian, C. "Beitraege zur Kritik der Metamorphosen des Apuleius." *Sitzungsberichte der Akademie der Wissenschaften zu Muenchen* (1881): 119-44.

Callebat, L. "L'Archaïsme dans les Métamorphoses." *REL* 42 (1964): 346-61.

Campbell, J. *The Inner Reaches of Outer Space: Metaphor as Myth and as Religion.* New York, 1986.

_____. *The Hero With a Thousand Faces.* New York, 1973

_____. *The Power of Myth.* New York, 1988.

Carr, J. "The View of Women in Juvenal and Apuleius." *Classical Bulletin* 58 (1982): 61-64.

Cassirer, E. *An Essay on Man.* New Haven, 1948.

Colin, J. "Apulée en Thessalie: fiction ou vérité." *Latomus* 24 (1965): 330-45.

Cooper, G. "Sexual and Ethical Reversal in Apuleius: The Metamorphoses as Anti-Epic." *Latomus Collection* 168 (1980): 436-66.

Cumont, F. *The Oriental Religions in Roman Paganism.* New York, 1956.

Defradas, J. "Études psychanalytiques sur la mythologie grecque." *IL* 10 (1958): 159-65.

Derchain, P., and J. Hubeaux. "L'affaire du Marché d'Hypata dans la 'Métamorphose' d'Apulée." *AC* 27 (1958): 100-104.

Dietrich, D. "Die Ausbreitung der alexandrinischen Mysteriengoetter Isis, Osiris, Serapis und Horus in griechisch-roemischer Zeit." *Das Altertum* 14 (1968): 201-11.

Dodds, E. *The Greeks and the Irrational.* Berkeley, 1951.

_____. *Pagan and Christian in an Age of Anxiety.* Cambridge, 1965.

Dornseiff, F. "Lukios' und Apuleius' Metamorphosen." *Hermes* 73 (1938): 222-33.

Dowden, K. "Ass-men and Witches." *Classical Review* 99 (1985): 41-43.

_____. "Eleven Notes on the Text of Apuleius' 'Metamorphoses.'" *Classical Quarterly* 30 (1980): 218-26.

_____. "Apuleius and the Art of Narration." *Classical Quarterly* 32 (1982): 419-36.

_____. "Psyche on the Rock." *Latomus* 41 (1982): 336-52.

Drake, G. "Candidus—A Unifying Theme in Apuleius' 'Metamorphoses.'" *Classical Journal* 64 (1964): 102-109.

————————. "The Ghost Story in 'The Golden Ass' by Apuleius." *PLL* 13 (1977): 3-15.

————————. "Lucius's 'Business' in the 'Metamorphoses' of Apuleius." *PLL* 5 (1969): 339-61.

Dunand, F. *Le culte d'Isis dans le bassin oriental de la méditerranée.* Leiden, 1973.

Ebel, H. *After Dionysus: An Essay on Where We Are Now.* Rutherford, New Jersey, 1972.

————————. "Apuleius and the Present Time." *Arethusa* 3 (1970): 155-76.

Ehrlich, E. *Der Traum im Alten Testament.* Berlin, 1953.

Eisenbud, J. *Paranormal Foreknowledge.* New York, 1982.

Eitrem, S. "Die Vier Elemente in der Mysterienweihe." *Symbolae Osloenses* 4 (1926): 39-59 and 5 (1927): 39-59.

Eliade, M. *Myths, Dreams and Mysteries.* New York, 1960.

————————. *Shamanism: Archaic Techniques of Ecstasy.* Princeton, 1974.

Elovitz, P. "Dreams as a Psychohistorical Source." *The Journal of Psychohistory* 16, 3 (Winter, 1988): 289-96.

Englert, J., and T. Long. "Functions of Hair in Apuleius' 'Metamorphoses.'" *Classical Journal* 5 (1972-73): 236-39.

Erbse, H. "Griechisches und Apuleianisches bei Apuleius." *AP*, pp. 370-81.

Ferguson, J. "Apuleius." *G&R* 8 (1961): 61-74.

Festugière, A. *Personal Religion among the Greeks and Romans.* Berkeley, 1954.

————————. "Vraisemblance psychologique et forme littéraire chez les anciens." *Philologus* 102 (1958): 21-42.

Fick, N. "Du Palais d'Eros à la robe Olympienne de Lucius." *REL* 47 (1969): 378-96.

————————. "La Symbolique Végétale dans les Métamorphoses d'Apulée." *Latomus* 30 (1971): 328-44.

Frazer, J. *The Golden Bough.* 12 vols. London, 1907-15.

Franz, M. von. *Interpretation of Fairy Tales.* Irving, Texas, 1978.

————————. *Problems of the Feminine in Fairytales.* Irving, Texas, 1979.

————————. *A Psychological Interpretation of the Golden Ass of Apuleius.* Zurich, 1970.

Freeman, K. "Vincent and the Donkey." *G&R* 14 (1945): 33-41.

Freud, Sigmund. *Standard Edition of the Complete Psychological Works of Sigmund Freud.* Trans. J. Strachey (London, 1981).

Friedlaender, L. "Das Maerchen von Amor und Psyche." *AP*, pp. 16-43.

Fromm, E. *The Forgotten Language.* New York, 1957.

Galen. *On the Usefulness of the Parts of the Body.* 2 vols. Trans. and introd. by M. May. Ithaca, New York, 1968.

Gardiner, A. *Hieratic Papyri in the British Museum.* London, 1935.

Garson, R. "The Faces of Love in Apuleius' 'Metamorphoses.'" *Museum Africum* 6 (1977-78): 37-42.

Gennep, A. Van. *The Rites of Passage.* Chicago, 1960.

Giangrande, G. "On the Origins of the Greek Romance: The Birth of a Literary Form." *Eranos* 60 (1962): 132-59.

Ginsberg, G. "Rhetoric and Representation in the 'Metamorphoses' of Apuleius." *Arethusa* 10,1 (1977): 49-63.

Girardot, N. "Initiation and Meaning in the Tale of Snow White and the Seven Dwarfs." *Journal of American Folklore* 90 (1977): 274-300.

Glenn, J. "Psychoanalytic Writings on Greek and Latin Authors, 1911-1960." *Classical World* 66 (1972): 129-45.

Godwin, J. *Mystery Religions in the Ancient World.* London, 1981.

Gollnick, J. *Dreams in the Psychology of Religion.* Lewiston, New York, 1987.

_____. *Flesh as Transformation Symbol in the Theology of Anselm of Canterbury.* Lewiston, New York, 1985.

_____. "The Dream as Medium of the Divine." *Dialogue and Alliance* 1, 4 (Winter, 1988): 65-73.

_____. "Jungian Reflections on Transformation in St. Anselm's Theology." *American Benedictine Review* 36, 4 (1985): 353-71.

Goss, J., and L. Martin. *Essays on Jung and the Study of Religion.* New York, 1985.

Grant, M. *Myths of the Greeks and Romans.* New York, 1962.

Griffiths, J. "Allegory in Greece and Egypt." *The Journal of Egyptian Archaeology* 53 (1967): 79-102.

_____. "The Flight of the Gods Before Typhon: An Unrecognized Myth." *Hermes* 88 (1960): 374-76.

_____. "The Horus-Seth Motif in the Daily Temple Liturgy." *Aegyptus* 38 (1958): 3-10.

_____. "Isis in the Metamorphoses of Apuleius." *AA*, pp. 141-66.

Grimal, P. "A la recherche d'Apulée." *REL* 47 (1969): 94-99.

_____. "Die Bedeutung der Erzaehlung von Amor und Psyche." *AP*, pp. 1-15.

_____. "Le calame égyptien d'Apulée." *REA* 73 (1971): 343-55.

_____. "Le conte d'amour et Psyché." *Vita Latina* 71 (1978): 2-9.

_____. "L'originalité des Métamorphoses d'Apulée." *LL* 9 (1957): 156-62.

Haight, E. *Apuleius and his Influence.* London, 1927.

_____. *Essays on Ancient Fiction.* New York, 1966.

Halliday, W. *Greek and Roman Folklore.* New York, 1927.

_____. *Greek Divination: A Study of its Methods and Principles.* London, 1913.

Hammond, M. "Roman Africa." *Classical World* 53 (1959): 83-85.

Hani, J. "L'Âne d'or d'Apulée et l'Égypte." *RPh* 47 (1973): 274-80.

Harding, M. *Woman's Mysteries: A Psychological Interpretation of the Feminine Principle as Portrayed in Myth, Story and Dreams.* New York, 1955.

Harrauer, C. "Lector, intende, laetaberis." *Wiener Studien* 17 (1983): 126-36.

Hawthorne, J. "Cenchreae: Port of Corinth." *Archaeology* 18 (1965): 191-200.

Heine, R. "Picaresque Novel Versus Allegory." *AA*, pp. 25-42.

——————. *Untersuchungen zur Romanform des Apuleius von Madaura.* Goettingen, 1962.

Heinrici, G. "Zur Geschichte der Psyche." *AP*, pp. 56-86.

Heller, S. "Apuleius, Platonic Dualism, and Eleven." *AJP* 104 (1983): 321-39.

Helm, R. *Der antike Roman.* Goettingen, 1956.

——————. "Ceterum bei Apuleius." *Wiener Studien* 70 (1957): 131-47.

——————. "Das 'Maerchen' von Amor und Psyche." *AP*, pp. 175-234.

Herrmann, L. "L'Âne d'or et le christianisme." *Latomus* 12 (1953): 188-91.

——————. "Le dieu-roi d'Apulée." *Latomus* 18 (1959): 110-16.

——————. "Le fragment obscène de l'Âne d'or.'" *Latomus* 10 (1951): 329-32.

——————. "Légendes locales et thèmes littéraires dans le conte de Psyché." *AC* 21 (1952): 13-27.

Herzog, R. *Die Wunderheilungen von Epidauros.* Philologus, Supp. Bd. 22, Heft 3. Leipzig, 1931.

Hesky, R. "Zur Abfassungszeit der Metamorphosen des Apuleius." *Wiener Studien* 26 (1904): 71-80.

Heyob, S. *The Cult of Isis Among Women in the Graeco-Roman World.* Leiden, 1975.

Hicter, M. "L'Autobiographie dans l'âne d'or d'Apulée (I)." *AC* 13 (1944): 95-111.

——————. "L'Autobiographie dans l'âne d'or d'Apulée (II)." *AC* 14 (1945): 61-68.

Hijmans, B., R. van der Paardt, E. Smits, R. Westendorp Boerma, and A. Westerbrink. *Apuleius Metamorphoses IV*, 1-27. Groningen, 1977.

Hijmans, B., and R. van der Paardt, eds. *Aspects of Apuleius' Golden Ass.* Groningen, 1978.

Hijmans, B., R. van der Paardt, V. Schmidt, C. Settels, B. Wesseling, and R. Westendorp Boerma. *Apuleius Metamorphoses VIII.* Groningen, 1985.

Hijmans, B. "Haemus, the Bloody Brigand (or What's in an Alias?)." *Mnemosyne* 31 (1978): 407-14.

——————. "Significant Names and Their Function in Apuleius' 'Metamorphoses'." *AA*, pp. 107-22.

Hillman, J. *The Dream and the Underworld.* New York, 1979.

——————. *The Myth of Analysis.* Evanston, Ill., 1972.

Hoevels, F. "Wer ist die Regina Caeli?" *Hermes* 102 (1974): 346-52.

——————. *Maerchen und Magie in den Metamorphosen des Apuleius von Madaura.* Amsterdam, 1979.

Holzberg, N. "Apuleius und der Verfasser des griechischen Eselromans." *WJA* 10 (1984): 161-77.

Hooker, W. "Apuleius' 'Cupid and Psyche' as a Platonic Myth." *Bucknell Review* 5 (1955): 24-38.

Hooper, R. "Structural Unity in the Golden Ass." *Latomus* 44 (1985): 398-401.

Houston, J. "Psyche and Eros." In *The Search for the Beloved*, pp. 151-88. Los Angeles, 1987.

Hubaux, J. "Deiphobe et la Sibylle." *AC* 8 (1939): 97-109.

Huet, G. "Le Roman D'Apulée." *Le Moyen Âge* 22 (1909): 23-28.

Ifie, J., and L. Thompson. "Rank, Social Status and Esteem in Apuleius." *Museum Africum* 6 (1977-78): 21-36.

Ingenkamp, H. "Thelyphron zu Apuleius, 'Metamorphoses' II, 20ff." *Rheinisches Museum* 115 (1972): 337-42.

Iversen, E. *The Myth of Egypt and its Hieroglyphs in European Tradition.* Copenhagen, 1961.

Jacobi, J. *The Psychology of C.G. Jung.* London, 1943.

Jacobsohn, H. "Das Gegensatzproblem im altaegyptischen Mythos." In *Studien zur analytischen Psychologie C.G. Jungs*, pp. 171-98. Zuerich, 1955.

Jacques, H-P. *Mythologie et psychanalyse.* Ottawa, 1969.

Jahn, O. "Abhandlungen: Variarum lectionum fasciculus." *Philologus* XXVI (1877): 1-17.

——————. "Die Cista Mystica." *Hermes* 3 (1869): 317-34.

James, P. *Unity in Diversity.* Hildesheim, 1987.

——————. "Serviles Voluptates (Apuleius, Metamorphoses 11, 15)." *LCM* 8.2 (1983): 29-30.

James, W. *The Varieties of Religious Experience.* New York, 1958.

Janousek, J. "Die Komposition und die Zeit in den 'Metamorphosen' des Apuleius." *Listy Filologicke* 107 (1984): 69-76.

Johanson, C. "Was the Magician of Madaura a Logician?" *Apeiron* 17 (1983): 131-34.

Johnson, L. *The Writings of the New Testament.* Philadelphia, 1987.

Johnson, R. *She: Understanding Feminine Psychology.* New York, 1976.

Joly, R. "Curiositas." *AC* 30 (1961): 33-44.

——————. "Notes sur la conversion d'Augustin." *AC* 35 (1966): 217-21.

Jung, C. *Collected Works.* 20 vols. Trans. R. Hull. Princeton, New Jersey, 1978.

Junghanns, P. "Die Erzaehlungstechnik von Apuleius' 'Metamorphosen' und ihrer Vorlage." *Philologus Suppl.* 24. Leipzig, 1932.

Katz, P. "The Myth of Psyche." *Arethusa* 9 (1976): 111-18.

Kawczynski, M. "Ist Apuleius im Mittelalter bekannt gewesen?" In *Bausteine zur romanischen Philologie*, pp. 193-210. Halle, 1905.

Kenny, B. "The Reader's Role in the Golden Ass." *Arethusa* 6-7 (1973-74): 187-209.

Kerenyi, K. *The Gods of the Greeks.* London, 1974.

——————. *Die griechisch-orientalische Romanliteratur in religionsgeschichtlicher Beleuchtung*. Darmstadt, 1973.

——————. "Urmensch und Mysterien." *Eranos Jahrbuch* 15 (1947): 41-74.

Kiell, N. *Psychoanalysis, Psychology and Literature: A Bibliography*. Madison, Wisc., 1963.

Krafft, P. "Apuleius' Darstellung der providentia tripertita." *Museum Helveticum* 36 (1979): 153-63.

Kranz, G. "Amor und Psyche." *Arcadia* 4 (1969): 285-99.

Kroll, W. "Das afrikanische Latein." *Rheinisches Museum* 52 (1897): 569-90.

Labhardt, A. "Curiositas—Notes sur l'histoire d'un mot et d'une notion." *Museum Helveticum* 17 (1960): 206-24.

Lancel, S. " 'Curiositas' und spirituelle Interessen bei Apuleius." *AP*, pp. 408-32.

Lavagnini, B. *Il significato e il valore del romanzo di Apuleio*. Pisa, 1923.

Leclant, J. "Reflets de l'Égypte dans la littérature latine d'après quelques publication recentes." *REL* 36 (1958): 81-85.

Lehner, H. "Orientalische Mysterienkulte im roemischen Rheinland." *Bonner Jahrbuecher* 129 (1924): 36-91.

Lesky, A. "Apuleius von Madaura und Lukios von Patrai." *Hermes* 76 (1941): 43-74.

Levy-Bruhl, L. *La mentalité primitive*. Paris, 1976.

——————. *The Notebooks on Primitive Mentality*. Trans. P. Rivière. Oxford, 1975.

Lévi-Strauss, C. "The Structural Study of Myth." In *Myth: A Symposium*, pp. 81-106. Bloomington, Ind., 1955.

L'Orange, H. "Das Geburtsritual der Pharaonen am roemischen Kaiserhof." *Symbolae Osloenses* 21 (1941): 105-16.

Lowe, E. "The Unique Manuscript of Apuleius' Metamorphoses and its Oldest Transcript." *Classical Quarterly* 14 (1920): 150-55.

Mackay, L. "The Sin of the Golden Ass." *Arion* 4 (1965): 474-80.

Mackay, P. "Klephtika—The Tradition of the Tales of Banditry in Apuleius." *G&R* 10 (1963): 147-52.

Maehler, H. "Lucius the Donkey and Roman Law." *MPL* 4 (1981): 161-77.

Mahe, J-P. "Quelques remarques sur la religion des Métamorphoses d'Apulée et les doctrines gnostiques contemporaines." *Revue des Sciences Religieuses* 46 (1972): 1-19.

Martin, L. *Hellenistic Religions*. New York, 1987.

Martin, R. "Le sens de l'expression *asinus aureus* et la signification du roman Apuléien." *REL* 48 (1970): 332-54.

Mason, H. "Fabula Graecanica: Apuleius and His Greek Sources." *AA*, pp. 1-15.

——————. "Lucius at Corinth." *Phoenix* 25 (1971): 160-65.

——————. "The Distinction of Lucius in Apuleius' Metamorphoses." *Phoenix* 37 (1983): 135-43.

_____. "Physiognomy in Apuleius' Metamorphoses." *Classical Philology* 79 (1984): 307-309.

Medan, P. *La Latinité d'Apulée dans les Métamorphoses*. Paris, 1926.

Meier, C. *Ancient Incubation and Modern Psychotherapy*. Evanston, Ill., 1967.

Merkelbach, R. "Der Eid der Isismysten." *ZPE* 1 (1967): 55-73.

_____. "Eros und Psyche." *AP*, pp. 392-407.

_____. "Inhalt und Form in Symbolischen Erzaehlungen der Antike." *Eranos-Jahrbuch* 35 (1966): 145-75.

_____. "Der Isiskult in Pompei." *Latomus* 24 (1965): 144-49.

_____. *Roman und Mysterium in der Antike*. Berlin, 1962.

Messer, W. *The Dream in Homer and Greek Tragedy*. New York, 1918.

Mette, H. "Curiositas." In *Festschrift Bruno Snell*, pp. 227-35. Muenchen, 1956.

Misch, G. *Geschichte der Autobiographie*. Vol. II. Bern, 1950.

Monceaux, P. "Apulée magicien." *Revue des deux mondes* 85 (1888): 571-608.

Morenz, S. "Aegyptische Nationalreligion und sogenannte Isismission." *ZDMG* 111 (1961): 432-36.

Morford, M., and R. Lenardon. *Classical Mythology*. New York, 1977.

Mortley, R. "Apuleius and Platonic Theology." *AJP* 93 (1972): 584-90.

Mueller, D. "Review of J. Bergman's Ich bin Isis." *OLZ* 67 (1972): 118-30.

Nehring, A. "Don't Monkey with the Donkey!" *Classical Weekly* 45 (1952): 229-30.

Nethercut, W. "Apuleius' Literary Art: Resonance and Depth in the Metamorphoses." *Classical Journal* 64 (1968-69): 110-19.

_____. "Apuleius' Metamorphoses—The Journey." *Agon* 3 (1969): 97-134.

Neumann, E. *Amor and Psyche—The Psychic Development of the Feminine*. New York, 1956.

_____. *The Great Mother*. Princeton, New Jersey, 1974.

_____. "Die Mythische Welt und der Einzelne." *Eranos Jahrbuch* 17 (1949): 189-254.

_____. *The Origins and History of Consciousness*. Trans. R. Hull. New York, 1954.

Nilsson, M. "Lampen und Kerzen im kult der Antike." *Opuscula Archaeologica* 6 (1950): 96-111.

Nock, A. "The Christian *Sacramentum* in Pliny and a Pagan Counterpart." *Classical Review* 38 (1924): 58-59.

_____. *Conversion*. Oxford, 1933.

Norden, F. *Apuleius von Madaura und das Roemische Privatrecht*. Darmstadt, 1974.

Norwood, F. "The Magic Pilgrimage of Apuleius." *Phoenix* 10 (1956): 1-12.

Oldfather, W., H. Canter, B. Perry. *Index Apuleianus*. Middleton, 1934.

Opeku, F. "Physiognomy in Apuleius." *Latomus Collection* 164 (1979): 467-74.

Otto, R. *The Idea of the Holy.* New York, 1969.

Paardt, R. Van der. *Apuleius. The Metamorphoses III.* Amsterdam, 1971.

—————. "The Unmasked 'I': Apuleius' Metamorphoses XI, 27." *Mnemosyne* 34 (1981): 96-106.

—————. "Various Aspects of Narrative Technique in Apuleius' Metamorphoses." *AA*, pp. 75-94.

Pausanias. *Guide to Greece.* 2 vols. Trans. P. Levi. Singapore, 1984.

Penwill, J. "Slavish Pleasures and Profitless Curiosity. Fall and Redemption in Apuleius' Metamorphoses." *Ramus* 4 (1975): 49-82.

Perry, B. *The Ancient Romances.* Berkeley, 1967.

—————. "An Interpretation of Apuleius' Metamorphoses." *TAPA* 57 (1926): 238-60.

—————. "On Apuleius' Metamorphoses II, 31-III, 20." *AJP* 46 (1925): 253-62.

—————. "The Significance of the Title in Apuleius' Metamorphoses." *Classical Philology* 18 (1923): 229-38.

—————. "Some Aspects of the Literary Art of Apuleius in the Metamorphoses." *TAPA* 54 (1923): 196-227.

—————. "The Story of Thelyphron." *Classical Philology* 24 (1929): 231-38.

—————. "Who was Lucius of Patrae?" *Classical Journal* 64 (1968-69): 97-101.

Pfister, F. "Review of H. Riefstahl's Der Roman des Apuleius." *Philologische Wochenschrift* 60 (1940): 533-41.

Pollitt, J. "The Egyptian Gods in Attica: Some Epigraphical Evidence." *Hesperia* 34 (1965): 125-30.

Purser, L. *The Story of Cupid and Psyche.* London, 1910.

Rahner, H. *Greek Myths and Christian Mystery.* London, 1963.

Rank, O. *The Myth of the Birth of the Hero: A Psychological Interpretation of Mythology.* New York, 1964.

Reardon, B. "The Greek Novel." *Phoenix* 23 (1969): 291-309.

—————. "Aspects of the Greek Novel." *G&R* 23 (1976): 118-31.

Regen, F. *Apuleius philosophus Platonicus. Untersuchungen zur Apologie (De magia) und zu De mundo.* Berlin, 1971.

Reik, T. *Dogma and Compulsion: Psychoanalytic Studies of Religion and Myths.* Westport, Conn., 1973.

Reitzenstein, R. "Eros und Psyche." *AP*, pp. 159-74.

—————. "Die Goettin Psyche in der hellenistischen und fruehchristlichen Literatur." *Sitzungsberichte der Heidelberger Akademie der Wissenschaften*, 1917, n. 10.

—————. "Das Maerchen von Amor und Psyche bei Apuleius." *AP*, pp. 87-158.

—————. "Noch Einmal Eros und Psyche." *AP*, pp. 235-92.

—————. *Zwei religionsgeschichtliche Fragen.* Strassburg, 1901.

Riefstahl, H. *Der Roman des Apuleius: Beitrag zur Romantheorie.* Frankfurt am Main, 1938.

Riklin, F. *Wishfulfillment and Symbolism in Fairy Tales.* Trans. W. White. New York, 1915.

Robertson, D. "The Assisi Fragments of the Apologia of Apuleius." *Classical Quarterly* n.s. 6 (1956): 68-80.

——————. "A Greek Carnival." *JHS* 39 (1919): 110-15.

——————. "Lucius of Madaura: A Difficulty in Apuleius." *Classical Quarterly* 4 (1910): 221-27.

——————. "The Manuscripts of the Metamorphoses of Apuleius I." *Classical Quarterly* 18 (1924): 27-42.

——————. "The Manuscripts of the Metamorphoses of Apuleius II." *Classical Quarterly* 18 (1924): 85-99.

Roeder, G. "Die Blumen der Isis von Philae." *ZAS* 48 (1910): 115-23.

Rohde, E. *Der griechische Roman und seine Vorlaeufer.* Leipzig, 1914.

——————. "Zu Apuleius." *Rheinisches Museum* 40 (1885): 66-113.

Roheim, G. "Fairy Tale and Dream." *The Psychoanalytic Study of the Child* 8 (1953): 394-403.

——————. *The Gates of the Dream.* New York, 1952.

——————. "Mondmythologie und Mondreligion." *Imago* 13 (1927): 442-537.

Rose, H. *Handbook of Greek Mythology.* London, 1953.

——————. *Religion in Greece and Rome.* New York, 1959.

Rubino, C. "Literary Intelligibility in Apuleius' Metamorphoses." *Classical Bulletin* 42 (1966): 65-69.

Ruch, M. "Psyché et les quatres vertus cardinales." *IL* 23 (1971): 171-76.

Ruediger, H. "Curiositas und Magie: Apuleius und Lucius als literarische Archetypen der Faust-Gestalt." In *Wort und Text: Festschrift fuer Fritz Schalk*, pp., 57-82. Frankfurt am Main, 1963.

Salles, C. "Assem para et accipe Auream Fabulam." *Latomus* 40 (1981): 3-20.

Samuels, A. *Jung and the Post-Jungians.* London, 1985.

Sandy, G. "Book 11: Ballast or Anchor?" *AA*, pp. 123-40.

——————. "Foreshadowing and Suspense in Apuleius' Metamorphoses." *Classical Journal* 68 (1973): 232-35.

——————. "Knowledge and Curiosity in Apuleius' Metamorphoses." *Latomus* 31 (1972): 179-83.

——————. "Recent Scholarship on the Prose Fiction of Classical Antiquity." *Classical World* 67 (1974): 321-59.

——————. "Serviles Voluptates in Apuleius' Metamorphoses." *Phoenix* 28 (1974): 234-44.

Sauneron, S. "Les songes et leur interprétation dans l'Égypte ancienne." In *Les Songes et leur Interpretation*, pp. 17-61. Paris, 1959.

Scazzoso, P. *Le Metamorfosi di Apuleio: Studio critico sul significato del romanzo.* Milano, 1951.

Schlam, C. *Cupid and Psyche: Apuleius and the Monuments*. University Park, Penn., 1976.

_____. "The Curiosity of the Golden Ass." *Classical Journal* 64 (1968): 120-25.

_____. "Platonica in the Metamorphoses of Apuleius." *TAPA* 101 (1970): 477-87.

_____. "Scholarship on Apuleius since 1938." *Classical World* 64 (1971): 285-309.

_____. "Sex and Sanctity: The Relationship of Male and Female in the 'Metamorphoses.'" *AA*, pp. 95-105.

Schmidt, V. "Apuleius Met. III. 15f—Die Einweihung in die Falschen Mysterien." *Mnemosyne* 35 (1982): 269-82.

_____. "Der Viator in Apuleius' Metamorphoses." *Mnemosyne* 32 (1979): 173-76.

Schroeder, J. *Het Sprookje van Amor en Psyche in het licht der Psychoanalyse*. Baarn, Netherlands, 1917.

Schubart, W. "Rom und die Aegypter nach dem Gnomen des Idios Logos." *ZAS* 56 (1920): 80-95.

Schuman, V. "A Second-Century Treatise on Egyptian Priests and Temples." *Harvard Theological Review* 53 (1960): 159-70.

Schwartz, G. "Apulei Metamorphoses I.2: desultoriae scientiae." *Latomus Collection* 164 (1979): 462-66.

Scobie, A. *Apuleius and Folklore*. London, 1983.

_____. *Apuleius Metamorphoses (Asinus Aureus)* I. Meisenheim am Glan, 1975.

_____. *Aspects of the Ancient Romance and Its Heritage: Essays on Apuleius, Petronius and the Greek Romances*. Meisenheim am Glan, 1969.

_____. "The Influence of Apuleius' Metamorphoses in Renaissance Italy and Spain." *AA*, pp. 211-30.

_____. "The Influence of Apuleius' Metamorphoses on Some French Authors." *Arcadia* 12 (1977): 156-65.

_____. "The Structure of Apuleius' Metamorphoses." *AA*, pp. 43-61.

Scranton, R., and E. Ramage. "Investigations at Corinthian Kenchreai." *Hesperia* 36 (1967): 124-86.

_____. "Investigations at Kenchreai, 1963." *Hesperia* 33 (1964): 134-45.

Simon, M. "Apulée et le christianisme." In *Mélanges d'histoire des religions offerts à Henri-Charles Puech*, pp. 299-305. Paris, 1974.

Simpson, D. *Cassell's New Latin Dictionary*. New York, 1960.

Smith, W. "The Narrative Voice in Apuleius." *TAPA* 103 (1972): 513-34.

Snell, B. "Das I-ah des Goldenen Esels." *Hermes* 70 (1935): 355-56.

Snowden, F. "Ethiopians and the Isiac Worship." *AC* 25 (1956): 112-16.

Sokolowski, F. "On the Rules Regulating the Celebration of the Eleusinian Mysteries." *Harvard Theological Review* 52 (1959): 1-7.

Solmsen, F. *Isis Among the Greeks and Romans.* Cambridge, Mass., 1979.

Souter, A. "'Zatchlas' in Apuleius." *JTS* 37 (1936): 80.

Spiegelberg, W. "Ein Denkstein auf den Tod einer heiligen Isiskuh." *ZAS* 43 (1906): 129-35.

Stabryla, S. "Functions of the Tale of Cupid and Psyche in the Structure of the Metamorphoses of Apuleius." *Eos* 61 (1973): 261-72.

Stephenson, W. "The Comedy of Evil in Apuleius." *Arion* 3 (1964): 87-93.

Stevenson, S. "A Comparison of Ovid and Apuleius." *Classical Journal* 29 (1933-34): 582-90.

Strub, C. "Die 'Metamorphosen' des Apuleius als Tiergeschichte." *WJA* 11 (1985): 169-88.

Summers, R. "Apuleius' Juridicus." *Historia* 21 (1972): 120-26.

——————. "A Note on the Date of the Golden Ass." *AJP* 94 (1973): 375-83.

——————. "Roman Justice and Apuleius' Metamorphoses." *TAPA* 101 (1970): 511-31.

Swahn, J. *The Tale of Cupid and Psyche.* Lund, 1955.

Tatum, J. "Apuleius and Metamorphosis." *AJP* 93 (1972): 306-13.

——————. *Apuleius and the Golden Ass.* Ithaca, N.Y., 1979.

——————. "The Tales in Apuleius' Metamorphoses." *TAPA* 100 (1969): 487-527.

Tegethoff, E. *Studien zum Maerchentypus von Amor und Psyche.* Leipzig, 1922.

Thiel, H. van. *Der Eselsroman: Synoptische Ausgabe.* Muenchen, 1972.

——————. *Der Eselsroman: Untersuchungen.* Muenchen, 1971.

Thompson, L. "Notes on Apuleius' Apologia." *Museum Africum* 6 (1977-78): 1-8.

Thompson, S. *The Folktale.* Berkeley, 1977.

Todd, F. "The Golden Ass." In *Some Ancient Novels,* pp. 102-40. London, 1940.

Tran Tam Tinh, V. *Le culte des divinités orientales à Herculanum.* Leiden, 1971.

——————. *Le culte d'Isis à Pompei.* Paris, 1964.

Trembley, J. *The Beloved Self: Erotic and Religious Themes in Apuleius' Metamorphoses and the Greek Romance.* Ph.D. Diss. Princeton, 1981.

Turcan, R. "Review of C. Schlam's Cupid and Psyche." *Latomus* 37 (1978): 240-42.

Ulanov, A. *The Feminine in Jungian Psychology and Christian Theology.* Evanston, Ill., 1971.

Ullman, M., and C. Limmer, eds. *The Variety of Dream Experience: Expanding our Ways of Working With Dreams.* New York, 1987.

Ullman, M., S. Krippner, and A. Vaughan. *Dream Telepathy.* New York, 1973.

Vanderlip, V. *The Four Greek Hymns of Isidorus and the Cult of Isis.* Toronto, 1972.

Veyne, P. "Apulée à Cenchrées." *Revue de Philologie* 39 (1965): 241-51.

Vignoli, T. *Myth and Science.* New York, 1882.

Visser, E. "Louis Couperus and Apuleius." *AA*, pp. 239-45.

Vliet, J. van der. "Die Vorrede der Apuleischen Metamorphosen." *Hermes* 32 (1897): 79-85.

Von Grunebaum, E. *The Dream and Human Societies.* Berkeley, 1966.

Vries, A. de. *Dictionary of Symbols and Imagery.* Amsterdam, 1984.

Wagenvoort, H. "Apuleius' Maerchen von Amor und Psyche." *AP*, pp. 382-91.

Walsh, J. "Galen's Writings and Influences Inspiring Them." *Annals of Medical History* N.S. VI: 1-30, 143-49.

Walsh, P. "Lucius Madaurensis." *Phoenix* 22 (1968): 143-57.

——————. "Petronius and Apuleius." *AA*, pp. 17-24.

——————. *The Roman Novel: The Satyricon of Petronius and the Metamorphoses of Apuleius.* Cambridge, 1970.

——————. "Was Lucius a Roman?" *Classical Journal* 63 (1968): 264-65.

Wapnick, K. "Mysticism and Schizophrenia." *Journal of Transpersonal Psychology* 1,2: 49-67.

Ward, P. *Apuleius on Trial at Sabratha.* New York, 1969.

Weinreich, O. "Eros und Psyche bei den Kabylen." *AP*, pp. 293-300.

——————. "Zu Apuleius." *Hermes* 56 (1921): 333-34.

——————. "Zur hellenistisch-aegyptischen Religionsgeschichte." *Aegyptus* 11 (1931): 13-22.

Weyman, C. "Studien zu Apuleius und seinen Nachahmern." *Sitzungsberichte der Akademie der Wissenschaften zu Muenchen* (1893): 321-92.

Whitmont, E. "Reassessing Femininity and Masculinity: A Critique of Some Traditional Assumptions." *Quadrant* 13,2 (1980): 109-22.

Winkler, J. *Auctor and Actor: A Narratological Reading of Apuleius' Golden Ass.* Berkeley, 1985.

Winterstein, A. "Die Pubertaetsriten der Maedchen und ihre Spuren im Maerchen." *Imago* 14 (1928): 199-274.

Witt, R. "Isis/Hellas." *PCPS* 192 (1966): 48-69.

——————. *Isis in the Graeco-Roman World.* London, 1971.

Wlosok, A. "Amor and Cupid." *HSCP* 79 (1975): 165-80.

——————. "Zur Einheit der Metamorphosen des Apuleius." *Philologus* 113 (1969): 68-84.

Woods, R., and H. Greenhouse, eds. *The New World of Dreams.* New York, 1974.

Wright, C. "No Art at All: A Note on the Proemium of Apuleius' Metamorphoses." *Classical Philology* 68 (1973): 217-19.

Wright, J. "Folk Tale and Literary Technique in the Tale of Cupid and Psyche." *Classical Quarterly* 21 (1971): 273-84.

Youtie, H. "The Kline of Serapis." *Harvard Theological Review* 41 (1948): 9-29.

Index

169

SR SUPPLEMENTS

Note: Nos. 1 to 8, 10, 13, 15, 18 and 20 in this series are out of print.

STUDIES IN CHRISTIANITY AND JUDAISM / ÉTUDES SUR LE CHRISTIANISME ET LE JUDAÏSME

Note: No. 1 and Vol. 1 of No. 2 in this series are out of print.

THE STUDY OF RELIGION IN CANADA / SCIENCES RELIGIEUSES AU CANADA

DISSERTATIONS SR

EDITIONS SR

Note: Nos. 1, 3, 6 and 9 in this series are out of print.

2. *The Conception of Punishment in Early Indian Literature*
Terence P. Day
1982 / iv + 328 pp.

4. *Le messianisme de Louis Riel*
Gilles Martel
1984 / xviii + 483 p.

5. *Mythologies and Philosophies of Salvation in the Theistic Traditions of India*
Klaus K. Klostermaier
1984 / xvi + 552 pp.

7. *L'étude des religions dans les écoles : l'expérience américaine,*
anglaise et canadienne
Fernand Ouellet
1985 / xvi + 666 p.

8. *Of God and Maxim Guns: Presbyterianism in Nigeria, 1846-1966*
Geoffrey Johnston
1988 / iv + 322 pp.

10. *Prometheus Rebound: The Irony of Atheism*
Joseph C. McLelland
1988 / xvi + 366 pp.

11. *Competition in Religious Life*
Jay Newman
1989 / viii + 237 pp.

12. *The Huguenots and French Opinion, 1685-1787:*
The Enlightenment Debate on Toleration
Geoffrey Adams
1991 / xiv + 335 pp.

13. *Religion in History: The Word, the Idea, the Reality /*
La religion dans l'histoire : le mot, l'idée, la réalité
Edited by / Sous la direction de Michel Despland and/et Gérard Vallée
1992 / x + 252 pp.

14. *Sharing Without Reckoning: Imperfect Right and the Norms of Reciprocity*
Millard Schumaker
1992 / xiv + 112 pp.

15. *Love and the Soul: Psychological Interpretations of the Eros and Psyche Myth*
James Gollnick
1992 / viii + 174 pp.

COMPARATIVE ETHICS SERIES / COLLECTION D'ÉTHIQUE COMPARÉE

Note: No. 1 in this series is out of print.

2. *Methodist Education in Peru: Social Gospel, Politics, and American*
Ideological and Economic Penetration, 1888-1930
Rosa del Carmen Bruno-Jofré
1988 / xiv + 223 pp.

Available from / en vente chez :

Wilfrid Laurier University Press

Wilfrid Laurier University
Waterloo, Ontario, Canada   N2L 3C5

Published for the
Canadian Corporation for Studies in Religion/
Corporation Canadienne des Sciences Religieuses
by Wilfrid Laurier University Press